Biographies

IN AMERICAN FOREIGN POLICY
Joseph A. Fry, University of Nevada, Las Vegas
Series Editor

The Biographies in American Foreign Policy Series employs the enduring medium of biography to examine the major episodes and themes in the history of U.S. foreign relations. By viewing policy formation and implementation from the perspective of influential participants, the series seeks to humanize and make more accessible those decisions and events that sometimes appear abstract or distant. Particular attention is devoted to those aspects of the subject's background, personality, and intellect that most influenced his or her approach to U.S. foreign policy, and each individual's role is placed in a context that takes into account domestic affairs, national interests and policies, and international and strategic considerations.

The series is directed primarily at undergraduate and graduate courses in U.S. foreign relations, but it is hoped that the genre and format may also prove attractive to the interested general reader. With these objectives in mind, the length of the volumes has been kept manageable, the documentation has been restricted to direct quotes and particularly controversial assertions, and the bibliographic essays have been tailored to provide historiographical assessment without tedium.

Producing books of high scholarly merit to appeal to a wide range of readers is an ambitious undertaking, and an excellent group of authors has agreed to participate. Some have compiled extensive scholarly records while others are just beginning promising careers, but all are distinguished by their comprehensive knowledge of U.S. foreign relations, their cooperative spirit, and their enthusiasm for the project. It has been a distinct pleasure to have been given the opportunity to work with these scholars as well as with Richard Hopper and his staff at Scholarly Resources.

Volumes Published

Lawrence S. Kaplan, *Thomas Jefferson: Westward the Course of Empire* (1999). Cloth ISBN 0-8420-2629-0 Paper ISBN 0-8420-2630-4

Richard H. Immerman, *John Foster Dulles: Piety, Pragmatism, and Power in U.S. Foreign Policy* (1999). Cloth ISBN 0-8420-2600-2 Paper ISBN 0-8420-2601-0

Thomas W. Zeiler, *Dean Rusk: Defending the American Mission Abroad* (2000). Cloth ISBN 0-8420-2685-1 Paper ISBN 0-8420-2686-X

Edward P. Crapol, *James G. Blaine: Architect of Empire* (2000). Cloth ISBN 0-8420-2604-5 Paper ISBN 0-8420-2605-3

David F. Schmitz, *Henry L. Stimson: The First Wise Man* (2001). Cloth ISBN 0-8420-2631-2 Paper ISBN 0-8420-2632-0

Thomas M. Leonard, *James K. Polk: A Clear and Unquestionable Destiny* (2001). Cloth ISBN 0-8420-2646-0 Paper ISBN 0-8420-2647-9

James E. Lewis Jr., *John Quincy Adams: Policymaker for the Union* (2001). Cloth ISBN 0-8420-2622-3 Paper ISBN 0-8420-2623-1

Catherine Forslund, *Anna Chennault: Informal Diplomacy and Asian Relations* (2002). Cloth ISBN 0-8420-2832-3 Paper ISBN 0-8420-2833-1

ANNA CHENNAULT

Anna Chennault, circa 1970s, from Flying Tiger Lines Public Relations

ANNA CHENNAULT

Informal Diplomacy and Asian Relations

CATHERINE FORSLUND

Biographies
IN AMERICAN FOREIGN POLICY

Number 8

to belinda—
thanks for being
a great inspiration!
Catherine
Forslund

SR BOOKS

A Scholarly Resources Inc. Imprint
Wilmington, Delaware

First published 2002
Printed and bound in the United States of America

Scholarly Resources Inc.
104 Greenhill Avenue
Wilmington, DE 19805-1897
www.scholarly.com

Source for Illustrations
All illustrations were provided by Anna Chennault

Library of Congress Cataloging-in-Publication Data

Forslund, Catherine, 1955–
Anna Chennault : informal diplomacy and Asian relations / Catherine Forslund.
p. cm. — (Biographies in American foreign policy ; no. 8)
Includes bibliographical references (p.) and index.
ISBN 0-8420-2832-3 (alk. paper) — ISBN 0-8420-2833-1 (pbk. : alk. paper)
1. Chennault, Anna. 2. Women diplomats—United States—Biography. 3. Diplomats—United States—Biography. 4. Chinese American women—Biography. 5. United States—Foreign relations—China. 6. China—Foreign relations—United States. 7. United States—Relations—Asia. 8. Asia—Relations—United States. 9. United States—Foreign relations—20th century. 10. Cold War. I. Title. II. Series.

E748.C524 F67 2002
327.73'0092—dc21 2001042678

∞ The paper used in this publication meets the minimum requirements of the American National Standard for permanence of paper for printed library materials, Z39.48, 1984.

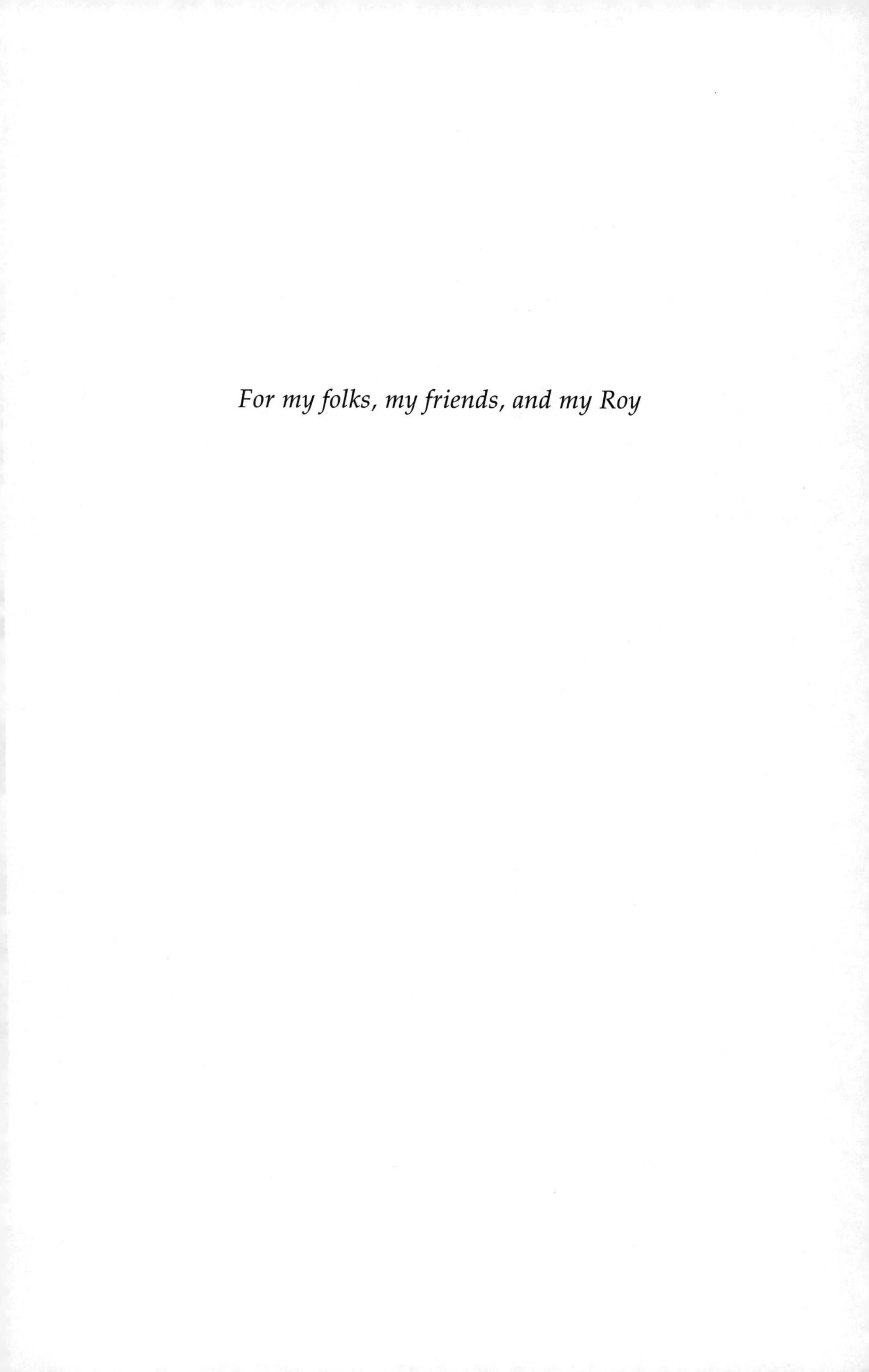

For my folks, my friends, and my Roy

About the Author

Catherine Forslund earned her doctorate from Washington University in St. Louis. This book is based on her doctoral dissertation. She contributed entries on Anna Chennault and Clare Boothe Luce for the forthcoming *Encyclopedia of U.S.-East Asian Relations, 1784–2001* and has presented her work at annual meetings of the American Historical Association and Society for Historians of American Foreign Relations. Her current work includes examinations of editorial cartoons' reflection of American diplomacy and culture in the twentieth century. She is an assistant professor of history at Rockford College in Illinois.

Contents

Acknowledgments

This book was possible only through the contributions of many individuals and institutions. I consider myself blessed to have received such generous support. All their names cannot be mentioned here, and most of them know what they have done and share my success. However, any deficiencies herein are mine alone.

I owe an intellectual debt to my graduate experience, to Dr. Henry Berger and to the many colleagues who helped shape my historical sensibilities and my skills as a historian. Dr. Nancy Grant did not live long enough to see this work come to fruition, but she planted the seed from which it grew; others were there for support (academic, emotional, official) and guidance. Thanks to Dr. Kun-shuan Chiu, Dr. James Shih, and Willie Li who helped me understand the Chinese context necessary for my work.

For research funding, I must thank the Gerald R. Ford and Lyndon Baines Johnson Foundations as well as Washington University in St. Louis, whose grant awards supported vital doctoral research. At all the Presidential Libraries where I worked, the staffs were exceptionally helpful and went out of their way to assist me. In addition, two years of summer grant funding from College Misericordia in Dallas, Pennsylvania, made possible the time and space for revising my dissertation into this manuscript. The friendship and scholarly companionship of Cathy Turner and Kylie Shafferkoetter made life there worthwhile.

As for the support of academic colleagues and other friends in the "real" world, I must thank them all. Margaret Ries started me on the road to being a scholar, but others kept me going: Padraic Kennedy, Fabian Hilfrich, Lynn Johnson, Barbara Krauthamer, Betsy Kellerman, Jodie Kreider, and Kylie Hansen deserve special mention. My friends outside the hallowed halls gained a glimpse inside through my experience; I learned the better nature of friendship and especially thank them for their support and patience. Tim and Adrienne Boyer, Cheryl Brown, Caitlin MacAgy, Debbie Rabeor, Linda Scheuerman, Lana Stein, Ron and Maren Yeska, and others make life in the academy better because of the grounding they give to the rest of life. Two women went beyond the call of duty to read my entire dissertation: the efforts of Krista Camenzind and Madhuparna Mitra greatly improved this project.

The willingness of Anna Chennault and Irving Kaufman to allow me into their lives and into Mrs. Chennault's papers made this project a reality. It is said to be dangerous for a writer to get too close to her subject, but in this case I was enriched beyond my scholarly pursuits. Thanks to them for trusting me, and also to David Yao, who was invaluable with critical details and more.

Everyone at SR Books and my editor, Andy Fry, were very supportive in this effort. In particular, Andy's editorial hand had just the right amount of push and polish. His invaluable improvements are greatly appreciated. Thanks to Edward Crapol for being my connection from dissertation to publisher and for encouraging me when we meet at each summer's SHAFR conference.

My parents stood behind me when the twinkle of graduate school first glinted in my eyes. Raymond U. and Jacquelyn M. Forslund have my thanks and love for being as supportive and encouraging as any parents could be. Even with all this, nothing could have been done without my best friend and husband, Roy Roncal. His continued love, patience, reassurance, and steadfastness sustained me in my darkest hours and shined with me in joyous triumph. He knows how much I need him.

Introduction

In recognition of her career and to promote its own purposes, the Republican Party invited Mrs. Anna Chen Chennault to speak at its 1996 national convention in San Diego. Once the GOP's most prominent Asian-American woman member, Chennault stood astride a lengthy career of fundraising, donating, organizing, and vote-getting for the party. To ethnic Republicans she represented fulfillment of the dream that drew immigrants to America. To female Republicans she represented the possibilities for advancement within a major political party. To the GOP leadership she represented an opportunity to show how color- and gender-blind, how embracing the party was by showcasing an ethnic woman at its most important quadrennial event—something they had also done in 1976. To Chennault, however, the invitation was easy to refuse; she recognized the unfavorable time slot proposed for her speech as a veiled insult.

The GOP wanted to present an image of inclusive equality across color and gender boundaries, but from her longtime insider's perspective, Chennault knew it was more illusion aimed at generating votes than reality. During her career as an informal diplomat in business, political, and social spheres, Anna Chennault's own agenda followed that of American Cold War foreign policy—swinging from ardent anticommunism, to détente, and beyond. Once a person regularly in the spotlight in the United States and Asia, more recently she shunned the limelight, preferring quiet, private transactions to shield her actions from judgments concerning motives and goals. She was a pre-eminent citizen-diplomat, conducting informal diplomacy that advanced the larger goals of official American foreign policy. That is why she was important enough for the Republican Party to want to parade her across its stage even though she had been largely disconnected from it since 1989.

Informal Diplomacy

The increasingly complex nature of formal, state-to-state relations now includes multinational corporations, multilateral treaties, international terrorism, and natural and ecological disasters in addition to the usual trade, diplomacy, and tourism. In such a world, the value of informal diplomats has risen greatly. The composite connections that citizen-diplomats command expand any government's official ties within another nation and thus cannot be ignored. Indeed, any leaders not taking advantage of such opportunities to control policy and build influence are wasting a valuable national resource.

Scholars have left the subject of informal diplomacy largely unexamined. Its very nature necessitates that many of its activities go unrecorded, causing it to be mostly invisible in the written record. Understanding informal diplomacy requires not only definition but also the teasing out of its realms and inner reaches. Anna Chennault's career provides a lens for observing both.

Informal diplomacy may be defined as any exchange between citizens or groups of citizens from two or more nations outside the boundaries of the official governmental institutional apparatus (ambassadors, ministers, secretaries, et al.). It includes activities by persons or groups with commercial, social, labor, scientific, humanitarian, or cultural interests who operate within private or nongovernmental organizational forums in domestic or international settings—in other words, everything outside official state-to-state connections. Of course, not every tourist traveling to an international destination is an informal diplomat. The definition's scope must be limited to those who represent interests beyond their own and who seek to influence events or attitudes of governments. The career of Anna Chennault embodies an unusual case study of an informal diplomat, one woman who became active in the field well before women were prominent in foreign affairs and who functioned extensively between two worlds of several kinds: Asian and American, political and economic, private and public.

Former president Harry Truman expressed his aggravation when a spate of U.S. citizens in the late 1950s privately attempted to smooth the increasingly rough relations between the United States and the Soviet Union. Truman denounced these "diplomatic tourists" in a *New York Times* op-ed piece. He viewed their "diplomacy by press interview, special audiences or fishing expeditions" as interference in "an already complicated situation."[1] Truman acknowledged, however, that some benefit might come from exchanges between American and Soviet individuals and groups as long as they left the true diplomacy to the professionals.

Truman's reaction captured the mixed feelings often generated by such activity. Its perceived value ranges from positive to negative; from informal diplomats as either "go-betweens . . . diplomats without portfolio [or as] . . . meddlers."[2] This disparity results from success or failure rates and how their actions assist or impair the efforts of formal policymakers. Certainly, those informal diplomats who are knowledgable about issues and policy goals, who keep government officials informed of their efforts, and who act discreetly are more acceptable to the formal diplomatic establishment than those who operate indiscriminately with little or no regard for the consequences of their actions.

Historian George L. Ridgeway described those informal diplomats of the business world who endeavored to promote international cooperation through exchange of trade, capital, and industry as "merchants of peace." He concluded that commerce was "an ancient institution of peace." Anna Chennault would agree. She believed that American-Asian relations could be strengthened by what Ridgeway called "private internationalism," the direct connection achieved by the "exchange of goods, services, and ideas" between people, and nongovernmental activities.[3]

Important opportunities for contact arise in international business dealings when business leaders meet with their foreign counterparts and/or government officials who control specific fields such as transportation, manufacturing, or trade. International commerce was Chennault's largest sphere of activity. This venue of informal diplomacy has been important to American policymakers since the eighteenth century's cries of "free ships, free goods, free men" made obvious the nation's dependence on foreign trade. An early example of Chennault's informal diplomatic efforts was her negotiation of Flying Tiger Lines' landing rights in Southeast Asia in the late 1960s. While clearly a business transaction, the timing of such negotiations coincided with the U.S. regional strategy of supporting non-Communist regimes in an effort to prevent more "dominoes" from falling into the Communist bloc. Chennault went beyond policymakers' primary interests in the mercantile aspects of business by recognizing its value for expanding political and social contacts between Asians and Americans. In this regard, she agreed with another citizen-diplomat, industrialist Armand Hammer, who described the benefit of such activities by declaring that "peace, stability, and prosperity in the world are not necessarily created by [diplomats] so much as . . . promoted by day-to-day contacts and commerce among the peoples and institutions of nations through trade."[4] This belief was a guiding principle in her entire career as an informal diplomat.

The scant, existing literature about the realm of informal diplomacy examines almost exclusively the activities of individuals working with international organizations such as the United Nations, the Red Cross, or church groups such as the Quakers. In addition, figures who made their reputations in multinational business ventures, politics, journalism, or as scholars are included as participants in unofficial diplomacy.

Anna Chennault carved her own niche distinct from sole loyalty to any one organization, base of operation, or center of power. When she became involved in causes and events, she acted on her own, rather than at the behest of a particular agency or organization. Until at least the 1980s, she was an ardent Cold Warrior and anti-Communist, an ideological posture that originated with her life in war-torn China. Her marriage to General Claire Lee Chennault (the commander of the World War II Flying Tigers), his ties to Jiang Jieshi (Chiang Kai-shek), his staunch anticommunism, and her status as his widow reinforced these positions. She carried forward the General's legacy. Her links, originally through him, to the China Lobby and other like-minded Americans and Asians reinforced her *weltanschauung*. But her independence from any formal organization is part of what made her distinct from other informal diplomats and what makes her career worth examining as an example of free agency on the international scene.

Chennault's pursuits illustrate the essential nature of informal diplomacy: it is conducted in unconventional settings by individuals who are unconnected to government and whose activities generally remain unseen by the public. Such an environment for international contact allows for exploration of possibilities between nations without the pressure and glare that usually accompany more formal meetings. This combination of attributes—confidential access, detachment from government, and limited public exposure—makes informal diplomacy a valuable component of any nation's diplomatic apparatus. Chennault's career provides a clear insight into this interplay between informal diplomatic arenas and the formal goals of U.S. foreign policy. Over the years, she served as a link between the United States and Asia—whether as a cross-cultural representative, business negotiator, philanthropist, reporter, messenger, or peacemaker. This role extended through the Cold War and Vietnam War, the reopening of U.S. relations with the People's Republic of China (PRC), and current attempts to create "one China" and bring it into the family of nations.

Successful informal diplomats must meet certain criteria. They must possess good connections, specialized expertise, prominence, and anonymity. Also vital are acquaintance with key decision makers, availability, disposability, discretion, and influence. Frequent opportunities for contact with individuals, in public, on business, or socially, are also important. Chennault had all these traits. In addition, her numerous meetings with American and Asian leaders allowed her to discuss current events and policies and make her views known.

Through her positions within the international aviation field and the Republican Party, Chennault was connected to top party leaders in Congress and the White House (especially during the Nixon, Ford, Reagan, and George H. W. Bush administrations). A number of high-level U.S. officials have asserted, "You can't work on China and not be aware of Anna Chennault."[5] Her cachet as General Chennault's widow and as an author also gave her entrée at the highest levels of society within Asia's non-Communist powers—countries prominent in U.S. Cold War foreign policy concerns. Interviewing such men as South Vietnam's President Nguyen Van Thieu, South Korea's President Park Chung Hee, Philippines' President Ferdinand Marcos, and Taiwan's Chief Executive Chiang Ching-kuo for various English and Chinese publications gave Chennault some of her best top-level contacts with Asian leaders. Such pursuits also gave her opportunities for contact, whether to negotiate a business deal, conduct an interview, or attend a formal dinner, all of which often appeared on Chennault's foreign itineraries.

She certainly had the specialized expertise required of an informal diplomat. Men on both sides of the Pacific considered her an important connection to their counterparts as well as an excellent analyst of Asian and U.S. leaders and their policies. She was well and widely read and up on all the current events of the day. That knowledge combined with her work with General Chennault's airline, her life in Asia, and her business and political connections made her a valuable expert to both Asian and American policymakers.

As a famous widow, well-known Chinese journalist, author, and businesswoman, Chennault was prominent enough to have doors open for her, yet she could be anonymous when necessary. Her frequent business trips to Asia gave her the occasion to visit foreign leaders while at the same time providing useful cover to disguise her informal diplomatic endeavors in foreign settings. So, for example, while meeting with some foreign minister to negotiate the sale of jet aircraft, it was an easy matter also to discuss the importance of that nation's continued friendship and cooperation with the U.S. government.

Being disposable is an important characteristic that permits leaders to make use of citizen-diplomats with little risk. Since their undertakings appear to be private and not part of government policy, their actions can be easily denied when necessary. In Chennault's case, her gender may have enhanced the disposability factor. The ease with which American political leaders dismissed her as "that woman" with her own agenda, or attached to her the "Dragon Lady" image of a pestering, scheming figure, is evidence of one way a negative view of her gender enabled her to turn a liability to her own advantage.

As the friend of many political and business leaders, Chennault was sensitive to the value of discretion in her dealings. Being anonymous and discreet was something of which she was particularly proud. While open and forthright in her discussions with various leaders, and fairly public with the identity of her acquaintances and their frequent attendance at her parties, when it came to conversational details or the gist of meetings, she drew the line, kept things to herself, and only communicated what was prudent to any higher-ups or others who "needed to know." Most policymakers who spoke of Chennault's career acknowledged this valuable trait.

Finally, being influential is important for an informal diplomat. Scholar James Rosenau has identified two measures of influence: first, having the "opportunities to [transmit opinions] to unknown citizens [and] to . . . wield influence in government circles"; and second, to have "access to the channels of communication . . . [with] effectiveness . . . [being] founded upon some notion of the size and nature of the audience."[6] Rosenau thus limits influence to those who can communicate their opinions to others beyond their own acquaintances, and Chennault communicated with many audiences. In addition to the Asian and American policymakers to whom she had access, she also had the ear of large numbers of Asians, Chinese Americans, ethnic minority Republicans, and American businessmen living in the United States and abroad. Through her books, columns, and speeches she reached even larger Asian and American communities of citizens with a variety of messages over the years. As for the size and nature of her audience, Chennault was able to sit down privately with heads of state. Her appointment book also listed cabinet secretaries and ministers, legislative leaders, military commanders, and corporate chief executives among her international circle of friends.

Chennault derived influence in two principal ways: her ability to connect with others, and her access. She succeeded through the sheer volume of her contacts, in which effects of character and charisma defined her impact. Liked or not, she made her views known and was heard. And her access reached from the top governmental leaders down to ordinary citizens. But this was not a contradiction of her ability to remain anonymous because she presented two personas. One featured the public Chennault, the writer and speaker known to many Asian and American intellectuals and political activists who followed her appraisals of Asian politics and her entreaties to become politically involved. The other was the private Chennault, seen only by business leaders and policymakers who knew her as discreet, shrewd, and businesslike. The two personas met the needs of two audiences: the public face helped those who sought a voice in the halls of power, and the private face facilitated policymakers' demands for prudence.

While it is clear her influence was not such that she, for example, could keep President Richard Nixon from going to China, it was, however, important enough for him to discuss with her in 1972 the ways in which the Taiwan government might react to friendly U.S. approaches to the People's Republic of China. Her advice was not always heeded, but it was sought and heard at the top. Numerous interviews reinforce this conclusion. No one ever wanted to offend her. Those with whom she came into contact generally welcomed whatever insights she offered for use in their policy-making process, and the number of ordinary Americans and Chinese who are aware of her career demonstrates the wide range of her audience.

Her social activities in Washington and major Asian capitals illustrate how congenial and comfortable settings can "grease the wheels" of international relations and foreign policy initiatives. While often denigrated as an unimportant woman's task, entertaining with a purpose is an important part of successful diplomacy. Chennault followed a historical line of women known for their skill in this art which, it can be argued, resulted in some highly favorable environments for the exchange of culture, ideas, and perspectives. A comparison would be the salons of France's *ancien régime* hosted by Madame de Pompadour and others, which were well known for their contribution to intrigue and politics. It has always been easy for men to dismiss women who excel in this realm as mere hostesses, but their skills encourage diplomatic engagement.

The extent of Chennault's endeavors in business and politics is what makes her such an ideal model for the examination of the multiple aspects of unofficial diplomacy. She operated at the highest levels, engaging top executives, politicians, and elected officials in America and Asia and sharing observations, strategies, and outcomes of business negotiations, political developments, and official actions. Her level of access guaranteed a certain amount of influence, the effects of which on the general tenor of U.S.-Asian relations cannot be ignored.

A Chinese Woman in American Foreign Policy

Chennault's activities also add the dimension of ethnicity to the role of women in American foreign policy. In the past, studies of women in diplomacy have almost exclusively surveyed women connected with the nation's formal diplomatic apparatus either by virtue of their own position or by that of a spouse. The contribution of a private citizen-diplomat such as Chennault operating within her own sphere of influence and access shows what levels of success they can achieve. With the success of Madeleine Albright as the first female U.S. secretary of state, women's careers worthy of study for their contributions to diplomacy are surely multiplying.

As a result of their historic invisibility, women in American foreign policy have received little scholarly attention. The earliest works focus only on the roles of women in the State Department and foreign service. Another view is provided in oral histories that focus on diplomatic spouses and women ambassadors. These works are replete with specific examples of women in roles that highlight some gender-specific factors involved when they enter the male-dominated world of diplomacy.

Gender factors are part of the "sociological" examination of women in foreign policy. This perspective includes evaluating such issues as gender stereotypes, societal and cultural obstacles to women, behavior and management-style differences between genders, the peace movement's historical association with women and its impact on foreign policy, gender-related obstacles to women's entry and advancement in the field, and organizational impediments. These sorts of analyses provide contextual bases for understanding how, why, and where women are positioned in the foreign relations apparatus. Generally, sociological perspectives do not acknowledge or offer insight into informal diplomacy. They do, however, recognize that diplomacy is susceptible to external influences—usually those from the larger society or a segment thereof.

The career of Eleanor Lansing Dulles utilized the same kind of connections as Chennault, but in the formal diplomatic arena. The sister of John Foster and Allen Dulles, Eleanor was "well-connected and superficially on the threshold of power" in her highly successful positions planning the financial reconstruction of Austria and Germany after World War II, yet she was frequently reminded by her male colleagues that she was working in "a boys' club." For example, in postwar Austria, Eleanor Dulles, a lieutenant colonel in the military, was sent to board with the secretaries instead of being housed with her fellow staff members. In order "to circumvent the restraints on her effectiveness [she] installed herself in a large home, where she frequently entertained small groups of public officials, students and women. . . . She discovered in [Europe] that if she acted and entertained as if she had rank, Europeans responded. Thus she found a way to outmaneuver the boys' club and established her own influence within the bureaucracy."[7] Dulles's tools to do so included persistence along with social, personal, partisan, and business connections, which, when played in combination, afforded her a unique position within a hierarchy that labored to shut her out because of her gender.

Historian Joan Hoff has stated that because women in diplomacy operate in gendered environments, extra skills are required for them to navigate successfully through roles and relationships and to master techniques. Chennault can be clearly distinguished from these women in the formal diplomatic structure who were restrained by the sexual politics of that system. While she, on the one hand, functioned outside the male bureaucracy, on the other hand she operated in other highly gendered environments of business in general and aviation in particular. In the 1960s, when she was beginning her informal diplomatic career, women outside the secretarial pool were rare in the business world.

Hoff noted that despite the numerous claims of the women she studied "that their success owed little to their gender and much to their ability to become one of the boys," they also "expressed frustration with their male colleagues" and exhibited what other sociological observers have called "typical . . . feminine 'behind-the-scenes' *modus operandi*" to achieve their objectives. Her interpretation of this apparent contradiction was "that [basic] gender socialization made women foreign policy specialists sensitive to sexism; at the same time they had no choice but to rely on stereotypical female skills to rise professionally." Her women subjects saw themselves as playing in a man's field by men's rules ("becoming one of the boys") even while their appropriation of men's rules was done in a "typically female" manner.[8]

In fact, Chennault's gender never seemed to her to be a hindrance, nor a part of her consciousness. She believed that, if anything, it made her more persuasive. Chennault and other effective women in any field succeed because they go beyond the bounds of their femininity; the most accomplished women bring together the best attributes and styles of both genders. This approach, with whatever other favorable circumstances surround them, allows such women to excel within male-dominated hierarchies such as that of diplomacy.

The "role of male mentors" has been "essential" for women, as it is also for men, to rise on the diplomatic ladder, according to Hoff. What, of course, is different for women is that they sometimes marry their mentors, thereby "mingl[ing] the intimate with the international."[9] Chennault credits much of her success to her mentor, Thomas G. Corcoran, the Roosevelt Democrat who was a friend and ardent supporter of General Chennault. Corcoran was a close friend and social escort for Anna Chennault after the General's death. He also taught her the secrets of Washington influence. They never married, but his assistance and encouragement until his death in 1981 significantly increased her effectiveness.

Women faced a double standard of behavior when they tried to negotiate the "old boy network" of foreign relations. Hoff described them as often being "singled out for behavior unbecoming women, *but not men*, in carrying out their foreign policy jobs . . . such a double standard led to criticisms of amateurism or abrasiveness," criticisms that were not applied to men in similar positions.[10] This situation echoes a general pattern for career women who are often criticized for exhibiting the very characteristics for which men are lauded, such as toughness, tenacity, or aggressiveness. Similar judgments were also visited upon Chennault by her critics over the years, although most people considered her very competent and professional.

Finally, Hoff considered most models to be "strongly male identified, often trying to steer a middle course between warring [male] factions or [just] adopting views of various male mentors."[11] This assessment applied to Chennault, particularly when she was younger. She was heavily influenced by the views of General

Chennault and his political allies. Eventually she relied more upon her own instincts, even though they usually followed the lead of various policymakers. Her ideological views mirrored those of American foreign policy leaders, although she often accepted major changes in policy more slowly.

During the 1950s her life differed from that of many American women or at least from common perceptions of their lives. A woman of some means, she was often covered in and spoke out from the women's pages of the newspapers and gave public lectures about the least feminine of topics—politics and diplomacy. American society in the 1950s and 1960s expected a petite and delicate Chinese American such as Anna Chennault to behave in ways quite different from how she actually functioned. By the 1970s, however, Americans had begun to accept women in nontraditional roles, and she was thereafter more easily able to succeed as an informal diplomat.

A Chinese woman participating in American diplomacy coupled gender and ethnic culture. Chennault certainly recognized the stigma on daughters in China when she wrote that she and her five sisters meant "misfortune bordering on tragedy" for her parents, who had no male offspring in a society that valued boys more than girls.[12] Her determination to rise above such gender inferiority is seen in her choice of journalism as a career and her success in obtaining her first job in a largely male news organization. Moreover, marriage to an American—one for whom such a cultural prejudice did not exist—was another way to demonstrate her rejection of the traditional Chinese gender preference. Choosing to live in the United States following the General's death was the final disavowal of cultural submission, for there, rising above her gender was easier than in her homeland. Taiwan's former Ambassador to the United States Konsin Shah noted this by saying that she "was too outspoken" to have survived and prospered in China; "the United States was a better place for her."[13]

Her status as the Chinese widow of an important American gave her entrée on both sides of the Pacific, especially in Taiwan and later in mainland China. Yet, in Taiwan, she was and still is seen as an American first, and her activities, particularly with reference to the PRC, are viewed in that context. Her inside track with American policymakers was largely due to the fact that her "Chineseness" gave her insight, connections, and thus importance. As a woman she could be held at arm's length more easily than male Asians when America's superiority complex regarding Asia demanded it, yet her dual-ethnic status was important to her success as an informal diplomat.

One particular example illustrates how gender and ethnicity were combined in Chennault's career. In 1962, when the human crisis of the PRC's Cultural Revolution sent refugees streaming into Hong Kong and elsewhere, she was tapped to head Chinese Refugee Relief, a private philanthropy organized to assist the refugees. When President John F. Kennedy met with Chennault to give his support to her and the cause, the event was a cover story in *Parade* magazine.[14] As a Chinese woman in this role, her appeals on behalf of thousands of starving Chinese were especially meaningful to the American public, whose sympathies were crucial to success. She played the woman's part by touching the hearts of Americans and Chinese alike—especially those of the children and families who found or were offered new homes in the United States.

Her well-honed speaking skills and a new-found aptitude for fundraising, however, made her more than just an eye-catching female figurehead for relief work. No prima donna, she also did the tough sides of the job—writing and getting publicity for the cause, soliciting funds, and embarking on fact-finding missions to Asia. Her career went beyond any restrictions that her gender and ethnicity might have imposed on her because of her own determination and the opportunities that society offered her at the particular time in which she played an active role in diplomacy. Gender and ethnicity are, however, only one of the contexts in which to consider Chennault and informal diplomacy. Her connections through General Chennault and Thomas Corcoran gave her access to the informal diplomatic arena, but, once inside and established there, she made herself successful beyond any advantages that gender and ethnicity initially gave her.

In public, her skills as a hostess allowed her to take advantage of an arena where her gender played a vital, positive role. It facilitated and enhanced this aspect of her career because women are traditionally more accepted than men in the role of social organizer. Chennault's parties, routinely covered in the society pages of Washington's newspapers, linked many domestic and international leaders to her and enhanced her popular image. As American politicians met and talked policy with each other and with international leaders who shared common interests with her and her friends, her reputation rose among the guests as well as with the general public.

Sources

The issue of sources for this book deserves attention. Because of its very nature, informal diplomatic activity is often not explicitly recorded. It must be extracted from documents, media coverage, and interviews. Policymakers will not usually admit to being influenced by, or engaging, an informal diplomat to achieve success in foreign relations. The drawbacks of this reality for historians are fairly obvious. Thus, other sources must be used to account for the contributions of informal diplomats. In addition, the challenge of writing modern biography with a living subject involves obtaining sources from witnesses and others who prefer to keep matters hidden.

The record of Anna Chennault's family and early life is available primarily through two autobiographical books and personal interviews with her. Her papers are extensive but do not contain material from her childhood. Since her family was forced to move by the advance of the Sino-Japanese War, all of their records were lost. What survived was either destroyed by PRC government authorities during the Cultural Revolution or eliminated to protect the family from self-incrimination. The mere dozen years that Anna and General Chennault spent together did not produce any publicly available collection of correspondence, so only her recollections of their relationship exist from which to work. The General did, however, express his beliefs publicly and included them in correspondence with others.

There are obvious dangers inherent in relying on autobiographical sources when composing a historical narrative. The pitfalls of self-service, selective memory, or embellishment that accompany personal recollections have been ameliorated, whenever possible, by corroborating Chennault's childhood and adolescence with examples described in the secondary literature. Autobiographical information can in itself, however, be an extremely revealing source. One biographer has noted that autobiographical material is useful to see how the subject "remembered her past [more] than as a story of how she actually lived it." Moreover, a person's choice of material, of emphases, and of detail can offer significant insights into his or her own view of the important elements of personal and career development.[15]

As Mrs. Chennault's life progressed in time, following her husband's death in 1958 into the late 1960s, the variety of sources expands beyond personal recollections to include government documents. The narratives and recollections of others add greater dimension to the analysis. Her activities in business, politics, and as a prominent hostess—all areas critical to the conducting of informal diplomacy—are found in her papers, which provide in-depth documentation of her high-level contacts to both Asian and U.S. business and government leaders as well as evidence of her contributions to the advancement of American foreign policy in Asia during the Cold War.

Notes

1. January 19, 1959, 1, cited in Maureen R. Berman and Joseph E. Johnson, *Unofficial Diplomats* (New York: Columbia University Press, 1977), 1.
2. Ibid., v.
3. George L. Ridgeway, *Merchants of Peace: The History of the International Chamber of Commerce* (Boston: Little, Brown & Co., 1959), 287.
4. Armand Hammer, "Private Diplomacy at the Highest Levels," in *Private Diplomacy with the Soviet Union*, ed. David D. Newsom (Lanham, MD: University Press of America and The Institute for the Study of Diplomacy, Georgetown University, 1987), 55.
5. David Laux, July 21, 1994, Senator Ted Stevens, June 27, 1994, and other interviews by author.
6. James N. Rosenau, *National Leadership and Foreign Policy: A Case Study in the Mobilization of Public Support* (Princeton, NJ: Princeton University Press, 1963), 6, 133.
7. Lynne K. Dunn, " 'Joining the Boys' Club': The Diplomatic Career of Eleanor Lansing Dulles," in Edward P. Crapol, ed., *Women and American Foreign Policy: Lobbyists, Critics, and Insiders* (Wilmington, DE: Scholarly Resources, 1992), ix, 122–23.
8. Joan Hoff-Wilson, "Conclusion: Of Mice and Men," in Crapol, *Women and American Foreign Policy*, 182–83.
9. Ibid., 183.
10. Ibid., 184, Hoff's emphasis.
11. Ibid.
12. Anna Chennault, *The Education of Anna* (New York: Times Books, 1980), 11.
13. Ambassador Konsin C. Shah, interview by author, November 10, 1994, Taipei, Taiwan, Republic of China.
14. "A young refugee finds a HOME IN AMERICA," *Parade* (August 5, 1962): cover and 12–13.
15. Alice Wexler, "Emma Goldman and the Anxiety of Biography," in Sara Alpern, Joyce Antler, Elisabeth Israels Perry, and Ingrid Winther Scobie, eds., *The Challenge of Feminist Biography: Writing the Lives of Modern American Women* (Urbana: University of Illinois Press, 1992), 40.

Chronology

1893

Claire Lee Chennault born in Texas

1900

Boxer Rebellion in China

1910

Death of Chen Zi-yen (Anna Chen's paternal grandfather)

1911

Fall of Qing dynasty in China

1918

Marriage of Isabelle Liao to Sam Chen

1925

Death of Sun Yatsen
Death of Liao Chung-kai (Anna Chen's great-uncle)
Rise of Chiang Kai-shek to power in China
Anna Chen (née Chen Hsiengmei) born—June 23

1935

Sino-Japanese War begins
Sam Chen leaves his family to work in Chinese consular office in Mexico
Anna, her mother, and five sisters move to Hong Kong; Anna's first exposure to Chinese Communists along the way

1939

Isabelle Chen dies

1940

China Lobby organized

1941

American Volunteer Group ("Flying Tigers") formed—July
Japanese capture Hong Kong—December

1942

Anna Chen attends Lingnan University in Guilin, China

1943

Anna and sisters separated during refugee flight
Family reunited by men of U.S. Fourteenth Air Force led by General Claire Chennault

1944

Anna Chen begins work for China Central News Agency
She covers U.S. Fourteenth Air Force
Sam Chen brings daughters to United States; Anna refuses to go

1945

General Chennault leaves China—July
Anna Chen transferred to Shanghai
Chennault returns to China as civilian—December

1946

Chennault and Chen renew acquaintance

1947

CNRRA Air Transport (CAT) begins operations—January
Marriage of Chennault and Chen—December

1948

Chinese Communist advances force CAT to retreat and Anna to move to Canton

1949

Claire Anna Chennault born—February
General Chennault testifies before Senate Armed Services Committee—May
CIA funding to support CAT first approved
State Department issues"China White Paper"—August
Chinese Communist forces proclaim People's Republic of China (PRC)—October

1950

Cynthia Louise Chennault born—March
CAT moves headquarters to Taiwan
Korean War breaks out—June
CIA purchases CAT and starts supply operations for UN forces fighting in Korea

1951

Chennault family begins spending annual time in Monroe, Louisiana

1954

Chennaults give reception in Taiwan for Vice President Richard Nixon

1955

Anna Chennault addresses Dallas, Texas, Public Affairs Luncheon Club

1956

General Chennault diagnosed with lung cancer and has lung removed

1958

General Chennault dies—July

Anna and her daughters move to Washington, DC

Anna begins work at Georgetown University Chinese Section of Machine Translation Research

1960

Mrs. Chennault involved in Richard Nixon's presidential campaign

1961

General Claire Lee Chennault Foundation started

1962

President Kennedy supports Mrs. Chennault and Chinese Refugee Relief

She testifies before Senate committee on Chinese refugee issue

1963

Mrs. Chennault's first Voice of America broadcast to China

1964

Mrs. Chennault works in Barry Goldwater's presidential campaign

Nixon and Mrs. Chennault meet again in Taiwan

1967

Nixon asks Mrs. Chennault to be his "connection" to South Vietnam's leaders

She carries message from Nixon to South Vietnam's President Nguyen Van Thieu

1968

Peace talks to end Vietnam War begin in Paris
Mrs. Chennault becomes vice president of international affairs for Flying Tiger Lines (FTL)
Nixon meets with South Vietnam's Ambassador Bui Diem and Mrs. Chennault
She chairs Women for Nixon-Agnew Advisory Committee; member of Republican National Finance Committee
Johnson administration orders surveillance of Anna Chennault—October
North Vietnam agrees to expanded peace talks in exchange for bombing halt
Mrs. Chennault encourages South Vietnam's leaders' belief that Nixon will give them more support
South Vietnam's government refuses to join peace talks in Paris

1969

Story of Nixon-Anna Chennault-Thieu connection first breaks
She serves as special adviser to chairman of Nixon Inaugural Committee
All parties deny existence of Nixon's connection to South Vietnam's leaders
Mrs. Chennault negotiates Asian landing rights for FTL

1970

Mrs. Chennault appointed to United Nations Educational, Scientific, and Cultural Organization (UNESCO)

1971

Republic of China (Taiwan) expelled from United Nations
U.S. table tennis team competes in Beijing
National Security Adviser Henry Kissinger goes secretly to PRC

1972

Mrs. Chennault meets with President Nixon to discuss Taiwan's possible reaction to U.S. relations with PRC
Nixon becomes first American president to visit PRC
Mrs. Chennault and National Republican Heritage Groups Council involved in Nixon reelection
She chairs U.S. Citizens in Asia for Nixon

1973

Mrs. Chennault reelected co-chair of National Republican Heritage Groups Council

1975

Irregularities charged against Anna Chennault, Northrop, and FTL in government billing

She assists South Vietnamese leaders' entry into United States after fall of Saigon

1979

United States recognizes People's Republic of China

Mrs. Chennault and Thomas Corcoran prevent transfer of Taiwan's Twin Oaks embassy property in Washington, DC, to PRC

Passage of Taiwan Relations Act

1980

Mrs. Chennault invited to visit PRC by Deng Xiaoping

She is active in Ronald Reagan's election campaign

1981

Mrs. Chennault returns to mainland China for first time since 1949

Senator Ted Stevens and Mrs. Chennault meet with Deng Xiaoping and other Chinese leaders

She helps secure congressional approval for AWACS plane sales

She is appointed to President's Export Council (PEC)

1983

PEC first-ever trade mission, led by Mrs. Chennault, goes to Asia

1984

President Reagan's state visit to PRC

PEC trade mission led by Mrs. Chennault includes trip to China

1988

Taiwan legalizes investment in PRC

Mrs. Chennault abandons Republican Party political activities

1989

Federal Express purchases FTL

Chinese student protests take place in Tiananmen Square, Beijing

Mrs. Chennault organizes trade mission of Taiwanese businessmen to PRC

1990

Mrs. Chennault organizes second Taiwanese trade mission to PRC

1991–Present

Mrs. Chennault continues promoting U.S.-PRC relations through educational and business activities in addition to consulting with PRC and ROC leaders

Abbreviations

AFA	Fourteenth Air Force Association
AIT	American Institute of Taiwan
AVG	American Volunteer Group—Flying Tigers
CAF	Chinese Air Force
CAT	CNRRA Air Transport, later Civil Air Transport
CATC	Central Air Transport Corporation
CATF	China Air Task Force
CCNAA	Coordination Council for North American Affairs
CCP	Chinese Communist Party
CDS	China Defense Supplies
CIA	Central Intelligence Agency
CNA	China Central News Agency
CNAC	China National Aviation Corporation
CNRRA	Chinese National Relief and Rehabilitation Administration
COOM	Committee of One Million
CRR	Chinese Refugee Relief
DRV	Democratic Republic of Vietnam—North Vietnam
Fedex	Federal Express
FOFC	Friends of Free China
FTL	Flying Tiger Lines—air cargo shipping company
GMD	Guomindang—Nationalist Party/Government
GVN	Government of Vietnam—South Vietnam
NLF	National Liberation Front—South Vietnamese insurgents supported by DRV
NRHGC	National Republican Heritage (Nationalities) Groups Council
NSC	National Security Council
OPC	Office of Policy Coordination—part of CIA
PRC	People's Republic of China
ROC	Republic of China—Taiwan
TRA	Taiwan Relations Act of 1979
UNRRA	United Nations Relief and Rehabilitation Administration

1

The Importance of Character

Anna Chen Chennault (née Chen Hsiengmei) was born on June 23, 1925, in Beijing, China. Her parents, Chen Ying-yung (Sam) and Isabelle Liao, came from urban, upper middle-class families of merchants, scholars, and diplomats who embraced both Chinese traditions and modern Western ideas and practices. Thus, Anna's childhood drew on China's rich cultural legacy as well as its emerging political context and new social mores. In the Chen family, for example, Confucian familial relations were coupled with formal schooling for Anna and her sisters. The combination of the modern and the traditional gave Chen, and others of her generation, new opportunities for life and work unknown to those who preceded them, yet instilled in them a pride in their country's culture that also shaped their future.

Both of her parents' families participated in the tumultuous events that culminated in the Republican period of Chinese history. Her maternal and paternal grandfathers joined the large numbers of urban elites who formed the backbone of resistance to continued Qing dynasty rule in the early twentieth century. Anna Chen perceived changes in China through the prism of her class and family—a view colored by the elites' preference for nationalistic change in the direction of capitalist development, economic stability, and constitutional democratic reform. This view became her adolescent understanding of events in China during the late 1930s and early 1940s.

The Sino-Japanese War (1937–1945) was the formative event of Chen's youth. Her wartime experiences convulsed her life, accelerated her maturation, and built for her a tough, determined, and tenacious character. She came of age while China struggled to validate itself in the family of nations, institute a government, establish order, and fend off the long-entrenched Western powers and the Japanese. Changes she underwent in her first two decades of life mirrored those of the nation around her: slipping away from a sheltered comfortable position, going through difficult circumstances and times of serious hardship and obstinate survival, then finally rebuilding with expectant optimism. The woman who, as an adult, entered into American business and politics and Washington society, carving herself a place as an unofficial diplomat, was made by the culture, family, and world in which she matured.

The Setting

China's history has been shaped by the rise and fall of successive dynasties. Anna Chen grew up in the aftermath of the last imperial dynasty and the concomitant social and political changes that accompanied the downfall and overthrow of the Qing dynasty. Increasing numbers of foreign missionaries and expanding Western trade zones throughout the nineteenth century had accelerated the social and cultural changes already evolving within Chinese society. The consequences of the European, American, and Japanese presence compounded Chinese internal problems, particularly those of corruption and inefficiency. In a desperate attempt to quell domestic dissatisfaction over its inability to control foreign advantage and solve deepseated internal problems, the Qing government undertook modernization efforts. Qing policies were aided by foreign powers that recognized their own interests in perpetuating a stable, unified government able to assume national responsibilities and maintain order.

Qing success was, however, severely tested when Japan attempted to control Korea, China's important tributary. Chinese resistance to Japanese actions resulted in war from 1894 to 1895, in which China was quickly and decisively defeated by Japan. The resulting national disillusion with the inept and beaten government compounded the difficulties of the rapidly deteriorating Qing dynasty. The development of alternative forms of nationalism and antiforeign sentiment exploded at the century's end in the Boxer Rebellion (1898–1901) across North China. Directed at missionaries, their converts, and eventually the foreign legation quarter in Beijing, the rebellion led to the deaths of thousands of Chinese Christians and 250 foreigners. Though finally suppressed by foreign troops, the rebellion further undermined the Qing government when the victorious foreign powers inflicted punishment on the dynasty, including an immense indemnity payment.

These continued indignities hastened the rise of what noted historian John King Fairbank has called a "reformist urban elite," which desired "provincial development, local self-government, and constitutionalism" along with an end to foreign influence, and a place for China in the emerging power structure of Asia.[1] This elite was historically composed of landowners and officeholders; by the turn of the century it also included merchants, scholars, and professionals. The charismatic revolutionary leader Sun Yatsen (and others) promoted global initiatives among Chinese expatriates to fund and popularize the cause of republican nationalism. Chinese overseas merchants sought to support domestic elite and bourgeois elements who increased their calls for political change. The domestic elites, funded and ideologically supported by the expatriates, finally generated and consolidated enough power by 1911–12 to overthrow the by-then impotent Qing dynasty, thus commencing the Republican era of China's history. It was among these groups that Anna Chen's grandfathers were active.

The Family

The maternal side of Anna Chen's family had the greater impact on her life, both as a child and as an adult. Her maternal grandfather's family belonged to the Chinese Hakka minority, descendants of northern migrant farmers who moved south to escape Qing dynasty persecution in the eighteenth century. The Hakka were recognized in Chinese society as a very industrious, proud, and earnest people. Because of their diligence, by the mid-1800s, Hakka males were among the most literate of any group of laborers in the country, succeeding "disproportionately" in the imperial examination system, yet mostly being too poor to advance in the bureaucratic ranks.[2] Chen's grandfather Liao Fung-shu's family managed, however, to send him to be educated in France and England early in the twentieth century.

Liao Fung-shu returned from Europe to witness a China struggling to develop a cohesive government and throw off the last remnants of imperialist bonds. Its society faced new challenges as the age of representative government and newly opened commercial opportunities unfolded. Liao Fung-shu, as a scholar and poet, participated in the expansion of Chinese scholarship and bureaucratic mechanisms. He also joined the young Republic's diplomatic apparatus as it expanded to facilitate China's entry into the family of nations, serving as a customs inspector as well as being posted in Cuba, Panama, and Japan.

In contrast to the more intellectually elite background of her mother's family, Chen's father's family were long-standing members of the merchant class of Canton. Anna's paternal grandfather, Chen Zi-yen, achieved his greatest success at age thirty when he became president of the China Merchants' Steam Navigation Company. He subsequently lost his fortune as a result of a bad investment in the new Hong Kong streetcar company. According to Anna's recollections of the family's account of events, the turn-of-the-century provincial Chinese were xenophobic and superstitious of the foreign, mechanized contraptions and therefore refused to ride in the cars. The company failed. Unable to face the impending new year with its requisite gift giving and credit reckoning, Chen Zi-yen committed suicide on New Year's Eve of 1910. In the wake of his death, the eldest son, thirteen-year-old Sam (Ying-yung), was sent abroad by his mother to study as well as to shield him from the family's disgrace. Sam was educated in England and the United States while his mother maintained the extended family household in China.

Eight years after Chen Zi-yen's death, Liao Fung-shu, an old friend of Chen's who was then on diplomatic service in Havana, remembered a pledge they had made to each other years earlier. Both men were activists during the revolutionary period, "cutting off their . . . queues in defiance of the degrading [Qing] ordinance" requiring all males to wear the long braid of hair.[3] While still bachelors, Liao and Chen had vowed to tie their families together through the marriage of two of their future children. Both men went on to raise large families. In 1918, Liao's oldest daughter, Anna's mother Isabelle, was ordered to Cuba by her father. She left her studies in London to be an unwilling participant in a prearranged marriage to a stranger, Chen's son. Sam arrived in Havana to marry Isabelle Liao in December 1918. The newlyweds settled in the United States for three years, during which time Sam finished his schooling at Columbia University and Isabelle gave birth to their first daughter, Cynthia, in 1921.

By the early 1920s, when Sam and Isabelle Chen returned to China, the nation had fallen into political chaos—a period of factional infighting and war-lordism. Sun Yatsen, who had mobilized men like Anna's grandfathers, Liao Fung-shu and Chen Zi-yen, in the cause of revolution and had aided the overthrow of the Qing dynasty was, by the 1920s, trying to hold together the fractious elements of the Republican revolution. When Sun died in 1925, growing division among several Chinese leaders already existed. They struggled over governmental structure. Political splits occurred along numerous lines: within Sun's own party (the Guomindang, or GMD), between it and the Chinese Communists, and with the various warlords who sought to protect their own fiefdoms.

Anna's maternal family divided over the path to China's future. Her grandfather, Liao Fung-shu, supported the overthrow of the Qing dynasty in 1911–12. Following Sun Yatsen's death, numerous factions within the GMD struggled for party domination. Liao Fung-shu supported the military leader, Chiang Kai-shek, who consolidated the more conservative GMD elements. Liao Fung-shu's brother, Liao Chung-kai, was part of the overseas Chinese community that supplied funding, leaders, and participants to the Republican revolution. Liao Chung-kai was a close colleague of Sun Yatsen and head of the GMD's left wing. He orchestrated the GMD-Communist alliance in 1924 and played a key role in the effort to establish a cohesive government in China. Considered by some to be Sun's heir apparent, Liao Chung-kai was assassinated in August 1925, about six months after Sun's death, most likely by rightwing GMD elements.

At the time of Liao Chung-kai's death, both Liao brothers supported different wings of the same party. But as the elements of the GMD split apart in the ensuing struggle for party leadership, the Liaos and innumerable other families were divided by their ideological differences. In the case of the Liao family, Chung-kai's wife and children maintained their allegiance to the leftist elements within the GMD and eventually joined the Chinese Communist Party (CCP) when it split from the GMD in the late 1920s. Anna's parents and her grandfather, Liao Fung-shu, however, remained tied to the GMD, which governed the country until 1949. The dual allegiances of her extended family members shaped Chen's activities after World War II and influenced her outlook on China thereafter.

Double Fifth in the Year of the Ox

Anna's father, Sam Chen, who had departed China in the wake of his father's suicide, remained away from home for a total of ten years studying at Oxford and Columbia Universities. When he returned with his wife and daughter around 1921, he taught law at

Beijing National University and became chief editor of the *New China Morning Post*, an English-language newspaper. In a nod to the political turmoil at the time, Anna's autobiography records the historic significance of her birth year, 1925, because it coincided with "the year of Sun Yatsen's death and Chiang Kai-shek's rise to power." She pointed out that, according to Chinese astrology, her birth in the Year of the Ox signified "a life of hard effort." In addition, she emphasized that her arrival occurred on the fifth day of the fifth moon of the Chinese calendar—the Double Fifth—which coincided with the annual Dragon Boat Festival. This date portended the destiny of a writer, a third-grade teacher later told her, for the festival honored a poet. Chen took to heart both of these prophetic signs. Throughout her life she defined herself as a writer above all the other occupations to which she would lay claim.

Anna Chen spent her earliest years living with her parents in the household of her maternal grandparents. Their antiques-filled home in an exclusive residential area of Beijing provided warm childhood memories for Anna, many of which centered on her grandfather. They shared a bond that Chen remembered well: "Like many another man of money and influence, he was at times a little lonely. I like to feel that in my innocent childish way I was able to bring him the kind of comfort and companionship of one who was not old enough to ask too many questions; someone who loved him in the unquestioning, adoring way of a little girl."[4]

Their attachment illustrated relationships based on customs of Confucian filial piety. These customs dictated familial bonds across generations and still hold sway in China at some level today. Unlike a child's relations with her parents, which were more formal, aloof, and constrained, Anna and Liao exemplified the relations between grandchildren and grandparents. Sam Chen personified the distant father common among the elite and prescribed by Confucian filiality. Anna's "intimacy" with him was "limited to a polite question-and-answer exchange at the dinner table."[5] She later wrote that on his return from studying abroad, her father was "a severe young man . . . bookish, withdrawn, and melancholy."[6] The bond she shared with her grandfather Liao gave her the "father figure" she needed together with positive emotional support. Her affinity for her grandfather represented her strongest attachment to a male family member.

In the retelling of her life, it is clear that she resented the diminished value of daughters in Chinese society. Anna was the second of what would be six daughters, a fate "constituting misfortune bordering on tragedy" for her family, as she described it. Her family's shame at the birth of a second daughter was recounted to her: "Your Grandmother Chen even suggested to your father that he take a concubine," to increase the possibilities of having a son.[7] Anna recalled that the role of the first daughter was to be obedient, but that the second daughter was always seen as less important in Chinese families. Her resentment and determination to be more than "just a second daughter" was a driving factor in her reach for success.

As a child, Anna enjoyed the comforts of an elite lifestyle in Beijing. She was surrounded by a large household of servants and family and lived with a profusion of books, social events, and holidays. Her autobiography tells of many celebrations from the wealth of cultural occasions that fill the Chinese calendar. Anna and her older sister Cynthia often spied on the frequent parties that spun by below the marble staircase where they hid to watch the guests. Elegantly dressed men and women arrived in carriages, cars, rickshas, or sedan chairs, ate delicious multicourse meals, and danced beneath dazzling crystal chandeliers.

Despite the many Western influences, Anna grew up in a traditional style that emphasized China's familial, cultural, and social heritage. Because Sam believed that his own education and maturation experiences outside of the country were disadvantageous to him when he returned, he stressed Chinese traditions in their household so that his daughters would be comfortable in their homeland. Anna's schooling included the Chinese classics in addition to modern subjects. The existence of a public school where she could obtain an education that included an array of courses was a direct legacy of the social changes that occurred in the Republican era. Despite hard work, she fondly remembered the joys of childhood, particularly her early school years and the third-grade teacher who put her on the path to becoming a writer.

Teacher Li Chieh, a graduate student from Beijing University, taught Anna's composition class. It was he who told her the legend of the Dragon Boat Festival that coincided with her birthday. She remembered him as "an energetic, overworked man . . . with ink brush eyebrows."[8] He prodded young Chen to improve her skills by telling her that with hard work she could become a good writer. He tutored her and a few select students each week in writing and in Chinese literature. They went for short excursions beyond the city of Beijing, which inspired the students to compose short verses. One such trip resulted in Chen's first published work. Teacher Li also encouraged her continued consumption of both Western and Chinese literature and movies. She recalled that by age twelve she had decided to be an author. Her life then changed dramatically, and the focus of a chosen direction helped guide her in the confusing years ahead.

The War

In 1937 the Sino-Japanese conflict disrupted the opulent life of twelve-year-old Chen, as it did the lives of most urban elite Chinese. The movement of Japanese invaders, from their initial incursion into Manchuria in 1931 to their advances to the Yellow and Yangzi Rivers by 1938 and beyond, put much of the nation on the run, starting a period of forced migration. The Nationalist government, headed since 1927 by Chiang Kai-shek, retreated from Nanjing to Wuhan, then finally to Chongqing (Chungking), where it held out until the war's end. Together with intellectuals and administrators, industries and whole colleges and universities joined the mass exodus, all trying to stay ahead of the Japanese invaders. The CCP, estranged from its former Nationalist partners in the GMD, completed in 1934–35 a retreat of its own —a six-thousand-mile trek across southwest and central China from Jiangxi to Shaanxi known as "The Long March."

As the danger of war with Japan increased in 1935, Anna's father chose to accept a position in the Foreign Ministry and was sent to the Chinese consular office in Mexicali, Mexico. Rather than take his large family along on his modest civil servant's salary, he sent his wife and six daughters to the relative safety of Hong Kong. There they could be comforted by relatives and servants and his daughters could continue to receive the Chinese education he deemed so important.

With this disruption in her family, Anna recalled perceiving a distance—both personal and geographic—developing between her parents. Sam and Isabelle were of very different temperaments, and their arranged marriage had not taken into consideration who they were or what they wanted in life. Her mother was a fun-loving socialite, her father a serious scholar/bureaucrat. Anna, too, grew apart from him. Her childlike fathoming of her father living half a world away created a gulf between them, with lasting repercussions.

Anna's trip with her mother and sisters to Hong Kong introduced her to two female relatives who made divergent but lasting impressions upon her. En route they stopped in Canton, where Anna met her paternal grandmother Chen for the first time. She lived in a rambling, labyrinthine dwelling like that of Grandfather Liao. The month-long visit created for the young Anna wonderful memories of another grand mansion of gates and courtyards. She also remembered her grandmother's traditionalism and piety that was demonstrated by worship at her private courtyard Buddhist shrine. Grandmother Chen had married at a time when centuries-old Confucian traditions still held sway—she was from the generation that witnessed the end of bound feet and concubines. Although Chinese culture no longer encouraged a widow to commit suicide, Grandmother Chen chose to follow other ancient mores that dictated she could never remarry following the death of her husband. Anna described her grandmother as being "full of ancient anecdotes and family lore . . . outspoken, stubborn, fanciful, warm, and generous," someone who earned a young girl's respect and adoration.[9]

Grandmother Chen stood in contrast to her great aunt, Ho Hsiang-ning, the wife of her grandfather's assassinated brother Liao Chung-kai, whom Anna first encountered upon the family's arrival in Hong Kong. Tradition and religion seemed absent from Ho's life, but she shared a certain strength with Grandmother Chen. Following her husband's assassination, Ho forced the GMD government to investigate the crime and bring the guilty parties to justice. The cursory inquiry was inconclusive and did little except settle some internal party disputes. GMD officials failed to prosecute the culprits. Unsatisfied, Ho subsequently thrust forward her son, Liao Chengzhi, for appointment to various GMD party positions. In this she was also disappointed. By 1938, when Anna, her mother, and sisters reached Hong Kong, Ho's family members were actively working as members of the CCP. After repeated frustrations with the GMD and its leader, Chiang Kai-shek, they had joined the CCP, believing that it most closely represented the ideals of Liao Chung-kai and Sun Yatsen.

This was Anna's earliest contact with communism. She recalled the mysterious comings and goings of her cousin Liao Chengzhi, in particular, during family dinners. Only years later, when Chen lived again in Grandfather Liao's home, did she learn what the intrigue had been about. Liao Chengzhi had participated in The Long March, but after the Sino-Japanese War began, he returned to Hong Kong to act as an agent and official of the CCP. He often traveled to the GMD's wartime capital in Chongqing to carry out CCP guerrilla operations. He was repeatedly detained by the GMD for his "underground activities" and was just as habitually released by authorities "in deference to his father."[10] He was finally captured by the GMD in 1942 and held until 1946. Chen's fleeting dinners in Hong Kong with her cousin Liao would not be her last contacts with him.

Ho was a severe woman who, Chen remembered, "lectured us on any visible signs of vanity or frivolity. . . . Everything that detracted from the cold, harsh purpose of Communism as she saw it was a felony." After the 1949 revolution, Ho became a distinguished leader in the Communist Party, but in the mid-1930s Chen saw only an angry woman who rejected her family's Catholic religion, who seemed to enjoy looking "frumpish," and who withheld the children's traditional New Year's money envelopes, denouncing them as a capitalist custom.[11] This early negative impression of Communists on the thirteen-year-old Anna was not grounded in any understanding of substantive issues. Later, her early views combined with those of others, especially Americans such as General Claire Chennault, in furthering her anticommunism.

Once established in Hong Kong, Anna's mother, Isabelle, transferred her active social life to a new bustling scene, but she still offered guidance and wisdom to her daughters in their father's absence. Chen later recalled her mother's belief that "a woman should be feminine and ladylike at all times." Also, Isabelle once told her that "it was not where one came from, or how far one came that counted—it was the direction that one took and whether one ever found the right road in life."[12] These insights seemed obscure to her at the time, but Isabelle's advice became a part of Anna's world view and character. Anna's childhood was not characterized by the hothouse glamour of her mother's upbringing; Isabelle had been surrounded by luxury, had been pampered by servants, had traveled to Europe for schooling and vacations, and "glowed with the refinements of privilege."[13] Even though Anna's childhood was limited to more moderate comforts, Isabelle's social circles were an instructive part of her daughter's youth. Anna followed her mother's advice and cultivated aristocratic feminine traits. As an adult, she chose her own highly feminine style—appearing among businessmen, fashion models, politicians, or military brass herself dressed in brightly colored skirts, dresses, and jackets (sometimes of her own design), while rejecting the mannish tailored suits that became the uniform of modern businesswomen.

Isabelle, Grandmother Chen, and Ho Hsiang-ning served as differing, but similarly strong, female role models for Anna. In addition, the legacy of female figures in Chinese literature and history showed her a combination of women's roles from the ancient matrilineal society to women writers to empress dowagers and even Empress Wu Chao, who led her own dynasty in 690–705. Young Chen soon decided that certain past roles of Chinese women—whose lives were often not their own—were not for her. Amid the myriad political and cultural changes occurring in her country as she matured, Chen learned that she could choose her own course, her own husband, and make of her own life what she wanted.

Her years in Hong Kong in the late 1930s revolved around home and school as Anna pursued dreams of becoming a writer. The war raging in distant parts of China had little direct effect on her as she studied, edited her school's newspaper, and learned the skills of a news reporter. Her decision to make journalism her career was followed by years of study with that goal in mind.

Her home life was relatively quiet until one morning in 1938, when she discovered her mother packing for a short stay in the hospital for tests. For six months, Anna visited her mother at the hospital daily and carried the burden of Isabelle's illness. With her elder sister Cynthia away at nursing school, Anna was the oldest child at home. Her four younger sisters could not understand the gravity of the situation or help shoulder the burden. It was a long time before the doctors diagnosed the illness as cancer. While Chen did not understand the extent of this disease, she did understand her anger, especially at her father for his refusal to return home during her mother's illness and decline.

After her mother's death, Chen became the head of the household, which compelled the fourteen-year-old to grow up fast as she managed the family finances and served as both mother and father to her younger siblings. The five girls survived on the monthly stipend that Sam Chen provided, but after a year the effort was too much. Chen received permission from her father for all of them to board at St. Paul's, the French Catholic convent school they were attending. Youthful innocence faded rapidly in the face of such duty, and Chen's leap into adult responsibility brought her a certain maturity. It also robbed her of a mother who would meet her adolescent needs—caretaking, security, and guidance. Long gone were carefree days playing in the garden courtyards and luxurious rooms of Grandfather Liao's home in Beijing.

By the time of Japan's December 7, 1941, attack on Pearl Harbor, Chen was completing her last years of high school. The news of the attack reached St. Paul's a day later when Japanese bombs began raining on Hong Kong. The bombing lasted until the British surrendered on Christmas Day, 1941. During those weeks, Anna and her sisters joined the other boarders and the nuns in the daily tedium of huddling in the dank basement shelter and eating meager rations in order to survive. School resumed after the Japanese captured the city, but St. Paul's survived on little food, with no heat or water for many months afterward.

In 1942, Chen was accepted at Lingnan University of Hong Kong, but, like most Chinese universities, Lingnan had moved inland away from the Japanese invasion. It was still the closest university—four hundred miles from Hong Kong near Guilin (Kweilin). The decision was made to move all the girls to Guilin. The Chen sisters—Cynthia, Anna, Connie, Sylvia, Theresa, and Loretta—departed Hong Kong, accompanied by friends, all joining the multitudes escaping to "free" or unoccupied China.

The journey to Guilin that Anna and her sisters thought would take two or three weeks instead took two arduous months. They traveled mostly by foot along bomb-cratered roads choked with refugees fleeing other areas occupied by the Japanese. Animals and humans trudged along together, all carrying heavy loads, pushing or pulling their worldly possessions as they went. In the midst of their journey, Anna became ill with dysentery, which halted the group's advance for a week until an acupuncturist finally worked what seemed like a miracle cure and restored her health.

Her experiences as a refugee fleeing from the Japanese were repeated by millions of Chinese during the war. She and her sisters combined some decent meals with those of weevil-ridden rice, contaminated water, and rotten vegetables. They often paid for a place to sleep inside a home or inn, cramped and dirty as it may have been. Their life, while unpleasant, was less difficult than that of a majority of Chinese uprooted in those years.

Anna's group finally reached the foothills of Guilin, which meant that they were nearing their destination's foggy, cool, mountainous setting. The sisters waited there for several weeks for money to arrive from their father. The respite allowed them their first real relaxation since the Japanese bombings of Hong Kong, almost eight months earlier. Members of the group soon went their separate ways, and Anna's life resumed some semblance of normalcy. Cynthia had finished nursing school and was recruited for a job with the U.S. Fourteenth Air Force before their Hong Kong departure, so she left for her assignment in Kunming. Connie, Sylvia, and Theresa settled in a boarding school near Guilin. Anna, keeping the youngest sibling, Loretta, with her, moved again to catch up with Lingnan University, which had relocated once more to avoid the Japanese. Anna's energy became focused on her university studies.

Her years at Lingnan University were anything but quiet as the school evacuated from village to village, dodging bombs while students lived and studied with no running water or electricity. The deprivations that she endured—lack of books, paper, and writing tools, minimal food supplies, frequent disease, and generally harsh living conditions—were shared by students all across "free" China. Exposure to these conditions, as well as the journeys that most of them were forced to make to get to wartime campuses, was more hardship than many of the Chinese students had ever experienced before. A usually privileged group, college students during the war underwent difficulties that were the norm for scores of less fortunate Chinese.

Many students offset their college expenses by working in surrounding communities. In Chen's case, she taught primary school off and on during her college years. The work gave her experience, extra money, and confidence that she could survive on her own if necessary. She was not exempt from an important feature of wartime study: heightened feelings of national loyalty. In classes, subjects such as classical Chinese literature, with its glimpses of life's diversities, were coupled with history and current events, which tied her to the global struggle against fascism and made her feel purposeful. She again edited her school paper. She published her first short story and had two job offers as a writer while still in college.

In the spring of 1943 continued Japanese advances and the university's movement required Chen to uproot her sisters and flee farther inland to Guiyang (Kweiyang). They traveled by truck and later transferred to a train packed with refugees. The train would stop along the track for undetermined amounts of time, starting up unannounced and leaving those stranded on the ground to catch up with their companions and families who were powerless to slow the train or help them aboard. Led by Anna, the Chen sisters stuck together and hoped to find enough nourishment to sustain themselves. They were relatively lucky in their travels and suffered only the usual refugees' distresses of hunger, exhaustion, and minor illnesses.

As the Chen sisters neared their destination in Guiyang, Japanese troops moved to take over the train. In the crowd's rush to escape from the car, Anna was pushed forward onto the platform and separated from her sisters, who remained trapped inside. As she described it, "Now I was one of the desperate masses running alongside the moving train, yelling and banging uselessly on its sides and falling back at last to wail and curse as it sped away—carrying my sisters with it."[14] Strangers comforted Chen, who was in despair over how to proceed. Some joined her temporarily in a village-to-village search in the hope that the girls would get off the train to wait for her.

Anna's efforts to find her sisters went on for a week until one day a group of American soldiers stopped to ask her if she needed help. She told them her story and added that Cynthia worked for the U.S. Fourteenth Air Force. Unexpectedly, the soldiers, who were members of the Fourteenth, drove her to Guiyang and sent a message to Cynthia in Kunming. Cynthia wired their father, still in the United States, about their predicament. He, in turn, wired General Claire Lee Chennault, the commander of the Fourteenth Air Force whom Sam Chen had met in San Francisco, to see if he could assist in the search. Soon, American soldiers bearing photographs searched trains between Guiyang and Kunming until they found four young girls huddled in a boxcar and thought one of them looked like Cynthia. They were right. The soldiers reunited Connie, Sylvia, Theresa, and Loretta with Anna and Cynthia in Kunming and took them to meet General Chennault, whose men were responsible for bringing them together. This was Anna's first encounter with the man who would play a large role in her life.

In the months that followed, Chen combined college classes, teaching, and, by 1944, a part-time job with the China Central News Agency (CNA). Women news reporters were not unheard of at this time in the GMD wartime capital of Chongqing, but most of them worked for the city's thirteen daily newspapers. CNA was the government's news bureau and wire service headquarters, and women reporters there were uncommon. A Chen family friend, Kao Chih-shih, referred Anna to the Chongqing bureau chief for the job. The day before her interview, Kao told her that CNA's "policy was to hire only men as correspondents," even though he was quite confident of her abilities.[15] She interviewed for the CNA job anyway, because she sought a position more prestigious than those with the local publications that had already approached her. The bureau chief, impressed with her writing, hired her on a trial basis.

She started as a junior assistant editor and learned the trade working the night shift while continuing her studies during the day. Often, the university moved back and forth between villages that were captured and retaken by the warring Japanese and Chinese forces. She frequently carried out her studies on a special assignment or an independent study basis since facilities for classroom work were at a premium, or even nonexistent. Once their classroom building was bombed by the Japanese while the students were in their dormitories. This upheaval was typical of a college education in China during wartime. Chen, like many other students, persevered because of her stubborn nature and determination. In the end, her journalism degree was awarded in 1945 by Lingnan University through the mail since the war precluded any possibility of graduation ceremonies.

Anna Chen, circa mid-1940s

On the job, she advanced to cultural and educational assignments and finally, after several months, was asked to cover the U.S. Fourteenth Air Force in Kunming partly due to her command of the English language. She found lodging in Kunming in 1944 with a local businessman in exchange for tutoring his sons. Her confidence was bolstered anew by being able to support herself. The difficulties that she survived toughened her, made her hungry for personal success, and gave her the skills that never could have come from a comfortable Beijing upbringing.

As the new CNA correspondent in 1944, Chen again encountered General Chennault. Her first press conference at company headquarters was followed by an invitation to join the General and his officers for afternoon tea. Chennault's dynamism and personal charm awed the nineteen-year-old, and they became casually acquainted during his remaining months in China. Chen gained great respect for the man more than thirty years her senior whom many in southern China saw as a savior of their nation in the struggle against the Japanese.

In the meantime, Sam Chen decided that his daughters should join him in the safety of the United States where he was living with his new wife. Cynthia, who had received some schooling in America, welcomed the chance to return there and resume a "normal" life. The younger sisters were excited by the prospect of coming to the States, but Anna had no desire to leave her homeland. During her wartime years in school, she had developed a strong, deep feeling of patriotism that kept her from any thoughts of abandoning China at such a critical juncture. In her as yet short life, she knew only of the need to repel the invaders and free China from foreign oppression. Issues of domestic rule would not attract her attention until after the war. As countless others around her yearned for an opportunity to escape to the relative calm of America, Anna believed her place was to remain and contribute to the war effort in her own way.

She was still angry and resentful that her father had let his wife die alone and then remarried only a year later. Her streak of independence and rebellion was piqued by her father's efforts at coercion. Sam Chen threatened to cut off his daughter's funds if she stayed in China. This deepened Anna's determination to stay and overcome the low expectations that Chinese culture prescribed for a second daughter. Relieved of caretaking responsibilities for her siblings, she knew she could survive on her own. In a conversation with General Chennault, he supported her decision to stay. This green light from someone whom she respected more than her father helped to make up her mind. Her sisters left China later in 1944 after making the complicated arrangements to go over the

Hump into India.[16] From there, they connected by train to a ship that took them across the Pacific to meet Sam and their stepmother Bessie in San Francisco. Anna did not see any of them for another three years.

This decision was bold for a young Chinese woman, but one that exemplified Chen's already determined character. The adversities she encountered, while not exceptional for the time, nonetheless represented hardship and created in her the appetite to "have enough money to live comfortably, [and] never budget again."[17] These early life events influenced her ideology, defined her motives, and foreshadowed her operating style.

Chen eventually made a place for herself in the informal diplomatic arena—a world and system different from, but not unknown to, that of her father and grandfather. Her ambition enabled her to gain the positions she wanted in later years, but the nuances and techniques acquired from her mother and grandfather eased her way into a domain that turned out to suit her well. Social graces, tact, determination, perseverance, and boldness all combined to create a woman who excelled in the complicated milieu of American politics and international relations. Anna already knew the value of having important friends; building on that knowledge naturally followed.

Her experiences as a refugee shaped her evolving attitudes about the status of women in China. Her recollections of the trip frequently included the fates of mothers and daughters along the way. She recounted episodes in which the loss of a female family member elicited not sadness but, instead, a man's relief that it was not a son who was lost. These narratives revealed her dissatisfaction with the predestined role that seemed to await her as an adult. Her own developing ideology included a personal drive to be strong and independent in order to avoid succumbing to the traditional fate that Chinese society prescribed for women.

Chen's ideology, which began solidifying as World War II ended, was shaped by her experiences until that time and reflected the conflicted nature of contemporary China. Changing postwar events and new people in her life also exercised great influence. At war's end, however, her strongest belief was that she would defy the female traditions of the country's past. While she took any advantage she could from being a woman, whether it meant a better place to sit or accepting an offer of a ride, she did not allow gender to stand in her way. Society and politics were changing around her, and she used those changes to advance herself in the world.

Notes

1. John King Fairbank, *China: A New History* (Cambridge, MA: The Belknap Press of Harvard University Press, 1992), 236.

2. Jack Gray, *Rebellions and Revolutions: China from the 1800s to the 1980s* (New York: Oxford University Press, 1990), 57.

3. Chennault, *Education of Anna*, 9.

4. Anna Chennault, *A Thousand Springs: The Biography of a Marriage* (New York: Paul S. Eriksson, 1962), 21–22.

5. Chennault, *Education of Anna*, 30.

6. Ibid., 9.

7. Ibid., 3.

8. Ibid., 26.

9. Ibid., 8–9.

10. Ibid., 33.

11. Ibid., 34.

12. Chennault, *A Thousand Springs*, 24.

13. Chennault, *Education of Anna*, 10.

14. Ibid., 83.

15. Ibid., 87.

16. "The Hump" was the name for the final leg of the route for all supplies coming into China. Because of Japanese occupation of all other routes, everything needed for China's war effort came in by air from India. Material arrived in India, usually by ocean passage, then was transshipped by both wide- and narrow-gauge railroads into the Assam Valley of India. From there it was flown over "the hump" of treacherous mountains into China.

17. Chennault, *Education of Anna*, 40.

2

A Model of Influence

In December 1947, Anna Chen married General Claire Lee Chennault. They lived and worked together until his death in 1958. Anna then went on to establish a career and reputation of her own beyond that of just the widow of a famous American war hero. Life with the General helped her propel herself from the relative obscurity of a China Central News Agency (CNA) pool reporter to a position within the circles of U.S. and Asian power. He provided her with an education in politics, business, and influence that expanded her existing skills when she reentered the workforce after a dozen years as primarily a wife and mother. The brief period that she spent with Chennault was significant not just for her evolving professional and personal character, but it was also when she became involved in matters of American foreign policy.

When Chen married the well-known Chennault, she instantly affiliated herself with the ideology and causes that he represented. His military career during the war and his activities as a postwar businessman tied him to certain segments of American and Asian leadership. Chen's marriage to him brought her to the attention of not only the Nationalist Government of the Republic of China (ROC—on mainland China until 1949, on Taiwan thereafter) and other Asian nations, but also made her visible to American businessmen, government officials, military leaders, and lobbyists concerned with U.S.-Asian foreign policy and relations. This wide range of personal contacts helped her, after General Chennault's death, to launch her own career in America, but it was through her own determination that she made a place for herself.

The diplomatic stage upon which Chen and Chennault appeared changed dramatically in the 1940s and

1950s. Washington's relationship with mainland China went from one of wartime alliance to diplomatic hostility and finally armed conflict during the Korean War. During this period a strong informal diplomatic network, widely known as the China Lobby, strenuously advocated continuing American support for the "free" or non-Communist China eventually established by the GMD on Taiwan. Within this network, Chen was initiated into American politics and diplomacy.

Independence

Before she married General Chennault, Anna Chen covered the end of the war and its aftermath. She celebrated V-J Day on August 10, 1945, in Kunming, but she was sad because the General, whose fight for China brought him great respect in the eyes of many, was not there to participate in the victory over the Japanese. He had resigned from the Army Air Corps on July 8. Her connections through her coverage of the U.S. Fourteenth Air Force paid their first dividends immediately after the war's end. She was offered a promotion and transfer from Kunming to CNA's Shanghai office if she could get there—not a simple task at the time. She secured a seat on an American military flight out of Kunming thanks to friends in the Fourteenth. She was glad to get the assignment, which provided the added bonus of allowing her to live once again with Grandfather and Grandmother Liao, who, by 1945, resided in Shanghai.

Chen saw this new start as an escape from deprivation. She made a commitment to herself "never [to] be poor again," promising herself hard work but also the luxuries that would be her reward: "soft comfortable beds with fresh linen [and] the luxury of being driven from place to place instead of . . . walk[ing]."[1] This promise was a motivating factor that propelled Anna's life forward. The war's end was a transformative time for her. She set her sights on a certain standard of success and resolutely prepared to do whatever was necessary to reach her goal.

Her days at CNA were hard and long. The friendship and guidance of an older associate helped her adjust to the male world in which they struggled together. Chen credited this friend with showing her "that the impossible is there to be challenged" through the example of success against great odds.[2] Already, she had demonstrated steely determination by her refusal to live with her father in the United States, yet her memory of this friendship shows how important it was to her still-developing character. Anna applied herself to her work, including a major assignment—that of covering the Shanghai war crimes trials. In that capacity, she was remembered by an American member of the War Crimes Commission as part of the tenacious "press pack" that covered the events. As a "very glib, good talker" among the group, she "tagged along" with the reporters following the commissioners and the trial story. The press corps, which was three-quarters Chinese, included about fifty percent women among the Chinese reporters,[3] an indication of the new career opportunities for modern, educated Chinese women.

Chen's duties also placed her in the group of reporters who met General Claire Chennault's plane when it arrived at Kiangwan Airport shortly after Christmas 1945, an event covered in the *New York Times*. Upon seeing his friend Chen from the old days, Chennault renewed their acquaintance. He was divorced when he returned to China and started seeing Chen and other women socially. Chennault, sharing a house with business associate Whiting Willauer and his wife, settled into a busy work and social routine. His housemates knew that he wanted to marry again and hoped he would find a woman to take care of him.

General Chennault and Anna, circa 1950

During the months she dated Chennault, Anna Chen met his friends and associates. To some of them, she gave the positive impression of a dynamic, intelligent, and determined woman. Others saw her vibrance as aggressive and considered it only the self-serving tactic of a social climber, merely interested in the General because of his fame. Decades later, feelings of either great respect or resentment toward Anna are obvious in people's recollections, whether recent or back to the postwar years in China. Yet, whatever his friends' impressions of her, Anna and Chennault were attracted to each other despite the thirty-two-year difference in their ages.

Chen's autobiography described an early proposal of marriage and a long courtship while she considered her answer. Her account of their relationship was heavily romanticized at the insistence of her editors to improve the love story for publication. Given Chennault's apparent desire to be married and his fame within China, he was a popular man. He is said to have proposed to five different women in the spring of 1947. Only Anna Chen said yes. Chen told a story, perhaps apocryphal, that explained part of her attraction for him. She was in the hospital with a bleeding ulcer. Unlike a prominent Chinese banker who had also proposed marriage and who sent her armfuls of flowers during her convalescence, Chennault visited daily, no matter what his busy schedule. The banker, also significantly older than Chen, did not have what she called the "personal touch, of which the General was master."[4] This, she said, was a key factor in her decision to marry Chennault.

The attraction between Chen and Chennault is not hard to understand when one considers their personalities, needs, and goals. Possibly she saw him as a strong, protective father figure. Grandfather Liao partially filled this gap, but only intermittently. Chennault's wisdom and experience easily cast him in this role for Chen, although it was, perhaps, an unconscious part of her interest in him. More obviously, Chennault's war efforts, combined with his love for China and its people, made him heroic to her. His connections to those in power, both in China and America, could not have been lost on Chen. He was a man who went after what he wanted, letting nothing stand in his way—a man as determined as she. As they courted, away from war and the battlefield, she encountered his renowned charisma. He had enough confidence for them both—not that she lacked any, but when the question of marriage to an American arose, she found herself unsure. His determination that their marriage would succeed reassured her.

Chennault's affection for Anna is less easily explained, but the allure of a young, attractive woman might have been a factor. If, indeed, he asked several other women to marry him around the time he proposed to Chen, it is impossible to be certain of his reasons for settling in with Anna, given the absence of any personal statements by Chennault on the subject. Her insight into China was an asset, so his recognition of her abilities would have been important to him. Biographer Martha Byrd noted Chennault's desire for a wife who would share his life experiences by his side, be a partner. The fact that Anna was articulate and fluent in English could only have been another positive factor in her favor. As Byrd put it, "Chennault became more and more receptive to [her] unabashed admiration."[5] Even someone who knew them both and admittedly did not like her, allowed that she was a good wife who made Chennault very happy and comfortable. If theirs was not necessarily a fiery passion, it clearly seemed to be a marriage born of respect, admiration, and shared goals.

The wedding was small, held in the General's home in Shanghai on December 21, 1947, with family and a few friends. Anna's father, Sam Chen, and his second wife were visiting from America when the wedding was announced and stayed for the event. The short time between the announcement and wedding made possible a quiet intimate affair, for given the General's celebrity, a friend remarked, "he would have had to ask everyone in China if he had any other kind of wedding." It was obvious to their friends that "Anna [was] genuinely in love with him as he [was] with her."[6]

Their marriage started off with the best wishes of loved ones despite any hesitations there might have been about Chen being Chinese and Chennault American or about the age difference (twenty-two and fifty-four, respectively). These factors might have lowered their chances, but instead, their compatibility was enhanced by the couple's similarities in vision, drive, and perhaps a certain recognition on their part that each advanced his or her own goals through union with the other.

The General and China

Born in 1893, Chennault spent much of his childhood alone, wandering, hunting, and fishing in the woods surrounding the family farm in northeast Louisiana.[7] His father supported the family by growing cotton.

Young Claire developed an early fascination with aviation while still in college after seeing a biplane at the 1910 Louisiana State Fair. He later enlisted in the U.S. Army and emerged from officers' training school as a first lieutenant to work as an infantry trainer in 1917 during World War I. Chennault gained flight experience haphazardly at his various posts, and finally received his commission in the Army Air Corps in 1920. He developed and promoted theories of air combat tactics that conflicted with the beliefs of a military hierarchy wedded to the technologically advanced bomber planes and the new doctrines of bomber invincibility. He published numerous articles and, finally, *The Role of Defensive Pursuit* in 1933, which outlined his theory that multiple fighter planes could isolate and shoot down individual enemy planes, whether bombers or fighters. Chennault's clashes with his superiors over tactics became legendary in the Air Corps. Eventually, years of rejection of his theories and health problems led to his retirement at the rank of captain in 1937.

In late 1935, Chennault was approached by international businessman William D. Pawley and members of China's Commission on Aeronautical Affairs to assist in building the Chinese Air Force (CAF). Chennault eventually accepted a two-year renewable contract with the Beijing government and, upon his formal retirement from the Army Air Corps in early 1937, began his relationship with China. When the Japanese attack at the Marco Polo Bridge and occupation of Beijing in July 1937 marked the beginning of full-scale Sino-Japanese war, Chennault volunteered to continue assisting the Chinese government's inadequate air force. Over the next two years he applied his training and tactical skills to the CAF to fight the Japanese as their fighter planes overwhelmed China's cities, towns, and air defenses. As civilian adviser to the Commission on Aeronautical Affairs, he developed a close and long-lasting relationship with Generalissimo and Madame Chiang Kai-shek. This connection to the GMD leader that had begun in wartime was passed on to Anna Chen years later through marriage. Chennault's herculean efforts helped diminish the terror that Japan wreaked on China's people from the air. It also endeared the General to the many Chinese with whom he worked. Conversely, he developed great respect for the defensive efforts mustered by both the military and civilians who accepted the unfamiliar methods of a foreigner in an effort to save their country from the invading Japanese.

While Chennault labored in China, American policymakers initiated only a limited response to Japan's aggression. Loans, sales of supplies, rhetoric, and eventually Lend-Lease materials appeared to be the extent of U.S. assistance to China before Pearl Harbor. In October 1940, Generalissimo Chiang approached Chennault with a scheme for stopping the Japanese air attacks. He wanted to buy late-model American planes and hire American pilots to fly them, thus creating a mercenary air force. Chiang sent Chennault to the United States to effect this plan.

In 1940, Washington's strategy in Asia has been described by one historian as "walk[ing] a very narrow line aimed at maintaining Chinese resistance and weakening Japan through selective trade embargoes while avoiding a general war and, especially, direct American involvement."[8] But, as Japan's military moved steadily southward through China toward French and British possessions in Southeast Asia, U.S. leaders wanted to do more to halt the advance. Chennault's proposal for an air corps provided the perfect vehicle for doing so. It was an "independent" operation with the pilots employed by a private Chinese company, forming the nucleus of a secret air force to defend China. This setup allowed the United States to both circumvent neutrality laws and avoid public explanations for any involvement in the Sino-Japanese conflict and to intervene in the theater without the whole nation becoming involved. By combining Chennault's air attacks with President Franklin D. Roosevelt's total trade embargo against Japan in July 1941, policymakers hoped that their dual strategy might frustrate Tokyo's plans. When Roosevelt allowed reserve officers and enlisted men from the Army Air Corps and Naval and Marine Air Services to resign and volunteer for Chennault's unit, the American Volunteer Group (AVG) was born in the spring of 1941.

The AVG constituted American informal diplomatic activity as well as a secret military campaign because it worked outside standard channels of government and was aimed at influencing relations with Japan. The pro-active nature of the AVG operation, out of the public eye until after U.S. entry into the war, was not the standard fare of unofficial relations between nations, but it was not unique. By his very presence as a private, civilian adviser to the Beijing government, Chennault provided not only the opportunity for secret American activity but also the expertise, personal commitment, and connections in China to assist the Chinese without any acknowledgment of official U.S. involvement. The fact that, in the end, the American goal of preventing war with Japan itself was not achieved is unimportant here. What is important for the study of informal diplomacy is that the AVG represented a willingness on the part of U.S. policymakers to engage in such activities to advance foreign policy objectives.

Once the United States entered the war, however, the AVG's days as "independent" were numbered. The China Air Task Force (CATF) of the U.S. Army Air Corps succeeded the AVG on July 4, 1942, and operated in China as an attachment to the Tenth Army Air Force based in Delhi, India. The CATF existed until March 1943, when it became part of the U.S. Fourteenth Air Force that was created under Chennault's command. Because of its evolutionary association to the AVG, the Fourteenth was also called the Flying Tigers. With sharp teeth (designed by an artist at Walt Disney Studios) painted on the front of the aircraft, the Flying Tigers and Claire Chennault continued to be world famous. In the early months of the war their triumphant exploits were heralded in American newspapers as the only positive news from either front.

The years of AVG and CATF operation were those of Anna Chen's escape from Hong Kong as a refugee. The Chinese who fled through the countryside to escape advancing Japanese troops greatly appreciated the Chinese and "American" air forces' responses to Japanese bombing attacks. When Chen moved from town to town with the faculty and students of Lingnan University avoiding enemy raids, she and her fellow students also were thankful for the relief from Japanese bombers.

The activities of the Flying Tigers generated great interest about China in the United States. This interest represented a significant change from the level of American awareness of events in China in the late 1930s, but it was a continuation of the historical fascination with China that had long existed among the American public, if not always among American policymakers. Since the mid-nineteenth century, China had been viewed as a key to Asian markets deemed necessary for continued American economic success. It was this kind of interest that later helped Anna Chennault bring attention to Chinese issues. Still, U.S. concerns about China were never deep enough to prompt direct intervention before Pearl Harbor. Even then, the demands of war in Europe created a split in the attention of Washington policymakers who managed battle fronts in two hemispheres.

Starting in 1940, this divided concern was manifested in the United States by two groups who saw the future of U.S.-China relations through different lenses. On one side of the debate were Americans who witnessed the negative effects of dynastic- and/or warlord-era China from the late nineteenth century until 1930 and supported missionary and educational efforts to "modernize" the Chinese and buttress their fight against Japan. Some American military leaders, such as General Chennault, believed that the GMD could defeat Japan (with enough support from Washington). Henry Luce, the wealthy publisher of *Time* and *Life* magazines who had been raised by American missionary parents in China, and journalists Roy Howard and Joseph Alsop agreed. Roosevelt administration officials Harry Hopkins, Henry Morgenthau, attorney Thomas Corcoran, and Ambassador to the Soviet Union Averell Harriman were among those who supported the GMD because they believed that "a China independent of Russia was essential" to U.S. security.[9] Many individuals with this perspective on Sino-American relations later became part of what was known as the

China Lobby, whose activities sustained and enhanced (and some say were directed by) the GMD.

The China Lobby, which later included General and Mrs. Chennault among its supporters, started in 1940 as part of the effort to obtain aid for the Chinese government, which was then fighting alone against Japan. During World War II, the group was limited primarily to those few who worked funneling American aid to China; it was not a formal organization but rather a loose association of individuals interested in seeing that America supported not only China's efforts against the Japanese but also aided Chiang Kai-shek's consolidation of power against the growing Chinese Communist Party (CCP). They either ignored or minimized growing charges and evidence of corruption within the GMD and spread their view of what America's role, or even duty, must be in China. Luce's publishing empire worked to advance this view, even naming Generalissimo and Madame Chiang Kai-shek "Man and Wife of the Year" in 1938.

Those on the other side of the American policy debate argued that a Chinese form of communism would eventually prevail in the country, no matter what Washington policymakers did. U.S actions during World War II should be carefully planned, they believed, so as not to alienate CCP leaders and thus risk a closer CCP alliance with and dependence upon Soviet Communists in the postwar period. Journalists and diplomatic representatives, but also some military leaders, were the principal proponents of this view. These individuals, such as Edgar Snow, Agnes Smedley, John S. Service, John Davies, Captain Evans Carlson, and General Joseph Stilwell, wrote numerous articles, books, and reports chronicling their observations and assessments. Such opinions rarely got through to the American public or policymakers because it was virtually impossible to penetrate the "aura of popularity" that had been created around the GMD and its leader, Chiang Kai-shek.[10] While the China Lobby painted a rosy picture of the GMD's effective use of American aid to prosecute the war, their opponents suspected that rather than engaging the Japanese directly, Chiang was stockpiling his American supplies and reserving his best troops for the fight he expected with the CCP for rule of China after Japan was defeated.

Against this backdrop of domestic policy debate, Chennault spent the last two years of the war battling American officialdom as well as the Japanese. Arguing strategy with the military leadership finally got him pushed from the line of command by the superiors with whom he disagreed. He knew his job in China was finished because "the enemy airfields were bare and the ground forces [had] beg[u]n their retreat to the north in mid-May [1945]."[11] Chennault saved face by resigning, for he believed his fate was an affront to the record of his flyers in the war and also a result of his highly vocal support of Chiang and the GMD.

By the time of Chennault's retirement in July 1945, his recognition as the commander of the Flying Tigers prompted a farewell tour before his departure. He was hailed as a hero by Chinese society, greeted by parades and large crowds in various cities, and given a wide array of gifts. In Chongqing, Generalissimo Chiang conferred on him the nation's highest honor, the Order of the White Sun and Blue Sky, and China theater commander General Albert Wedemeyer awarded him a second Oak Leaf Cluster on his Distinguished Service Medal. Chennault's anger and disappointment as he left China was tempered by the affection he had developed for the land, its people, and many of its leaders. It was this sentiment, combined with his fear of Communist expansion, that prompted his postwar involvement in China on behalf of the Nationalist regime.

V-J Day marked the beginning of China's long road to recovery as well as the resumption of competition between the GMD and CCP for postwar leadership of the nation. Their conflict had been merely interrupted by Japan, and even a common enemy failed to forge unity between them. U.S. Ambassador to China Patrick J. Hurley and Chiang Kai-shek eventually convinced FDR that China's future was tied to that of Chiang and the GMD. When the CCP recognized that the United States was incapable of convincing the GMD to grant equal partnership in a coalition government, it created a surge of "anti-American propaganda." Hurley responded by denouncing CCP leaders and throwing his government's support fully behind Chiang, much to the delight of the China Lobby and its supporters.

By late 1946, Washington policymakers finally recognized that saving China for the GMD would require direct U.S. military intercession. They were, however, unwilling to commit American troops because they were disheartened by Chiang's lack of leadership and dwindling support. American pro-GMD interests (such as the China Lobby) refused to accept the reality of GMD problems and CCP successes. The United States continued to support Chiang's government even in the wake of the CCP victory and the GMD retreat to Taiwan in late 1949.

When General Chennault arrived in Shanghai in January 1946, the fact that Anna Chen's employer, CNA, sent her to cover the event indicated the interest of the Beijing government in the war hero's postwar intentions. His personal relationship with Generalissimo and Madame Chiang Kai-shek was well known, as was his support of the ruling GMD party. Chinese supporters of the GMD's emerging struggles with the CCP considered Chennault a valuable friend. Their admiration was not misplaced; he proved to be of great assistance to the GMD cause.

Chennault returned to China for several reasons. One was his desire to keep an anti-Communist government in control. Along with other American allies of the GMD, he urged strong U.S. backing of the GMD in its struggle against the CCP for postwar control of China. Also, he wanted to participate in the postwar reconstruction and simultaneously increase his personal wealth. In Chennault's first few months back in China, after he toured the country and observed its devastation, he decided to "organize an emergency air lift of relief supplies into the interior."[12] He consulted with Anna Chen, his Chinese friends, and the GMD leadership, who encouraged his plan to return to the United States and obtain financial backing for an air transport business.

Like-minded Americans viewed Chennault's plan as a way to promote a strong Sino-American relationship—a partnership predicated on the existence of a stable, non-Communist China. The plan also corresponded with the postwar business plans of Thomas Corcoran and his corporate investment associates. "Tommy the Cork" was a disciple of Harvard law professor Felix Frankfurter, who served as a legislative adviser and aide to President Roosevelt. A member of FDR's so-called Brain Trust, Corcoran had been Chennault's "political advocate" generally, and of the AVG, CATF, and China aid particularly, within the Roosevelt administration. While Chennault was in the United States, Corcoran's group approached him with an offer. The new business partners gladly embraced the coincidental possibility that their enterprise might enhance the aims of U.S. policy (Asian stability and deterring the spread of communism) by helping Chiang Kai-shek's government strengthen itself through the successful rebuilding of China.

Chennault's connections secured approval of the new airline by Beijing officials, while Corcoran's ties in Washington assisted in the search for venture capital. The project remained uncertain until Fiorello La Guardia, then director-general of the United Nations Relief and Rehabilitation Administration (UNRRA), was persuaded to provide $2 million through its Chinese counterpart, CNRRA, to transport supplies to China's interior. Chennault returned to China and worked there with his partner, Whiting Willauer, to arrange for CNRRA Air Transport (CAT) to begin operations.

The personal relationship between Anna Chen and Claire Chennault evolved alongside the preparations for and beginning of CAT. She continued her reporting for CNA. Whenever possible, she would include favorable reports about the prospects and opportunities that CAT represented for the nation in any coverage of China's reconstruction and future. Antipathy still existed there toward foreign-owned businesses following over a century of humiliation under foreign-controlled trade; therefore, anything that Chen could do to cast CAT in a favorable light was welcome and valuable.

Anna and the General meeting with Chinese businessmen, circa 1950s

When CAT's operations began in January 1947, it flew relief supplies, relief officials, and technicians from Canton and Shanghai to various points inland, often using old AVG/Fourteenth airfields. Return flights ferried out raw and manufactured goods to earn much-needed cash and foreign exchange for the Chinese. As the civil war escalated, CAT's activities in China were subject to the pro-GMD bias of its owners and aided American policy aims by helping to sustain the GMD. In addition to routine cargo and passenger business, CAT flights supported GMD military operations, often flying against heavy CCP military opposition. Although

CAT's cargo flights contributed to the temporary stability of the GMD, the assistance was not significant enough to change the downward spiral of the GMD's fortunes.

Following their marriage in late 1947, by early 1948, Anna Chen Chennault was working in CAT's Shanghai offices as its public relations officer, reporting only occasionally for CNA. The General's business required him to make frequent trips. In the spring the couple went to the United States, and Anna first saw her adopted country as they traveled to California, Louisiana, New York, and Washington. The General addressed a congressional committee and made public appearances in an effort to alert Americans to the Communist threat in China—and, by extension, in all of Asia.

Once back on the Chinese mainland, Chennault hurriedly moved CAT offices and airfields to remain ahead of the enemy as CCP troops achieved steady military successes on the battlefield. In July 1948, Anna discovered that she was pregnant, and the General worried about her safety as Communist forces edged closer. She agreed to leave their home in Shanghai and go to Canton, farther from the battle lines.

For the next nine months, Anna and the General kept in touch through letters and calls. He remained at the helm of CAT's efforts to support GMD forces, and he was so tied to the war effort that he could not get away to Canton for their first anniversary or for Christmas at the end of 1948. Anna disliked the separations but accepted them as the price of marriage to a man as committed to his mission as Chennault. She understood his dedication and shared the fear of China's future under a victorious CCP that drove him. The civil war kept Anna and the General separated until his visit to Canton right after she gave birth to their first daughter, Claire Anna, in early February 1949.

While visiting his family, General Chennault received an invitation to return to Washington and testify before the influential Senate Armed Services Committee concerning the situation in China. He viewed this as a last-ditch opportunity to persuade American policymakers to provide more assistance to Chiang and the GMD in their losing effort to defeat the CCP. Anna accompanied her husband on his trip to Washington in May 1949 for her second visit to the United States.

Chennault hoped to influence policymakers and the public with his testimony. He articulated the China Lobby's argument that GMD losses were caused by the lack of U.S. support. Chennault depicted a domino effect resulting from the fall of China to the CCP: "If we do not act soon, all China will be lost. The Chinese Communists' government will be on the borders of Indochina, Siam, and Burma. . . . And the rich islands of Indonesia will also find their way into these new provinces of the Soviet Union's new Asiatic empire."[13] Here, Chennault advanced the argument that the CCP was tied to Soviet communism. Overall, his testimony expressed his long-standing view (and that of the China Lobby) that American action was necessary to save all of Asia from communism. In the end, skepticism that the United States had either the power or the will to affect the outcome of the civil war prevailed, and the Senate Armed Services Committee rejected Chennault's recommendations for direct joint Sino-American operations.

Enlisting the aid of his CAT partner Corcoran, Chennault pitched the plan around Washington to anyone who would listen, including to the Central Intelligence Agency (CIA). There, in Frank G. Wisner, "head of the Office of Policy Coordination (OPC)—the euphemistic designation that masked the government's covert action arm"—they found a sympathetic ear.[14] Chennault and Corcoran revealed that CAT suffered cash flow problems with the fall of more and more territory to the advancing CCP armies. With American foreign policy advocating Communist containment, the OPC considered the possibilities of funding covert operations by CAT in China to support the faltering Nationalist cause. It was Wisner who decided it was useful to keep CAT operational for future OPC work in China.

As GMD resistance to CCP forces crumbled, the CIA pushed ahead with its plan to secure funding to keep CAT flying. In October 1949, $75 million was appropriated for the "general area" of China.[15] American policymakers thus sanctioned the use of CAT to provide small-scale covert assistance to anti-Communist groups on the mainland, not to reverse the outcome of the civil war, which was by October 1949 a foregone conclusion. Rather, it was a way of showing continued support to the GMD and to maintain pressure on the new Chinese regime. The long-range benefit of keeping CAT afloat in order to have a seasoned airline on hand for any future anti-Communist needs in the region was not lost on policymakers in the State Department and the CIA.

Again, Chennault was at the center of American activities in China. Like his proposal for the AVG almost ten years earlier, this was a covert plan to achieve U.S. foreign policy objectives that could not be pursued openly because of external constraints. The audience whom Chennault mustered for both his 1940 and 1949 proposals was the segment of policymakers who believed it was in the United States's best interests to take some kind of action in foreign nations, regardless of such pesky deterrents as public opinion, formal diplomatic relations, or congressional approval. While not directly a part of the negotiation or operation of Chennault's plans with the CIA, Anna knew of the arrangements and how her husband's objectives were achieved. She supported his and Corcoran's maneuvers using CAT to aid the GMD in the civil war. She learned about using indirect methods to achieve one's goals when direct methods failed or were not an option—crucial lessons in the ways of informal diplomacy.

In the final months of the civil war, CAT launched a legal-diplomatic maneuver to deny the CCP possession of planes on the ground and belonging to two Chinese airlines when those companies' assets passed to the government of the new People's Republic of China (PRC) at the end of 1949. Both CAT and OPC officials recognized the danger in allowing these planes to pass into Communist hands. It would make full evacuations of GMD personnel almost impossible during final CCP assaults and would mean surrender of vital military equipment to the CCP. This episode would serve as a model for a similar maneuver by Anna Chennault and Corcoran over thirty years later.

Through complicated maneuvering, the plan required sale of the companies and their assets to an American corporation established by Corcoran just for this purpose. Also, various suits were filed in the British courts (since Hong Kong remained a British colony even after the CCP victory in China) that eventually conferred Nationalist Chinese ownership and possession in 1952. Successful lobbying by Corcoran through the State Department brought pressure on the British government to grant American registry of the planes. This move, plus additional advances of CIA funds to keep CAT flying, demonstrated Washington's support for such informal diplomatic operations.

In the end, CAT's efforts on behalf of the GMD were incapable of turning the tide against the CCP. The CIA's efforts through the OPC to spur anti-Communist guerrillas and overt U.S. financial and materiel aid were equally futile. Despite the best of intentions, much hard work, and covert American money, Chennault and CAT made much more noise than difference in the civil war.

After the civil war on the mainland ended, the General continued his activities to secure American aid for the GMD now ensconced on Taiwan. These efforts included radio interviews, newspaper articles, personal appearances, and appeals whenever he was in the United States. Though Anna sometimes accompanied him on these trips, she remained in the background. The dutiful wife watched her husband's tireless quest to rouse the American public from its seemingly calm acceptance of China coming under Communist control.

The General's Wife

The Chennaults' second daughter, Cynthia Louise, was born in March 1950 and shortly thereafter the family moved to Taipei, Taiwan, the site of CAT's new headquarters. The General traveled less often, mostly between the United States and Taiwan. He and Anna purchased a lot in his home state of Louisiana in 1949, had a house built in Monroe, where the General had good friends, and in 1951 began living there for a month or two each year. The Chennaults resided the rest of the time in Taipei, where two of Anna's sisters and their husbands also lived; one of them, Dr. Richard Lee, was the company physician for CAT. Anna resumed work at CAT headquarters, primarily editing the *CAT Bulletin*, an internal company monthly begun in 1947. The couple's social life in Taipei allowed Anna to meet many of the General's friends in the GMD government and military. Their circle included Madame Chiang Kai-shek, a favorite bridge partner of the General's and the godmother of his two daughters. The ties that Anna built in these years, through her social life in Taiwan and in the United States and through her peripheral role at CAT, established crucial relationships that lasted beyond the life of her husband.

With its mainland business eliminated, CAT struggled to survive after the civil war. In early 1950, Chennault and Willauer raised the possibility with their CIA partners that CAT might be forced to liquidate or sell off its assets (perhaps even to the Communists) because of its precarious financial situation. CAT secured not only short-term financial relief from the OPC but also an option agreement for the CIA to purchase the airline. Soon afterward, the OPC decided it needed a safe source of transportation, which could be disavowed if necessary, to support its Asian covert actions, so the CIA decided to buy the airline (later known as Air America) to keep it in friendly hands and available for OPC operations. The purchase was made through a front corporation whose directors were secretly employees of the CIA. The purchase price of $950,000 first paid off company expenses totaling over $190,000. In the end, the

General came away with a little over $101,000 for his ownership share after four years of effort.

Chennault's role in CAT changed after the CIA became the airline's owners. Though appointed chairman of the board, he effectively lost day-to-day operational control. The CIA, however, still needed Chennault's friendship with Chiang Kai-shek to ensure continuation of their operations and cooperation from the GMD government. With the outbreak of the Korean War in June 1950, CAT began supply operations for the UN forces, but Chennault was eventually eased out as the CIA took over complete control. He remained as chairman of the board but was relegated to figurehead status. The General then put his energy into the crusade of words that kept his concerns about communism in Asia before the American people.

Through the 1950s, Anna became more active in her husband's public anti-Communist campaign. In May 1955 she addressed the women members of the Dallas Public Affairs Luncheon Club on the topic of Taiwan. Anna had "opinions worth listening to," according to the *Dallas News*, as "a personage in her own right, by inheritance and by achievement, as well as by marriage."[16] In her speech, Anna "warned that the United States—for its own sake—must increase shipments of military supplies to the Chinese Nationalists on Formosa [Taiwan]." She added that "we have lost enough territory [to communism] already in Asia and the Far East and I do not think that we can afford [to lose] any more territory if we want to remain free."[17] On another occasion, Anna addressed the Kiwanis Club on the subject, "Formosa: Its Climate and People, Its Relations with the U.S., and Its Conditions Today."[18] She was seen as an articulate Chinese-American with unique qualifications to carry the anti-Communist message to the American public. Her heritage, writing, speaking, and ties to Chennault defined her identity in the United States.

In 1956 the chronic bronchitis that Claire Chennault had suffered for twenty years got worse. His annual check-up revealed a tumor in his lung. The lung was removed and the tumor was found to be malignant. Over the next twelve months he remained cancer free, and he and Anna took a long-delayed European honeymoon. Chennault's thirteenth-month check-up showed a spot in his remaining lung. Anna faced the same lingering march of death that she had witnessed in her mother.

The General's friend, Tom Corcoran, was a great help to Anna through the difficult last year. Anna's numerous letters to Corcoran in 1957 and 1958 indicate her increasing dependence on him. She wrote to Corcoran in December 1957: "During these past months of crisis you have no idea how much comfort and support you have given me. . . . Sometimes, show[ing] me that I am not alone; or holding my hand in yours to let me know you do care, all these have given me more courage, and I shall remember these days always with gratitude and love. . . . I am most fortunate to have a truly devoted husband, and a wonderful friend."[19]

General Claire Lee Chennault died on July 27, 1958. The *New York Times* carried the news on its front page. It reviewed his career, mentioning especially that "soon after his arrival [in China he] developed great fondness for the Chinese people, and the affection was mutual."[20] The funeral at Arlington National Cemetery was reported by the *Times* as well as by the Washington papers. The list of dignitaries in attendance included many American World War II generals and GMD government officials. Chairman of the Joint Chiefs of Staff General Nathan Twining led the procession, which also included Generals Albert Wedemeyer, Curtis LeMay, and Bedell Smith. Madame Chiang Kai-shek and ROC Ambassador Hollington Kong were among the five thousand attendees.

The life that Anna and the General shared not only influenced her personally but also had an impact on American-Asian foreign policy. Chennault was instrumental in creating prime incidents of informal diplomatic action through AVG and CAT. Anna learned valuable lessons from such enterprises and, through her husband, developed a friendship with a Washington insider involved in both ventures, Tom Corcoran. The General's unrelenting calls for American action in Asia bolstered the China Lobby and contributed to the political reaction among Chiang Kai-shek's supporters. In the aftermath of the Chinese civil war, Korea and Indochina were often characterized by U.S. policymakers as symbols of the free world's fight against communism. That fight allowed the Chennaults to gain an audience for their appeals to protect Asia from "falling" under Communist control. And by the time of her husband's death, Americans recognized Anna's ties to the China Lobby and support of Taiwan.

The end of her marriage raised many questions for Anna Chennault. She had to decide where to live (she had homes in Louisiana and Taiwan), what career to follow, and where to educate her daughters. Her husband's legacy required her attendance at various events soon after his death. She was present in November 1958 when Louisiana's Lake Charles Air Force Base was renamed for the General. A little over a year later a bust of Claire Chennault was unveiled in Taipei, the first erected by the Chinese on their soil to honor a foreigner. Upon his death, Anna was imbued with Chennault's status, alliances, and causes. With these, she started careers in American politics and business that enabled her to enter the world of informal diplomacy. Her career as a famous widow had begun, a role that Anna accepted with honor and enthusiasm.

Notes

1. Chennault, *Education of Anna*, 90.
2. Ibid., 91.
3. Colonel Ed Rector, telephone interview by author, January 24, 1996.
4. Chennault, *Education of Anna*, 123.
5. Martha Byrd, *Chennault: Giving Wings to the Tiger* (Tuscaloosa: University of Alabama Press, 1987), 300.
6. Louise Willauer to her family, January 12, 1948, copy from William Leary.
7. His birthdate is in dispute. His autobiography lists 1890, yet other sources—scholarly and otherwise—cite 1893.
8. Michael Schaller, *The U.S. Crusade in China, 1938–1945* (New York: Columbia University Press, 1979), 55.
9. Ross Y. Koen, *The China Lobby in American Politics* (New York: Octagon Books, 1974), 20. 29.
10. Schaller, *U.S. Crusade*, 60–61.
11. C. L. Chennault, *Way of a Fighter* (New York: G. P. Putnam's Sons, 1949), 351.
12. Ibid., 357.
13. William M. Leary, Jr., *Perilous Missions* (University, AL: University of Alabama Press, 1984), 67–68. See "Statement of Maj. Gen. Claire L. Chennault, United States Army (Retired)," *Congressional Record*, 81st Cong., 1st sess., vol. 95, pt. 4, May 3, 1949, 5480–82.
14. William M. Leary and William Stueck, "The Chennault Plan to Save China: U.S. Containment in Asia and the Origins of the CIA's Aerial Empire, 1949–1950," *Diplomatic History* 8, no. 4 (Fall 1984): 353.
15. "Mutual Defense Assistance Act of 1949," *United States Code: Congressional Service*, 81st Cong., 1st sess., 1949, Chapter 626—Public Law 329.
16. *Dallas News*, May 17, 1955.
17. *Dallas Times*, May 17, 1955.
18. Unidentified 1950s newsclipping, Anna Chennault Papers, Washington, DC.
19. Anna Chennault to Thomas Corcoran, December 5, 1957, Papers of Thomas Corcoran, box 104, folder 4, Manuscript Division, Library of Congress, Washington, DC.
20. "Gen. Chennault is Dead at 67; Headed Flying Tigers in China," *New York Times*, July 28, 1958.

3

Young Republican

By the middle of 1958, Anna Chennault faced the challenges of raising two daughters alone, finding meaningful, productive work, and locating in a congenial city. Her decision to move from Monroe, Louisiana, to Washington, DC, placed her in an environment where informal diplomacy thrived in a sea of international relationships. Entering those waters first as the General's wife and then as his widow in the 1950s, by the late 1960s she had positioned herself alongside the leaders of conservative foreign policy, established her network within the international aviation business, and acquired a reputation as a leading hostess for Republican politicians and their followers in a city where business, politics, diplomatic activities, and pleasure often intersected.

The Capital

For several reasons, Mrs. Chennault decided to relocate to Washington after the death of her husband. Living in Taiwan would "court sadness in a place that had once meant happiness and hope."[1] Besides, the General wanted their daughters educated in the United States, not Taiwan. As for staying in Louisiana, the home they had built there also brought melancholy reminders of their happy life together. Moreover, it is likely that Louisiana would have proved to be a racially uncomfortable place to raise two Amerasian girls in the late 1950s, particularly without the protection of their well-known father. During his life, the General tolerated no complications from his interracial marriage, but Anna faced those problems alone after his death. She remembered being teased about her own English-language faux pas and she wanted to spare her daughters.

Washington was certainly more cosmopolitan than Monroe, Louisiana, could ever be, and it offered a favorable setting for Anna's Asian-American family. The city's large Chinese community gave her a sense of familiarity, and its ethnic diversity allowed her daughters to attend schools filled with children from many backgrounds. Washington's international orientation also provided opportunities for challenging employment for a skilled, educated Chinese woman.

Mrs. Chennault had two further reasons for moving to Washington. First, she had both close and casual friends there. Many political, military, and aviation business leaders who knew the Chennaults resided in or frequently passed through Washington. The most prominent among them was Thomas Corcoran, whose status as a widower allowed him to be her frequent social companion over the next twenty years until his death in 1981. In addition to serving as the General's World War II champion, attorney, and friend, Corcoran, at the General's request, continued to safeguard the legal and financial interests of Anna and her daughters.

Second, since the General's will was probated in Washington, Anna needed to establish residency there for one year. Although the will may have been probated there because Corcoran's office was located in the city, it may have also been done to avoid Louisiana miscegenation laws that might have prevented Chennault's Chinese wife and their daughters from receiving their inheritance. General Chennault's brother Joe, an attorney, had at one point "cautioned him that Louisiana did not recognize his marriage to Anna and might not honor a will that included his Eurasian daughters."[2] A former AVG and CAT associate of the General's stated in an interview that Chennault chose Washington "on advice of counsel" (likely his brother and/or Corcoran) so that Anna "could not be disinherited."[3]

In the 1950s, Louisiana still had on its books an 1894 law that prohibited "marriage between white persons and persons of color" and declared any such marriages "null and void."[4] Considering this law and the South's racial climate in the 1950s, Claire Chennault and Corcoran would have avoided any legal obstacle that might have tied up the estate in court or caused a result unfavorable to Anna and her daughters. Even though the General's stature might have been enough to prevent the state from interfering, it seemed a risk he was unwilling to take. His estate was divided approximately in half between his first wife and eight children and Anna and their two daughters. The *New York Times* reported that out of a $406,500 estate, $362,000 was in securities. The first wife received $181,000, and Anna received the remainder totalling $225,500.[5]

General Chennault's estate provided Anna with a financially secure position from which to launch the next stage in her life. She initially entrusted her funds to Corcoran, but in time she became a shrewd investor in her own right. Anna's first home in Washington was a roomy apartment on Cathedral Avenue in the fashionable northwest section of the city. She enrolled the girls in a good primary school nearby. But she needed to work, to augment the family's income as much as to have a challenge in life.

Corcoran wrote to the president of Georgetown University on her behalf. "She has," he remarked, "evolved into an important symbol of the Chinese anti-Communist resistance as a diplomatic and self-controlled woman who has seen much, suffered much and learned."[6] Although Corcoran proposed that she be a Chinese language and literature instructor, her skills with several Chinese dialects and English (and lack of any advanced degrees) instead earned her a position in Georgetown's Chinese Section of Machine Translation Research, which was working on a mechanical method for writing Chinese characters, like a typewriter, in the days before computers. It involved creating simplified characters from the over 40,000 (at least 7,000 of which are needed to print a newspaper) that exist in classic calligraphic form. Mrs. Chennault's efforts on this project included devising the simplified forms (not unlike those instituted in the PRC to aid in the extension of literacy) as well as transcribing ideographic Chinese into phonetic English. She stayed there for five years writing Chinese-English dictionaries, eventually becoming head of the section.

Party and Other Politics

While Anna Chennault's life revolved around caring for her daughters, reading, writing, translating, and tutoring, she also became active in politics. In 1960 she was asked by Sylvia Herman, the chair of the Republican Women's Federation of Maryland, to help organize ethnic minority groups for Richard Nixon's presidential campaign. Mrs. Chennault had first met Vice President Nixon in 1954 when she attended a banquet in Taiwan given in his honor by President Chiang Kai-shek. The Chennaults also gave a reception for Nixon during that visit. When the General died, Anna was comforted by Nixon's note of condolence. According to her memoirs, she thanked him and kept up a periodic correspondence with him about Asian politics.

From later examples of their correspondence in Anna's files, the analysis of the Asian political scene that she shared with Nixon revolved around the theme of American support for its non-Communist Asian allies as the best way to stop the spread of communism and protect American interests in the region. This connection to the candidate delighted Herman, who put the eager Anna to work in the Washington campaign office. She organized and spoke to minority groups (Chinese and others), working devotedly for Nixon, learning the basics of American political organizing from the grassroots up. Nixon's loss to John Kennedy was an early political disappointment for her, but she found the campaign intoxicating and its excitement addictive. It was Anna's American political baptism.

In the years between elections, Anna kept her hand in various political circles through other functions. In 1961 she hosted a gathering that had become an annual ritual—a weekend reunion of AVG and Fourteenth Air Force members, plus other political and military friends, all assembled to reminisce and lay a memorial wreath on the General's grave. According to the *Baltimore News-Post*, Anna's dinner guests were four generals and their wives, including General and Mrs. Wedemeyer, plus Senator and Mrs. Jack Miller of Iowa, Nationalist Chinese Ambassador to the United States George Yeh, George Doole, Jr. (of CAT), the Fourteenth Air Force Association members, and wealthy socialite Mrs. Robert McCormick. The society pages reported that one hundred seventy-five people attended the wreath-laying ceremony at Arlington National Cemetery. The weekend's events also included an afternoon reception at the Chinese embassy and a banquet with Senator Miller, a former Flying Tiger member, as principal speaker.[7]

This gathering, and its coverage in the press, exemplified Anna's activities beginning in the early 1960s. The lists of attendees at her parties read like a "Who's Who" of Washington politics, business, and power. This was her specialty—bringing together people of similar interests but diverse backgrounds for conversation and the exchange of ideas. And while many of her friends were no longer on the front line of foreign policymaking, they were often connected to those who were. She herself described the role that she played: "In Washington, where politics and entertaining are as indivisible as two sides of the same coin, it was not surprising that I, who delighted in entertaining, should take on the role of political hostess. The progression was simple. I was considered sociable and well-connected, and was single, thus free to seek out and cultivate whomever I pleased, able to bring people out and put them at ease. . . . And, I came with a certain exotic Asian aura. . . . Politicians are forever eager to caucus and convene, and the more comfortable the locale the better."[8]

To honor the General's memory, a substantial group of his friends organized the General Claire Lee Chennault Foundation in 1961. Former president Herbert Hoover was honorary chairman; Corcoran, old hunting "buddy" and former Louisiana governor James Noe, Nationalist Chinese ambassadors Yeh and T. F. Tsiang, Ambassador Whiting Willauer, and General Wedemeyer were directors. Honorary Advisory Committee members included Richard Nixon (chair), General John Alison, former Flying Tiger and Hollywood producer Meriam Cooper, Senator Hiram Fong (R-CA), popular radio entertainer Arthur Godfrey, former Flying Tiger and founder of cargo carrier Flying Tiger Lines Robert Prescott, and three members of General Chennault's family.[9]

The Foundation supplemented the education of students from non-Communist Asian nations in the fields of medicine and aviation by giving them an opportunity to travel, meet Americans, and form friendships. The goal was for the Asians to "appreciate and understand the free society, culture, traditions, politics, and ideals of the American people, and to observe and absorb knowledge of [the] practical operation of America's free society." They would then "carry home . . . a well-balanced knowledge . . . of America's culture, idealism, and melting-pot genius for welding diverse elements into a homogenous nation."[10] In establishing this organization, Anna reiterated to Hoover the General's belief that "the greatest opportunities for the building of East-West 'friendship bridges' lay in the flow of Asian students to the United States."[11] She has served on the Foundation's board since its inception, and its goals still echo those that she adopted from the General.

Though affiliated with and active in the Republican Party, Mrs. Chennault extended her reach on behalf of her Asian interests across party lines to the Democratic administration of John F. Kennedy. On June 2, 1962, she met with the president at the White House. Accompanying her were columnist Jack Anderson and prominent Washington Chinese-American businessman David Lee, both active in a private organization, Chinese Refugee Relief (CRR), of which Anna served as president. A photo was taken in the Oval

Office following their brief meeting at which Kennedy gave his blessing and encouragement to the organization and its efforts. Working with her as co-chairmen of the CRR board were former presidents Hoover and Truman. Later that week, Mrs. Chennault testified on behalf of CRR before the Subcommittee on Escapees and Refugees of the Senate Judiciary Committee. She suggested ways in which the United States could aid the thousands of Chinese fleeing starvation during the Cultural Revolution and flooding into Hong Kong.

Her testimony, given as a citizen of the United States, drew on her own experience as a refugee. "I know the misery of physical privation of the homeless and the emotional privation of the forgotten," she declared. Introducing herself as General Chennault's widow, she characterized him as "the symbol of deliverance to the Chinese people from the cruelty of the Japanese"; now she was "engaged in his unfinished business of delivering the Chinese people from the cruelty of the Communists."[12] Anna spoke passionately about CRR's mission to raise and use private funds in coordination with the policies of the U.S. and other governments, and of international welfare and refugee organizations. These joint efforts placed orphans with (mostly American) families, fed and provided medical care for refugees, and aided resettlement efforts.

She also used her platform before the Senate committee to make various points about the nature of the PRC government, the role of the United States as a beacon of hope to those behind the so-called Bamboo Curtain, and the need for American aid to be given in such a way as to help the Chinese people, not their Communist government. To her, PRC leaders were "masters of Chinese slavery" who used food "as an instrument of life and death . . . to kill freedom." On this last point, she noted that the "Communist army guards . . . are well fed." She warned of the consequences if America did not respond accordingly: "We would be making the same mistake we made when under the pressure of scrap dealers we shipped scrap iron to Japan before Pearl Harbor. Such impossible appeasement would be shot back in our faces in Southeast Asia as it was shot back at Pearl Harbor and Korea. Do you put troops in Thailand and Vietnam to face Chinese Communists made strong with your own food?"[13] A Chinese-American woman was admonishing congressmen to uphold their nation's role as the global leader in the struggle against communism, much as her husband had done in years past.

Chennault carried her anti-Communist appeal beyond the halls of Congress to the American people. Articles in major newspapers covered the activities of CRR. For example, the plight of Chinese refugees and CRR efforts on their behalf were introduced to the American public in a *Parade* magazine cover story, "A young refugee finds a HOME IN AMERICA." She used her increasingly numerous speaking engagements across the United States during 1962–63 to deliver news of the refugee disaster resulting from PRC government failures.[14] From her position with CRR, she expanded the platform from which she delivered the General's message that she had made her own.

Arizona's Senator Barry Goldwater's unsuccessful bid for the presidency against Lyndon Johnson in 1964 drew Chennault's interest. Her ideological affinity with the Republican Party's right wing linked her directly to the leaders who advocated a staunch anti-Communist, pro-Taiwan policy, and her growing public visibility made her a welcome supporter. Her work as a GOP committeewoman in Washington since 1960 also connected her to the various grassroots levels of the party. By the time of Goldwater's campaign, Chennault described her Washington apartment as a "popular watering hole for ranking Republicans" and the site of "early strategy and program meetings."[15] Some participants in those meetings were Senators Goldwater, Miller, John Tower (TX), and Strom Thurmond (SC) along with various members of their staffs. Her efforts in Goldwater's campaign were much like those in Nixon's 1960 bid: ethnic minority organizing and fundraising.

In this capacity, she spoke at the Twelfth Annual Republican Women's Conference in Washington in April 1964, where she shared the podium with Senator Goldwater, two governors, two more senators, and a congressman. In the program, she was described as "Widow of the famous 'Flying Tigers' General. Author of many books in English and Chinese. . . . Lecturer, fashion designer, feature writer, newspaper correspondent, broadcaster. . . . President, Chinese Refugee Relief and General Claire Lee Chennault Foundation."[16] As a Republican and Chinese, she was a useful spokeswoman to attract minorities and show party support for their concerns. Anna's persistent efforts built her reputation as a can-do activist, gracious hostess, and tireless fighter for any battles she took on—including Goldwater's losing candidacy.

Mrs. Chennault learned a valuable lesson from the 1964 election—"that the courage of conviction, no matter how incandescent, cannot on its own capture the Presidency."[17] Winning a presidential campaign took more than a candidate's power alone, which Nixon may have also learned during his 1960 campaign. Anna took this message seriously. She recognized the value of assertive action in electoral politics. It also explained her willingness to participate in Nixon's dealings during the "October surprise" events of 1968.

Two other activities during the 1960s raised her visibility. In the middle of the decade, Anna was featured in a weekly radio broadcast sponsored by the U.S. Information Agency for the Voice of America—a Sunday morning commentary for the Asian division patterned, she said, after Eleanor Roosevelt's "My Day" broadcasts. The programs were presented in Chinese from scripts prepared in advance in English. From 1963 through 1966, Chennault interpreted American policy goals for listeners in the PRC.

In addition, traveling around the nation, Chennault remained active on the lecture circuit in the 1960s, speaking to a wide variety of audiences on Cold War topics such as "The Asiatic Mind and the Cold War" and "Crisis in Vietnam." A sample of contracts with her New York agent revealed sponsors such as the Pelham, New York, Men's Club; Newark, New Jersey, Archdiocese Apostolate for Youth; Manchester, New Hampshire, Institute of Arts and Sciences; Detroit Education Association; Canadian Broadcasting Corporation; Fine Arts Center of Colorado Springs; Woman's Athletic Club of Chicago; and Central Florida Executives Club. In 1964 she opened the 67th season of the Washington University Association's annual lecture series in St. Louis with a speech titled, "The Split between Peking and Moscow." This busy schedule kept her name and message in front of the politically aware public.

The Nixon Ties Tighten

Anna Chennault's position as president of Chinese Refugee Relief in the mid-1960s enabled her to return periodically to Asia. She also visited her sisters and friends living in Taiwan, Hong Kong, and Saigon, and her work for Chinese newspapers—such as special correspondent to the *Hsin Shen Daily News* and the Central News Agency—required trips to cover stories or conduct interviews in various Asian capitals. In addition, she met with editors, for she was becoming a well-known author in Taiwan, having already published by 1965 several books of Chinese fiction and poetry. (*A Thousand Springs* [1962] and *Chennault and the Flying Tigers* [1963] were both published in the United States.) She had ties to many leaders in the government of Chiang Kai-shek from CAT days, particularly those in aviation—both civilian and military. And within the community of other so-called free (non-Communist) Asian nations such as South Korea, South Vietnam, and the Philippines, her military and political associations grew with her increased travels.

These connections made her a valuable person for establishing relationships in Taiwan, which may be why Richard Nixon met with her when they were both there in the mid-1960s. Nixon was in Taiwan on business for one of his legal clients. Hearing he was in town, Chennault recalled "feeling somewhat sorry for his reduced political circumstances, [and] decided to call on him." According to her, Nixon was "overjoyed to hear a friendly voice" when she called to offer him a ride to the airport. As he got into her car, he smacked his head on the edge of the door, cutting his forehead. Anna gave him her handkerchief to stop the bleeding. He seemed quite concerned that the Chinese officials in the car behind them had witnessed this mishap. At the airport, he apologized for spilling blood on her dress, thanked her, and "promised to be in touch."[18]

With Richard Nixon in Taiwan, circa mid-1960s

The recollections of a former member of the American embassy staff in Taiwan, who served as Nixon's liaison, confirmed Chennault's account of the Nixon meeting. Overall, the embassy staffer concurred with her version. For example, both agree that Nixon stayed at the Grand Hotel in Taipei. Nixon, on the other hand, claimed in his memoir, *RN*, that he had been a "houseguest of Chiang Kai-shek." Since Madame Chiang owned the Grand Hotel, perhaps he stretched the truth. In addition, the staffer corroborated that Nixon and Chennault rode together to the airport, although he could not be certain in whose car.

The most interesting discrepancy concerned Nixon's attitude toward Chennault. On this, the staffer clearly described a Richard Nixon very unhappy to meet or be seen with her; Nixon said that he did not want to be indebted to Mrs. Chennault or have his stature or credibility diminished by being viewed as someone influenced by her. Jonathan Aitken's biography of Nixon recorded that on this same trip to Taiwan, Nixon instructed his aide, Pat Hillings, to "keep her away from me, she's bad news."[19] The embassy official recalled Nixon's vehement declaration that he would "be Goddamned if that woman is going to the airport with me," as out of character with his polite and controlled demeanor during the rest of his visit. The exchange recounted here invites an explanation of the former vice president's seemingly contradictory behavior and of Chennault's place in the American political spectrum.

The Taiwan encounter reflected both on Chennault as a political opportunist and on Nixon as a political manipulator. He was a star in the Republican Party, someone to whom she had previous connections. Her desire to assist him (and perhaps place him in her debt, if Nixon's view is to be believed) was not unusual. In looking toward her own political future, she knew that Nixon was a politician on the rise (again). Strengthening her relationship with him was useful for increasing her influence in Washington and Republican circles, and displaying her own connections in Taiwan to Nixon was a canny maneuver to enhance her own status.

With his politician's savvy, Nixon recognized that she had ties to some Asian centers of power that he lacked and hoped to use her connections in Asia, but on his terms. If indeed he was reluctant to have any contact with Mrs. Chennault, why not avoid her altogether? It is unlikely she could have gained access to him had he not allowed it. In Asia on business, Nixon sought to bolster his foreign policy credentials. Since Anna was in favor with Taiwan's rulers, Nixon's apparent warmth toward her would impress his hosts. He discriminated between his public and private dealings with her, knowing that any private contacts could never be confirmed.

Even if Nixon viewed her as a political liability because of her previous association with Barry Goldwater, with the far right wing of the Republican Party, or with the most rigidly anti-Communist foreign policy perspectives, and was willing to disparage her in front of State Department officials and his own entourage, he nonetheless permitted her contact and did so in such a way that she remembered their encounter positively. The reason for Nixon's negative personal view of her is not totally clear. As an example of their problematic relationship, Chennault said that two of Nixon's friends (Robert Hill and George Fuller) had approached her to help him get an appointment with Chiang Kai-shek. She recalled that Chiang was not particularly interested in meeting with him since Nixon, no longer vice president, was in no position to aid Taiwan. As a result, Chiang's office told Nixon that the Generalissimo could not see him. Anna appealed to Ambassador Konsin Shah (who was director of protocol at the Ministry of Foreign Affairs at the time), who confirmed that she requested that he make arrangements for the Nixon-Chiang meeting. The ambassador also said that Chiang did meet with Nixon at Sun-Moon Lake, a vacation retreat outside Taipei occasionally visited by President and Madame Chiang, a point confirmed by the embassy staff member.

If this were the case, Nixon may not have known of her actions on his behalf, and, if he did know, would not have wanted to admit he needed her assistance. Chennault attributed this to the fact that in the 1960s, conservatives were reluctant to acknowledge the contributions of women. The issue goes beyond that. Nixon's ego would have made it hard for him to admit he needed assistance from anyone. Moreover, his desire to keep the limelight on himself explains why he tried to stay away from Chennault, who was never shy about seeking and taking credit. The citizen-diplomat and the politician were beginning the cultivation of a long-term working relationship whereby each one would use the other.

Nixon fails to mention Chennault in his memoir either during this visit to Taiwan or at any other time. Despite his desire to publicly distance himself from her, his verifiable meetings and contacts with her throughout his administration prove that when necessary, she was important enough to keep their relationship active. Whether Nixon would admit it or not, as the 1960s progressed, Anna Chennault's myriad activities and connections made her a valuable ally in Washington and Asia—especially in "free" Asia, the focus of U.S. Cold War foreign policy. She used her influence to advance the government's anti-Communist argument to the American public, while at the same time facilitating the exchange of ideas and influence between Asian and American leaders and policymakers. When J. Edgar Hoover wrote her to say, "It was a pleasure to be a part of the delightful company you assembled last evening. Thank you for including me," he expressed the sentiment of many people in Washington who valued the role that she played in linking politics and business in a comfortable social setting.[20] Such skills made Mrs. Chennault a textbook example of an informal diplomat.

Notes

1. Chennault, *Education of Anna*, 156.
2. Byrd, *Chennault*, 364, citing interview with Joe Y. Chennault.
3. C. Joseph Rosbert, telephone interview by author, Franklin, North Carolina, September 7, 1995.
4. Acts of the General Assembly of the State of Louisiana, No. 54, July 5, 1894. In 1972 a bill was passed that "provid[ed] that there [wa]s no longer a prohibition of marriage between members of the white race and persons of color." House Bill 920, State of Louisiana, Acts of the Legislature, No. 256, July 5, 1972.
5. *Washington Post*, October 2, 1958; *New York Times*, October 2, 1958.
6. Thomas Corcoran to Rev. Edward B. Bunn, August 26, 1958, box 104, folder 4, Corcoran Papers.
7. Baroness Stackelberg, "Chennault Dinner Honors Hero's Memory," *Baltimore News-Post*, May 31, 1961.
8. Chennault, *Education of Anna*, 167.
9. Foundation letterhead, "Chennault Foundation" 1 of 3, Chennault Papers.
10. Certificate of Change of Purpose and Number of Directors, filed in New York, April 1962, ibid.
11. Anna Chennault to Herbert Hoover, April 19, 1961, "Chennault Foundation" 3 of 3, Chennault Papers.
12. Mrs. Claire L. Chennault before the Subcommittee on Escapees and Refugees, Senate Judiciary Committee, June 8, 1962, 87th Cong., 2d sess., *Congressional Record*, A4319.
13. Ibid., A4320.
14. While not available for 1962–63, Chennault's papers do include, by way of illustration, a folder of 1966 contracts with her agent, W. Colston Leigh, Inc., for speaking engagements indicating over twenty dates for that year. "1966 Contracts," Chennault Papers.
15. Chennault, telephone interview by author, July 7, 1996.
16. Papers of the Republican National Committee, Box RNC #32—Republican National Committee Women's Division, Office of Presidential Libraries, National Archives and Records Administration, Washington, DC.
17. Chennault, *Education of Anna*, 167.
18. Ibid., 169–70.
19. Jonathan Aitken, *Nixon: A Life* (Washington, DC: Regnery Publishing, 1993), 365.
20. J. Edgar Hoover to Anna Chennault, September 24, 1965, Chennault Papers.

4

"October Surprise"

The Rise of an Informal Diplomat

Within ten years of her husband's death, Anna Chennault was at the center of a major episode of informal diplomacy, the 1968 "October surprise." The basic story—that Mrs. Chennault, at the behest of Republican presidential candidate Richard Nixon, used her connections to the leaders of South Vietnam to prevent their participation in the peace talks announced by the Johnson administration six days before the election—has been covered by most studies of the period. Among her career activities, only this event has received any extensive examination. Yet, the perspectives from which it has been analyzed do not reveal its true significance.

It is not, as some have assumed, merely the story of presidential electoral machinations, a model of failed peace efforts, or a narrative of the personal ambitions of a woman on the political rise. All the participants, even President Lyndon Johnson and his advisers, took a rather simplistic view of Chennault's activities, judging only her impact on South Vietnamese President Nguyen Van Thieu while ignoring the repercussions within their own circles. This episode is foremost an illustration of the power of unofficial diplomacy on policymakers. Not at issue is the question of whether Johnson's efforts could have succeeded without the intrigues of Nixon's team; that possibility has been discounted by historians elsewhere and is less crucial than examination of how the episode launched Chennault's career as an informal diplomat.

Her ties to the leaders of the South Vietnamese government and to the Republican Party made her appear powerful to those wishing to use her for specific ends.

These ties also allowed her to advance her own ideological view—that of the necessity of continued U.S. support for the "free" nations of Asia in order to avoid the domino effect of Communist takeovers predicted since the Eisenhower administration. This was the legacy she carried forward from the General and made her own in the 1960s. Her importance was, in fact, subtle; while her actions were expected to greatly affect President Thieu, they influenced President Johnson's administration and American electoral politics even more. The final outcome earned her both gratitude and criticism. Anna moved beyond her famed husband and, over the next ten years, fashioned her own public identity. No longer Mrs. *Claire* Chennault, after the 1968 election she was more frequently referred to as Mrs. *Anna* Chennault. Thus, understanding Anna Chennault as a paradigm of informal diplomacy requires that the "October surprise" events be viewed in the contexts of American-Vietnamese foreign policy and her evolving career.

Making the Connections

By the time Nixon got back in touch with Chennault after the Taipei airport episode, his 1968 presidential bid was well under way. His position as an international affairs expert was well developed by 1966. Examples of his attempts to keep himself in front of the American foreign policy establishment were the publication in the *New York Times* of his critique of President Johnson's late-September 1966 Manila summit meeting with allied Asian leaders and a 1967 article in *Foreign Affairs* titled "Asia after Vietnam," in which he proposed a new U.S. approach to the PRC.[1] As he prepared for his presidential run, Nixon recognized the Vietnam War as the major campaign issue.

Chennault had firm ties within the political leadership of several "free" Asian nations such as South Vietnam, Taiwan, and the Philippines. She built on a base of acquaintances as the General's widow from his CAT days, then added her interview subjects as a Chinese freelance journalist and her contacts from a budding aviation consulting career. She continued her frequent visits to Saigon, Taipei, and other Asian capitals. From Nixon's perspective, any misgivings about working with her were overridden by his desire to use her unique connections to the South Vietnamese government for his own purposes. Knowing that she was a loyal Republican made it easy for him to secure her help. Thus, while lecturing in

Asia in the spring of 1967, she received a cable from Nixon asking her to meet with him as soon as possible.

They met in Nixon's New York apartment, where he asked her to become an adviser to his campaign on Southeast Asian affairs. "He had to rely on people like [her], well-informed, trustworthy, and with solid connections to the Vietnamese leaders, to supply him with reliable information," because he questioned the adequacy of the reports he received from the State Department. He told her that "[a]s a lecturer on Asian affairs, [she could] be of great help to [him]." Her inquiries as to his plans should he be elected were met with vague references to "end[ing] th[e] war with victory."[2] This promise was the single strongest factor in Chennault's decision to act as a liaison for Nixon. She recalled suggesting a meeting between Nixon and President Thieu, which Nixon readily agreed would be useful. As they parted, Nixon requested another meeting after her next Asian trip.

Later in 1967, Chennault met with President Thieu of South Vietnam (GVN, Government of Vietnam) in Saigon during a regular trip on behalf of an aviation client. She described the purpose of the meeting as "an informal presentation of credentials . . . delivering a message from Nixon requesting [that she] be recognized as the conduit for any information that might flow between [Nixon and Thieu]."[3] Until the presidential election in November 1968, she kept Nixon apprised of the attitudes of the GVN leaders about the war as well as the peace talks that commenced in May 1968 in Paris between the United States and North Vietnam (DRV, Democratic Republic of Vietnam).[4]

Early on, she recognized the intransigent attitude of the GVN leaders toward any negotiations. Their disinclination to participate was communicated back to Nixon, primarily through what became regular contacts between Chennault and John Mitchell, Nixon's campaign manager and future attorney general. She realized from Mitchell's comments that she was expected to convey the "Republican position" to the GVN: hold firm and do not participate in peace talks.[5] Identifying completely with the nonnegotiable attitude of the GVN leaders, she considered it akin to the circumstances she had witnessed in China during its civil war when she believed that U.S. abandonment of the Nationalists led to the PRC victory.

Anna Chennault's involvement with Nixon's campaign also meant service on an advisory "foreign policy task force." The weekly meetings at the Capitol Hill Club included influential

Republican leaders such as Texas senator John Tower, who served as chairman; Massachusetts governor John Volpe, Maryland congressman Rogers C. B. Morton (who in 1971 was named secretary of the interior by Nixon), Wisconsin congressman Melvin Laird (future secretary of defense), New York senator Charles Goodell, Ambassador to Spain Robert Hill, businessman Bryce Harlow (who became assistant to the president, then counselor), and occasionally the Senate Republican minority leader, Everett Dirksen of Illinois.[6] Anna's presence among such company was evidence that her position as a special expert on Asia was recognized by leaders within her party. Whatever else Nixon might have thought about her, it is apparent that she was deemed valuable enough to place her in positions designed to exploit her expertise.

Her great value to both American and Asian policymakers rested on her astute political observations, knowledge of national political realities, and personal relations with leaders. As a journalist, she was a trained observer of people and society. And in mid-1968, when she became the vice president of international affairs for Flying Tiger Lines (FTL), her connections to political and military leaders in the non-Communist nations of Asia and the United States expanded to include almost any government official related to the aviation industry in Asia. FTL was started in 1945 by former members of the Fourteenth Air Force as a domestic and international air cargo carrier, and her position there kept her moving in high-level circles on both sides of the Pacific. Chennault maintained her impressive political access over successive decades because both foreign and domestic policymakers believed she had similar connections in other capitals; leaders who wanted her continued assistance kept open their lines of access to her.

When the GVN ambassador to the United States, Bui Diem, arrived in Washington in the late 1960s to begin his assignment, Anna already had met him in Saigon in 1965 while he was an assistant to then Prime Minister Nguyen Cao Ky.[7] Bui Diem had sought her out during the Saigon visit because he was "eager then to know as much as possible about Washington"—a typical example of a foreign official recognizing her mastery of the American scene.[8] At the suggestion of the Nixon campaign, she arranged a meeting between Ambassador Diem and the Republican Party's presidential candidate.[9] While Diem and his staff hoped to influence the Vietnam War planks in both the Republican and Democratic Party platforms, the ambassador was reluctant to offend the Johnson administration, so he proceeded cautiously and informed the State Department of his intention to meet with Nixon.[10]

The most recent evidence indicates a single meeting in Nixon's New York apartment in July 1968.[11] The number of participants was very limited and the meeting itself was unknown to most of Nixon's staff—both Chennault and Diem record John Mitchell as the only other person present. During the cordial session at which they discussed the Vietnam War and politics in general, Nixon indicated that the ambassador "should rely on [Chennault] . . . as the only contact between" Nixon and the GVN.[12] In addition, she mentioned an hour-long portion of the meeting behind closed doors with only Nixon, the ambassador, and Mitchell.[13]

Bui Diem was only one connection to the government of South Vietnam. Chennault was well acquainted with President Thieu's brother, Nguyen Van Kieu, the GVN ambassador to Taiwan at the time, and one of her sisters was married to a ROC diplomat in Saigon. Both Mrs. Chennault's and Diem's memoirs noted that President Thieu sought independent sources of information whose loyalty to him was more assured than Diem's; Thieu was leery of those he believed were more loyal to Nguyen Cao Ky, so he used his brother and others to contact Anna.[14] In addition, she knew important men in the Vietnamese legislature and military hierarchy going back to her years with General Chennault and CAT. Her friendship with Vice President Nguyen Cao Ky and his wife began when she interviewed him in the early 1960s. She also maintained a solid relationship with Prime Minister Tran Thien Khiem and his wife; he was ambassador to Taiwan and then to the United States in the early 1960s. All these connections gave Chennault just what Nixon wanted—an insider's perch from which to observe and interpret GVN policy.

As time ticked away toward Election Day, Chennault busied herself with various duties for the campaign. She served as chair of the Women for Nixon-Agnew National Advisory Committee, which included Mamie Eisenhower, Shirley Temple Black, and Clare Boothe Luce as co-chairs, and she was a member of the Republican National Finance Committee, for which she raised $250,000.[15] In addition, she continued traveling to South Vietnam as a columnist for a leading Chinese newspaper, which kept her current with the GVN leaders' views.[16] She attended the 1968 Republican National Convention in Miami as a District of Columbia delegate and served as executive secretary to the Platform Committee.[17] Indeed, her participation in Nixon's campaign was important enough to earn her a spot at his headquarters for the private revelation, prior to the public announcement, that Spiro Agnew would share the party's ticket.[18] In summary, her position in the campaign was ensured through multiple levels of election work as well as the unseen channel that she maintained to the South Vietnamese government.

Meeting the press during Nixon's 1968 campaign

Peace Talks

Watching her native China fall to the Communists in the aftermath of World War II made Chennault particularly sensitive to GVN efforts to maintain U.S. support against its entrenched enemy. Like many Americans who advocated greater U.S. backing of Chiang Kai-shek during the civil war, Anna placed more blame for the CCP victory on the absence of greater U.S. patronage than on inherent weaknesses in Chiang's government. This bias, coupled with her own anti-Communist ideology, made her a willing participant in Nixon's Vietnam triangle (Nixon, Anna Chennault, and the GVN government) and helped her rationalize the merits of funneling information between a government she wanted to survive and the presidential candidate she believed would best defend its interests.

The Johnson administration's peace efforts placed the Saigon government in a very difficult position. The GVN feared that rather than pursuing the war to a military victory, the Americans might force it to accept a coalition government with the National Liberation Front (NLF), the southern insurgents supported by Hanoi. In March 1968, Johnson announced an end to bombing north of the 20th parallel with an invitation to Hanoi to begin peace talks. To the surprise of many, including the White House and the GVN, Hanoi agreed to begin negotiations in May.

Once official peace talks between the United States and North Vietnam began in Paris, American policymakers worked for DRV reciprocity in the war in exchange for U.S. actions. But the DRV's representatives in Paris seemed in no hurry to break the stalemate that ultimately developed, and little progress was made until October 1968. The Saigon government was highly suspicious of Hanoi's motives. According to Bui Diem, Thieu believed that by starting talks with the United States, "the North Vietnamese were achieving both a bombing halt and . . . [an] . . . ability to affect the [American presidential] election."[19] Thieu considered the Americans naive if they believed establishing a coalition government would protect GVN sovereignty. In fact, no discussion of a coalition government was part of American overtures in 1968.[20]

Chennault appreciated GVN apprehensions of the negotiations developing in Paris. One of the most critical components of the talks was the American effort to engage the GVN and DRV directly. The GVN refused to talk to representatives of the NLF, and the DRV resisted negotiating with Saigon, which the DRV viewed as a puppet government controlled by Washington. The Americans proposed an our-side, your-side formula whereby the United States and DRV each composed their own negotiating teams, thus allowing the GVN and NLF to participate without being recognized as independent entities.[21] Ultimately, this formula was unsatisfactory to the GVN leaders. They believed it represented an American effort to establish a coalition government with the NLF as an equal partner to the Thieu regime. From Thieu's perspective, "a [Hubert] Humphrey victory would mean a coalition government in six months; with Nixon at least there was a chance."[22] Chennault conveyed all these GVN reservations to Nixon.

She corresponded several times with Nixon during 1968.[23] Her records also include several return letters from him, most of which seem to have been form letters that went to many of his closest supporters, but one from late September with a handwritten signature was personal. On his own letterhead—not that of the campaign—the typed message read:

> Dear Anna:
>
> I have your letter of September 16 and again want to say how deeply grateful I am for your dedicated efforts in my behalf.
> You are doing just great!
> With best personal regards,
>
> Sincerely,
>
> Dick[24]

Without the September 16 letter for reference, this note could refer to any of a variety of "efforts" by Anna: minority organizing, Women for Nixon-Agnew, Republican Finance Committee, or liaison to the GVN government. However, it is possible that only the latter role was significant enough to warrant a special thank-you note; the others constituted her standard campaign activities.

On October 15, 1968, Chennault sent Nixon a lengthy memo marked "Confidential" on the issue of Vietnam. She discussed the war and peace talks, primarily the "bombing pause" and the "de-Americanization of the war." On the first point, she characterized the bombing halt as "a false issue" because it allowed the DRV "to [throw] upon the Americans the 'aggression charge' "—meaning the DRV could portray the United States as the war's aggressor because of its bombing policy. According to Anna, American war critics argued that the absence of a "complete [bombing] cessation . . . constitute[d] a stumbling block to . . . negotiations in Paris." But she saw "more cons than pros" from a bombing halt on the "military consequences . . . to the fighting men in Vietnam," believing that American soldiers were hurt by such a pause. Whether a bombing halt would really bring "fruitful negotiations in Paris . . . nobody knows."[25]

A main DRV tactic had been to "separate the war in *North Vietnam* from the one in the *South*," Chennault further noted. Thus, once bombing of the DRV stopped, Hanoi "would presumably tell the Americans that [it] ha[d] nothing to do with the war in [the South] and that if the [United States wanted] peace they would have to talk to the [NLF]," therein achieving for the DRV a safe sanctuary in the North "while the Americans would still be tied up by the war in the South." She argued that if the DRV really wanted to have "serious talks, there were thousands of ways available to them for discreet contacts." But they have "deliberately . . . avoided all such opportunities," so the DRV's actions proved that its leaders were "debating among themselves whether they have to enter into negotiations *now* or *later*." Here, she went beyond any mere reporting role for Nixon and delivered an analysis on the finer points of delicate negotiating issues. Her appraisal of DRV intentions revealed her anti-Communist bias, especially by discounting the DRV's willingness to join in peace talks, which they had already done in March of that year. These comments likely reflected some thinking of the GVN leadership as well, but were not put forward as such.[26]

On the "de-Americanization of the war," Chennault pointed out that everyone agreed that the questions were: "Through what procedures? How long will it last and in the meantime how can we gradually plan for the Vietnamese to take over?" She recognized that "it should be clearly understood that the [GVN] have to take care of the main fighting and that the Americans are only helping the Vietnamese to negotiate and to fight."[27] Finally, she highlighted a "vital" issue to "be remembered": "Whatever . . . the process [of] de-Americanization, . . . it should be . . . worked out in an atmosphere of confidence and cooperation between South Vietnamese and Americans (along with other allies) long in advance and discreetly in view of giving time for the [GVN] to psychologically prepare their public opinion of their own people to avoid giving the impression of a unilateral pull-out which would be disastrous for Asian morale in general and detrimental to the overall interests of Americans in the Pacific."[28]

This analysis of U.S. actions in withdrawing from the war, coupled with the necessity of maintaining a stable GVN and American influence in Asia, was nuanced. Chennault's assessment included the perspective of both GVN and DRV leaders, coupled with issues important for American leaders. She considered the larger picture of U.S. foreign relations, going beyond the view of the anti-Communist ideology with which she was identified and beyond only the issues of one, localized anti-Communist war. Nixon's eventual actions to end the war did reflect some of her suggestions on "de-Americanization" (which she claimed to have been the first to propose to him). His later escalations of bombing—in early 1969, and the famed Christmas bombings in late 1972—may also have stemmed from an agreement that bombing halts did not aid U.S. efforts. It is impossible to know how much this memorandum influenced Nixon, but the perspective articulated by Chennault was certainly part of the overall situational analysis that Nixon brought to his administration's war effort.

Simultaneous with Anna Chennault's reports on the GVN leaders was inside information received by Nixon from Henry Kissinger about the Johnson administration's efforts in Paris. His reports effectively kept the campaign apprised of the peace talks' progress in the critical final weeks before the election. Kissinger, a Harvard professor of government, originally served as Nelson Rockefeller's foreign policy adviser during Rockefeller's unsuccessful run for the 1968 Republican presidential nomination. When Nixon appropriated Kissinger by asking him to serve as a foreign policy adviser to his campaign, Kissinger declined a formal role, saying he could do "more if I work behind the scenes."[29] Although Kissinger never had contact with key Vietnamese players comparable to Chennault's, his credentials and access within not only the Johnson White House but also among its eventual negotiating team in Paris proved useful to Nixon.

Both Anna Chennault and Henry Kissinger were involved in high-stakes games where American domestic politics was concerned. Both acted as informal diplomats for Nixon on the international scene in a way that influenced domestic events. Both also used their positions within inner diplomatic circles for their own objectives—an unacceptable motive for shameless manipulation of diplomacy or domestic politics. Chennault's objective was to aid the presidential candidate whose views were closest to her own, whose plans seemed to best support GVN integrity, and who promised to end the war in a favorable manner for both the GVN and the United States. Kissinger's objective was to ingratiate himself with Nixon in order to gain a high-level position in the new administration. Kissinger never passed along (and likely never received) any truly sensitive information about the peace talks; however, in late September he warned the campaign that "something big was afoot regarding Vietnam," as Nixon later wrote. In October, Kissinger alerted the Republicans of Johnson's impending bombing halt announcement before there were any public revelations.[30] With Kissinger exposing the peace talks' progress and Chennault reporting the GVN's reluctant attitude, Nixon was in a powerful position to manipulate the situation for his political advantage.

The Johnson administration was accused of using the peace talks and bombing halt to aid Democrat Hubert Humphrey's presidential campaign. A close examination of the documents does not support such a conclusion. In late July the United States was still pressing Hanoi for reciprocity on the existing bombing halt, reiterating the same key requirements demanded since May. The Americans had no control over the timing of Hanoi's response and thus no way to manipulate the peace talks. The ice finally broke in Paris when, on October 11, the DRV representatives inquired if the bombing would stop if they agreed to include the GVN in the talks. At the same time the Soviet Union's embassy in Paris delivered a message to American negotiators that Hanoi would agree to GVN participation if the bombing stopped, and talks with all parties could resume the day after the bombing ceased.

Ellsworth Bunker, the U.S. ambassador in Saigon, kept President Thieu and his subordinates well informed of the terms that American negotiators set forth in Paris. Reams of cables between Paris, Saigon, and Washington recount the tedious negotiations carried on by the Americans with both the DRV and the GVN in an effort to bring about multilateral peace talks. When Hanoi's "feeler" came on October 11, Johnson instructed Bunker in Saigon to confer with President Thieu, who agreed to go along "so long as [the United States is] going to press the offensive in the South and in Laos, and . . . [is] prepared to resume the bombing if they [the North Vietnamese] violate the DMZ or attack the main cities."[31] This acceptance gave Johnson the green light to make final arrangements with DRV representatives. He methodically got the approval of all his "diplomatic and military authorities" to proceed. But, on October 14, when American negotiators in Paris reported back with news of the U.S. willingness to stop bombing in exchange for acceptance of the GVN at the peace talks, the North Vietnamese seemed to waver on their previous offer.

At this point, the Nixon camp had been alerted by Kissinger of the impending breakthrough in Paris. The information was relayed to Mrs. Chennault by John Mitchell, as were Kissinger's previous communications. Her steady contacts with the GVN kept her informed of its view of Paris events, particularly the dissatisfaction with some of the American positions. Ambassador Bui Diem wrote that Thieu viewed "the North Vietnamese offer [as] nothing but a ploy to influence the presidential race in favor of Humphrey, whom they much preferred to Nixon, with his cold war background." Even intelligence reports of the time indicated that the DRV leaders believed that the more dove-like stance of Humphrey would work to their advantage if he were elected.[32] Saigon's leaders did not need any persuasion from Anna Chennault to prefer Nixon's election to Humphrey's.

President Johnson decided to brief the three presidential candidates on the progress in Paris. On October 16, while campaigning in Kansas City, Nixon participated in a conference call with Johnson, Humphrey, and independent George Wallace. Nixon recalled that the president told them that "there had in fact been some movement by Hanoi, but that anything might jeopardize it." Upon assurance of American insistence on the same points necessary to halt the bombing, Nixon and the other two candidates said they "would support whatever arrangement Johnson could work out."[33] Nixon saw Johnson that same night in New York at the Alfred E. Smith Memorial Foundation dinner where Humphrey, Nelson Rockefeller, and other political luminaries were in attendance. Nixon wrote that there, Johnson asked him to "be careful about what I had to say on Vietnam."[34] It is clear that Johnson worried about the need for secrecy, coupled with a fear that the candidates might say something that would derail his administration's efforts to achieve peace before he left office.

Watching Mrs. Chennault

Much of the historical debate about the "October surprise" is dominated by such questions as the level of Anna Chennault's involvement, how much Nixon knew of or directed her actions, or how much she influenced the South Vietnamese. Another important issue is her domestic impact as a citizen-diplomat. There is no doubt that Thieu's government, on its own, was unwilling to take part in any peace initiative with an American government it did not trust to protect its political integrity. It is also certain that Chennault communicated these attitudes to Nixon, either directly or through Mitchell. What is left to evaluate is how these unofficial diplomatic events affected presidential politics as well as how Chennault's actions, as manipulated by Nixon, influenced not only the 1968 election but also the Johnson administration. This is the unexamined aspect of the "October surprise" and a major element of its importance to American foreign relations.

The Johnson administration became aware of Mrs. Chennault's activities several weeks before the election. According to Clark Clifford, then secretary of defense, this knowledge was gained "through the normal operations of the intelligence community . . . the FBI, the CIA, and the National Security Agency . . . [including] surveillance of the Ambassador of our ally [Bui Diem], and an American citizen with strong political ties to the Republicans."[35] Johnson and his advisers faced a terrible dilemma. They had evidence of an individual involved with the GVN leadership who purported to represent Nixon, but the information had been gathered by politically sensitive means that they could not reveal. Revelations of this type would arouse at least as much concern about the source of the information as about the activities. In the end, Johnson decided not to risk exposing Nixon and Anna Chennault.

During a pre-dawn meeting at the White House on October 29, Johnson discussed additional evidence of Chennault's activities—the contents of a note to National Security Adviser Walt Rostow from his brother Eugene. An "informant" told Eugene Rostow that

> he thought the prospects for a bombing halt or a cease-fire were dim, because Nixon was playing the problem . . . —to block [it]. [Nixon] was taking public positions intended to achieve that end. They would incite Saigon to be difficult, and Hanoi to wait.
>
> [This] would make it easier for Nixon to settle after January. Like Ike [Eisenhower] in 1953 [concerning Korea], he would be able to settle on terms which the President [Johnson] could not accept, blaming the deterioration of the situation between now and January or February on his predecessor.[36]

Additional information further confirmed Nixon's attempts to influence both the GVN and the DRV.[37] Johnson was so angered by these disclosures, which confirmed his suspicions about Chennault, that he ordered FBI surveillance of her.[38]

Written evidence of government observation of Mrs. Chennault has increased in recent years as more researchers gain access to formerly classified material. One view is contained in two memos from Rostow to Johnson written just before the 1968 election. In the first one, dated Sunday, November 3, Rostow cited an item from the November 1 *Washington Post* stating that Mrs. Chennault "intended to proceed to New York City where she would await the election results . . . with Presidential nominee Richard M. Nixon." The memo noted her car in the parking garage of her apartment building (the Watergate) that morning. She later left, with her chauffeur at the wheel, via the Baltimore-Washington Parkway "heading north." Rostow told the president that "arrangements have been made with the New York office of the FBI for them to observe the car en route and to undertake discreet surveillance with reference to her activities while in New York."[39] Rostow had accepted the news report, assumed that she was already headed to New York in her car, and planned to have her watched.

Chennault, however, remained in Washington until Election Day, when she voted in the early morning, then flew to New York to await the outcome. This is confirmed by the second memo written Monday, November 4, which detailed her movements the morning before Election Day. She was followed from her home to the South Vietnamese embassy, to a Nixon campaign office, back to the embassy, then to the Taiwan embassy before returning to her own downtown office.[40] These memos demonstrate not only the serious attention given to her activities, but also the scope of the surveillance directed toward American citizens by the federal government because of its concern about the peace process.

The Johnson administration had visual and taped evidence that Anna was meeting with the GVN ambassador and others. They knew she expressed sympathy for their difficult position and encouraged their inclination to avoid peace talks with Hanoi, and they knew she said that she represented the Nixon campaign. They did not know whether Nixon directed her actions, but they suspected he did. Johnson's concerns caused his staffers to engage in the same kind of extreme and often illegal actions that would ultimately bring about the downfall of Nixon's administration five years later.

Playing the Insider Card

Ambassador Bui Diem scrambled around Washington during October 1968 in an effort to keep his government's concerns before U.S. policymakers. He received volumes of cables from Saigon reporting the developments between Bunker and Thieu and spent countless hours meeting with Assistant Secretary of State for East Asia William Bundy and Walt Rostow.[41] At that time, the ambassador was unaware that American intelligence agencies were intercepting his communications to and from Saigon.[42] On October 23 he cabled his government that "many Republican friends have contacted me and encouraged us to stand firm. They were alarmed by press reports to the effect that you had softened your position." Then, four days later, he reported to Saigon that he was "regularly in touch with the Nixon entourage," whom he later identified in his book as Anna Chennault, John Mitchell, and Senator John Tower.[43] As the peace negotiations grew more tense with the approaching proposed bombing halt, such statements led Johnson administration officials to presume the worst about possible domestic interference in the diplomatic arena.

Initially, on October 28, the Johnson administration received word from Bunker in Saigon that he had worked out a joint announcement of the bombing halt with President Thieu. U.S. leaders planned to make the joint declaration on October 31, but it never happened. At the last minute, South Vietnam balked. Late on October 28, Thieu and his advisers insisted on several additional conditions necessary for their concurrence with the bombing halt and peace talks. Johnson believed that his worst nightmares about Anna Chennault's impact were coming true. Over the next two days, frantic efforts continued in Saigon to induce Thieu's government to join the peace talks.

In Washington, leaders decided to go ahead with the bombing halt "on the basis of the previously agreed joint position."[44] The Johnson administration thought it had to pursue the opportunity to start serious talks with the DRV in exchange for some halts in aggression, yet the president faced a problem if he proceeded without Saigon's participation. If the United States began substantive talks alone, it might fuel arguments that the move toward peace was purely political.

President Johnson and his advisers feared being accused of playing politics in peace talk efforts. He had decided not to run for reelection in 1968 and was trying to end the war before he left office. Suddenly, the chance was there, but its timing seemed very suspicious. But Johnson forged ahead. As Secretary of State Dean Rusk told him, "if you were doing this for political reasons you would have done this before the [national party] conventions."[45] Clifford advised, "As soon as the decision is made [to stop the bombing] don't let the date of the election concern you. The weight of public opinion is for this. . . . There is more benefit than detriment. It will leave not a single stone unturned in your quest for peace."[46]

As the administration debated, Nixon brought the issue into the open. With his background knowledge from Chennault and Kissinger, he stated, "I am told that top officials in the administration have been driving very hard for an agreement on a bombing halt. . . . I am . . . told that this spurt of activity is a cynical, last-minute attempt by President Johnson to salvage the candidacy of Mr. Humphrey. This I do not believe."[47] Nixon was careful to do nothing to arouse accusations that he was hindering peace. But his statement was designed to further raise suspicions of the Democrats and ascribe cynical, self-serving, political motives to the Democrats even as he denied that it was so.

It can be argued that the Johnson administration was manipulated as much by the machinations of the DRV in tandem with its ally, the Soviet Union, as it was by Richard Nixon through his minion, Anna Chennault. It was Moscow's early October initiative that restarted the peace mechanism, not any new proposals from the Americans. Clifford later said that "the decision to move at this time is not based on our initiative. It is based on Hanoi's initiative."[48] Clifford's statement highlighted an issue not generally raised in discussions of these events: the possibility that Hanoi and Moscow manipulated the 1968 election with the timing of DRV acceptance of talks with the GVN. Indeed, even Rostow recognized that the GVN leadership suspected that Hanoi and Moscow were trying to get Humphrey elected. Such intrigues, Saigon's leaders believed, justified their own use of leverage with respect to the peace talks—actions encouraged by "some in the Nixon entourage."[49] The DRV and the Soviets expected an easier opponent in Humphrey than in the well-known Cold Warrior Nixon. The interests of Communist policymakers seeking a Humphrey victory were as much at stake as those of an incumbent Democratic administration hoping to continue its partisan control of the presidency into the next decade.

On the morning of October 29, President Johnson learned "that people who claimed to speak for the Republican candidate were still trying to influence the South Vietnamese to drag their feet on the peace talks." American policymakers could only speculate whether Thieu and his advisers were swayed by Chennault's arguments that Nixon would be more friendly to their interests, or Thieu was having trouble within his own regime. Johnson thought that "both were probably true," yet he never specifically named her in public or in his memoirs. Whatever the case, he knew the agreement was unraveling.[50]

In the end, Johnson went ahead with the bombing halt and the negotiating arrangement with Hanoi. He wanted to issue a joint announcement with Thieu that the bombing would end on October 31 and talks would begin on November 6 or later—notably *after* the election. The disadvantage of the GVN's absence from the talks was outweighed by the fear that the talks might collapse altogether.

Rostow sent Johnson a memo on October 31, the day of his planned speech, which outlined possible actions if President Thieu refused to participate in the talks. He suggested that Johnson bring in Nixon "alone" to share with him their evidence of Thieu's plans and Chennault's participation, while "tell[ing] him flatly that you [Johnson] are confident that he has had nothing whatsoever to do with this." Rostow hoped to remind Nixon of the problems that Syngman Rhee had caused Dwight Eisenhower—and Nixon as his vice president—during Korean War negotiations. Rostow's remark that "we simply cannot let these inexperienced men [presumably Nixon, Thieu et al.] snatch defeat from the jaws of victory" demonstrated the administration's desperation.[51]

The president and his staff spent the day of October 31 notifying various political leaders of the impending announcement and preparing his speech. The speech draft had two endings—one announcing Saigon's participation, and one skirting the issue. Johnson held out hope all day that Ambassador Bunker could still persuade Thieu to join them in Paris. Finally, Johnson placed a conference call to the three presidential candidates to advise them of the coming announcement. He detailed the negotiations since their last conversation on October 16. After asking a few questions, all three candidates said that they would "back [him] up."[52] Clifford recalled that Johnson then said that "some old China hands are going around and implying to some of the Embassies . . . that they might get a better deal out of somebody that was not involved in this. Now that's made it difficult and it's held up things a bit, and *I know that none of you candidates are aware of it or responsible for it*."[53] In fact, Johnson was telling and warning Nixon that he knew about Republican activities in an effort to discourage further meddling. The president left unsaid what he would do with such information and thus hoped that his revelation to Nixon would result in Thieu's agreement to go to Paris.

On the night of Johnson's October 31 speech, Anna Chennault attended a dinner given by Perle Mesta, the venerable Washington hostess. As the guests finished dessert, John Mitchell phoned Chennault and asked her to call him back from an "anonymous number" due to his concern about tapped phones. She left the party with her escort, Tom Corcoran. When she returned Mitchell's call, she asked Corcoran to listen in on an extension phone because she "had a sense of needing moral support, or a witness, or both."[54]

Johnson's bombing halt announcement had prompted Mitchell's call. He told her, "I'm speaking on behalf of Mr. Nixon. It's very important that our Vietnamese friends understand our Republican position and I hope you have made that clear to them."

With Thomas G. Corcoran and J. Edgar Hoover in Anna's Watergate penthouse apartment, circa late 1960s

Chennault thought that "the instructions seemed to have changed from the ones I had been given, simply to keep Nixon informed of South Vietnamese intentions." She recounted the rest of the conversation:

> "Look, John, all I've done is relay messages. If you're talking about direct influence, I have to tell you it isn't wise for us to try to influence the South Vietnamese. Their actions have to follow their own national interests, and I'm sure that is what will dictate Thieu's decisions."

> But Mitchell sounded nervous, "Do you think they really have decided not to go to Paris?"
>
> "I don't think they'll go. Thieu has told me over and over again that going to Paris would be walking into a smoke screen that has nothing to do with reality."[55]

No direct accounts of the conversation from Mitchell or Corcoran exist. But, in an article after Anna Chennault's autobiography came out in 1981, Corcoran said, "people have used Anna scandalously, Nixon in particular. I know exactly what Nixon said to her and then he repudiated her."[56] Corcoran referred to Nixon asking her to convey the Republicans' "hold firm" message to Thieu and other GVN leaders and then denying it. In the final analysis, since Chennault is the only one left alive to recount the events, the conversation and Nixon's role in the episode must remain uncorroborated.

Chennault had read the GVN leaders accurately and knew their decisions were based on their own sense of national security. Her professed annoyance at Mitchell was out of place, however, considering her earlier recognition that communicating the Republicans' "hold firm" position was part of their expectations of her. Actually, she knew that, first, Thieu would act as the Republicans hoped without more prodding from her; and second, that GVN internal politics were best served if the decision was prompted by national interests, not concern about American domestic politics. She was confident that her goal of helping the GVN by electing Nixon would be aided when Thieu refused to go to Paris.

After Johnson's bombing halt speech, election momentum swung toward Humphrey because of rising hopes that the Democrats would soon end the war. On October 21, Nixon held an eighteen-point lead in the Gallup Poll. By November 2, his advantage had shrunk to only two points, but he was far from deflated by this turn of events. The former special assistant to President Thieu, Nguyen Tien Hung, described Nixon's pleasure at the Democrats' expense: "With his intimate knowledge of what Thieu was contemplating in Saigon, [Nixon] was glad to see the Democrats sinking into a self-created trap. Nixon knew that Thieu would not go to Paris [thanks to Chennault], yet the Democrats were inflating the prospects for peace by linking the bombing pause to expanded Peace Talks scheduled for November 6."[57] Nixon's knowledge gave him an advantage over his opponents. While these events appeared to favor Humphrey, Nixon worked to inflate Americans' hopes. In a Madison Square Garden speech on October 31, Nixon announced that neither he nor his vice presidential candidate (Agnew) would "say anything that might destroy the chance to have peace."[58] With his inside information that Thieu would not go to Paris, Nixon was, as Hung put it, "setting up Humphrey and Johnson for a fall."[59]

Following Johnson's October 31 bombing halt speech, Ambassador Bunker spent many more hours trying to build a consensus. Thieu told Bunker "privately . . . that he would not do anything to upset [Johnson's] initiative," and he confirmed this sentiment by telling Bunker at a diplomatic corps reception the night before his own speech that "everything is okay."[60] Thieu's final reply was given in his address to the Vietnamese National Assembly on the country's National Day, November 1. When he said that "the government of South Vietnam deeply regrets not being able to participate in the present exploratory talks," the chamber erupted in cheers and a standing ovation. Ambassador Bunker, seated in the Assembly Hall's front row, was stunned.

The response to Thieu's declaration was equally shocking to the audience in the White House. Johnson, in particular, feared that the initiative for peace had been lost and believed that Republican activities had contributed to the debacle. Rostow sent Johnson a lengthy memo on November 2, explaining that Ambassador Bunker thought that Thieu would not change his position until after the U.S. election. Rostow cited a supportive "cable to Nixon from a number of South Vietnamese Senators" as proof of GVN sentiment.[61] Rostow's memo also suggested challenging Nixon with the administration's information on Chennault's activities, but Johnson still resisted.

On the day after Thieu's speech, the FBI's tap on the embassy line picked up a call from Anna Chennault to the South Vietnamese embassy. She again "urged Saigon to hold firm: they'd get a better deal with Nixon." The embassy official asked if Nixon knew about her call. She said, "No, but our friend in New Mexico does."[62] Those listening in took this to mean vice presidential candidate Spiro Agnew, who was then campaigning in Albuquerque. President Johnson ordered phone records checked, but initial reports uncovered no calls between Agnew's campaign plane and Chennault.[63] A November 3 memo from Rostow to Johnson, which mentioned this conversation and other surveillance, confirmed that LBJ knew of these contacts.[64]

New material indicates that a call from Albuquerque did go to Anna Chennault, and that it could have been made by Agnew. However, it seems implausible that Nixon would have shared his most dangerous secret—an inside connection to the GVN leaders—

with Agnew. Late in the 1990s, Chennault wavered on these conversations while never faltering in her position that Nixon knew of and/or directed her actions. She once said that FBI wiretap technicians misunderstood her; she insisted that she said "New Hampshire," where John Mitchell was at the time, and anything Mitchell knew or told her to do would have been known or come from Nixon. When confronted directly with phone records indicating a call to her from New Mexico, she was less sure of her memory. The question of where and whether she spoke with Agnew, Mitchell, or another Nixon lieutenant is irrelevant for the purpose of understanding her as an informal diplomat. She operated within the context of Nixon's mission for her, not only on specific actions ordered directly by him. Her objective was to keep Nixon and GVN leaders informed of each other's intentions with whatever tactics she deemed best.

Nixon masterfully manipulated the fallout from Thieu's repudiation of the Paris talks over the last weekend of the campaign. He used his own November 3 "Meet the Press" television appearance to exempt himself from Republican charges that the bombing halt had political motives. While he did not say it, "many of my aides and many of the people supporting my candidacy around the country seem to share [the] view . . . that the bombing pause was politically motivated and was timed to affect the election."[65] In the same interview, Nixon offered to assist Johnson's peace negotiation efforts in any way he could if he were elected, even going to Saigon or Paris if the president "would consider it helpful."[66] Thus, Nixon, the man who had secretly encouraged Thieu's rejection of the peace talks and benefited thereby, publicly volunteered his services to Johnson in advancing negotiations. Historian Stephen Ambrose puts it best: "Nixon's pledge, with its implicit reminder of Ike's 1952 promise that if elected 'I shall go to Korea,' was as bold and brazen as anything he had done in a career marked by boldness and brazen effrontery."[67]

Nixon's television comments pushed Johnson to his limit, but, rather than challenging Nixon directly, the president summoned the highly respected Illinois senator, Everett Dirksen. Dirksen heard the accusatory speech that the president would have preferred delivering directly to Nixon, but Johnson settled for its filtering back to the candidate. The senator's report to Nixon reiterated Johnson's suspicions of Chennault's activities, but they presumed that the Democrats had nothing that incriminated Nixon personally since Johnson had not specified anything. If, however, Johnson or

Humphrey raised a suspicion against Nixon by making charges of complicity and naming a known Nixon supporter such as Anna Chennault, it might be enough to make a difference in what then appeared to be a dead-heat election.

Concerned that an upset of his carefully laid plans might be in the offing, Nixon placed a call to the president. Many sources claim that Johnson phoned Nixon, but records clearly indicate that the call was made by Nixon to the president at his Texas ranch.[68] Johnson quizzed Nixon about Chennault's activities. Nixon claimed that she was acting on her own and that his "only wish was to help Johnson achieve peace."[69] Nixon was not about to concede anything, and Johnson seemed to accept his denial, but he had no other choice without any conclusive proof of Nixon's direct contacts with Chennault. In the end, the president never—even in his memoirs—publicly stated that he suspected Nixon was personally involved in her activities. The evidence against her and, by association, against Nixon was, in the end, politically unusable.

By Monday, November 4, the day before the election, pollster Lou Harris had conducted two surveys: the first showed Humphrey ahead by three points, but the second revealed that Nixon was again in the lead.[70] Nixon had waited out the surge that peace prospects brought Humphrey and was rewarded when his manipulations brought public opinion back his way.

The election was incredibly close: according to final Associated Press compilations of voting totals, Nixon won by only 499,704 votes out of the over 73 million cast, or just 0.7 percent of the turnout.[71] Such a tight race might have been altered by the release of allegations of Chennault's and, by implication, Nixon's collusion in Thieu's actions. It cannot be proved that the bombing halt would have pushed Humphrey over the top even if the GVN had participated in the Paris talks. However, because the vice president's popularity had risen along with the approaching prospects for peace in the waning weeks of the campaign, Thieu's refusal to go to Paris can logically be judged the momentum stopper. Whether or not this was the "critical margin of difference," Nixon feared that margin enough to risk everything and use Anna Chennault as a link to South Vietnam's leaders.[72]

The decisions by Johnson and the Humphrey campaign not to make any revelation about Anna Chennault and the Republican candidate were fateful. Their decisions were prompted by two primary factors: lack of a conclusive connection between Nixon and Mrs. Chennault, and the Democrats' unwillingness to reveal their sources. Had the State Department known that she was a party to Ambassador Bui Diem's meetings with Nixon, the Johnson administration might have started its surveillance of her sooner and amassed the type of evidence necessary to make a public accusation. But the U.S. government was unwilling to admit that it spied on its allies and citizens, particularly since such activities were often conducted illegally. Exposure could have destroyed American credibility, even if such "eavesdropping" was a known practice—such as the alleged bugging of Thieu's Saigon office. Ultimately, unsubstantiated charges might have redounded against Humphrey, suggesting that his was a desperate campaign seeking any means, no matter how fantastic, to discredit his opponent.

In his memoirs, Clark Clifford suggested another reason for the Democrats' silence: underestimation of the "damage" to the U.S. negotiating position in Saigon from the Chennault-Nixon channel to GVN leaders.[73] It is worthwhile to speculate why Chennault's actions were minimized by the American delegation in Saigon when she created such great concern in Washington. First, Thieu and his advisers responded positively to Ambassador Bunker's frequent proposals for the peace talks, right up to the last minute. American representatives in Saigon saw no evidence of Chennault's efforts. Second, since 1960s diplomacy was still almost exclusively a male domain, the notion of a woman having such impact was perhaps unfathomable. If Armand Hammer (for example) had talked to the GVN leaders, would his influence have been so depreciated? Even Clifford's reference to Anna Chennault by the nickname "Little Flower" was a put-down. U.S. diplomats in Saigon probably asked themselves, "Could one woman's actions derail the long hours, weeks, and months of negotiations we have conducted?" Their answer was one of disbelief.

A third consideration was the close association of Thomas Corcoran to both President Johnson and Anna Chennault. Nguyen Tien Hung and Jerrold Schecter write that Humphrey tried to muzzle Chennault through one of his own major supporters, James Rowe, Corcoran's law partner. They claim that Rowe told Humphrey that "Thieu will hold on," meaning he would not go to the peace talks. They also claim that Johnson wanted to avoid hurting Corcoran by exposing Mrs. Chennault.[74] It is impossible to imagine that had the Democrats possessed useable incriminating evidence against Nixon, they would have kept quiet just to protect Corcoran. Rowe's oral history interview states that around November 3 he asked Johnson, "Do you want me to get Tommy to pull her off?" but the president replied, "It's too late."[75] Even had this strategy been tried, the Democrats' connections to Mrs. Chennault through Corcoran were not strong enough to override her personal desire to assist the GVN.

Whatever the reasoning (complicated and multifaceted as it was) behind the decision to keep Anna Chennault's activities out of the public view, the consequence was very probably Nixon's victory. Many observers suggest this outcome. The "October surprise" established a precedent that subsequent presidential candidates have attempted to duplicate to their advantage. Most definitely, the events demonstrate informal diplomacy in its most politically covert and dangerous form.

Denial and Repudiation

The final act in this diplomatic drama came after the election, when Nixon was pressured by Johnson to act on his professed support of the peace talks and join with Johnson in urging Thieu to come to Paris. Nixon cared less for the GVN going to Paris than having his victory sullied by Johnson raising charges against Anna Chennault, so the president-elect went along. Just a week after the election, Mitchell asked Chennault to "persuade [the GVN] to go to Paris." Incredulous, she demanded an explanation for the about-face and was told, "This, whether you like it or not, is politics."[76] She refused to carry such a message and stormed out of the meeting. Nixon then asked Senator Dirksen not only to deliver the message to Ambassador Bui Diem but also to "make sure that [Chennault] would not let anger get the better of [her] by talking to the press."[77] She received repeated calls and visits over successive weeks and months from "Nixon lieutenants" who urged her to keep silent about Nixon's use of her South Vietnamese connections.

Nixon's secret remained just that—for almost two months after the election. Stephen Ambrose claims that the connection "was widely known among the reporters covering the campaign, but it was up to Humphrey or Johnson to make it public, as none of the reporters had any hard information."[78] No news stories broke until January 3, 1969, when a front-page item appeared in the *St. Louis Post-Dispatch* under a picture captioned, ". . . Nixon campaigner talked to South Vietnamese." The lengthy story described events leading up to the election with reasonable accuracy. Everyone interviewed denied much of what had occurred. Chennault herself responded to questions by saying, "You're going to get me in a lot of trouble. . . . I can't say anything . . . I know so much and can say so little."[79]

Indeed, she knew far more than most Nixon campaign operatives. Years later she acknowledged that just Nixon, Mitchell, Tower, and Robert Hill, a long-time Nixon adviser—all now dead—knew of the campaign's connections to the GVN through her.[80] Thus, no unequivocal independent confirmation of her part in these events can ever be obtained. Few Johnson administration observers will talk about the matter. Rostow has said only that Chennault's writings on the subject were very accurate and could be "take[n] as gospel truth."[81] Another official confirmed that Johnson had "ample evidence" of her contacts with the Nixon campaign but gave no specifics.[82]

The *Post-Dispatch* printed a follow-up story, again on page one, "Tower Charges Coverup, Denies GOP Tried to Stall Paris Talks"; other papers around the nation and in several foreign countries reported on the events.[83] In early March 1969, Congressman Clement Zablocki (D-WI) called for an investigation by the State Department of Chennault's alleged actions. He suggested that she "could be in violation of a federal law which prohibits American citizens from meddling in this country's foreign policy."[84] Zablocki referred to the 1798 Logan Act, which outlawed private citizens negotiating with foreign governments. The law did not apply, for she never purported to represent the U.S. government. As author William Safire put it, "Mrs. Chennault had every right as an American citizen to urge other nations to do whatever she wanted them to do, which is why her surveillance was illegal; had she been breaking the [Logan Act], the surveillance would be admitted by now [1975] and action against her would have been taken."[85] Safire correctly identified a part of the Democrats' difficulty in exposing Nixon's Saigon connection.

Anna Chennault issued a press release denying any wrongdoing following Zablocki's statements on the episode. The issue sporadically reappeared throughout 1969, but popular attention never really focused on the story. Perhaps it all seemed too implausible to be true. Even when Chennault told the story in her 1980 autobiography, it drew little attention from a by-then cynical public no longer surprised by such political machinations.

Despite the fact that President Thieu's inclinations were only encouraged, not created, by Anna Chennault—and Richard Nixon, by implication—the reality of private citizens acting independently to influence the outcome of diplomatic events should not be overlooked. The "October surprise" illustrates best what is arguably the negative side of informal diplomatic activity. Mrs. Chennault's and others' manipulative actions affected U.S. diplomatic relations generally and the lives of war victims—civilian and military—specifically.

The circumstances of the 1968 election and the Vietnam War created a favorable and unusual milieu for such activity; domestic and diplomatic elements are rarely so aligned. Nixon and his team knew how to take advantage of the situation. Chennault used her connections to the GVN's leaders and her knowledge of their fear of U.S. abandonment to aid him. Kissinger used Nixon's fascination with foreign policy and thirst for information to ingratiate himself with a potential presidential employer. And Nixon used Chennault and Kissinger for knowledge with which to gain control over the diplomatic situation in Vietnam so he could manipulate it to his electoral advantage. In this manner, informal diplomacy affected foreign relations and domestic politics simultaneously.

The propriety of what Chennault, Kissinger, and Nixon did is highly debatable. Nixon's actions were personally and politically motivated, as were Kissinger's. As historian Ambrose puts it, "[Nixon] could not keep himself from trying to influence Thieu through Chennault," and he did it "in an effort to scuttle the peace prospects."[86] He wanted the presidency so badly that he risked all by using Chennault's ties to Thieu. Kissinger sought a position in the incoming administration from which to implement his own strategies for American foreign relations. Chennault acted not out of loyalty to Nixon, but from a desire to assist the GVN in its fight against communism. She truly believed that Nixon would do more to help Saigon's leaders, that he would not abandon them or force them to accept an unworkable coalition government, and that he would end the war soon.

She could not tolerate the American "abandonment" of Chiang Kai-shek in 1949 also becoming the fate of President Thieu. Nixon was best for South Vietnam, she thought, and thus best for the United States because she wanted America to have an anti-Communist ally in Asia, one uncompromised by any coalitions or forced unifications. This conviction motivated her and allowed her to think that she was doing nothing improper or harmful to either the GVN or her adopted nation. Nixon knew that her personal convictions would aid his cause. As she said, "I was young and naive, and believed that Richard Nixon meant it when he said he wanted to end the war honorably."[87] The strength of her belief in Nixon (at the time) equaled her commitment to aiding the GVN.

Any personal motives that Anna Chennault might have had are less discernable. She most certainly recognized the value of ensuring the election of the next president, yet she was never directly rewarded because the Nixon camp wanted to keep her under wraps. She was used to rubbing elbows with important leaders and policymakers, but the chance to make a difference through her own actions appealed to her, particularly given the strength of her wish to save the GVN. The flattery of being approached by Nixon to help him—to give him something that only she could provide—was hard to ignore. Her self-admitted naiveté shows that she was susceptible to flattery. From her perspective, there was no reason why she should not or could not be an important player in U.S.-Asian relations, especially when Nixon held out his hand and asked for her assistance. All her years of experience and work appeared to have come to fruition.

Regardless of the motives of the participants, the ethics of their actions must be assessed. If Thieu had been less certain of his decision to stay away from the Paris talks, his friendship with Anna Chennault could have made her opinions decisive and thus made her a king-maker in the 1968 election. One could argue that she may be excused because her actions were driven primarily by the (arguably) more altruistic motive of halting communism's spread in Southeast Asia, and because she believed that Nixon would soon end the war "honorably." But that argument is too simplistic.

She could and should have known that Nixon's Cold Warrior exterior was cracking as he recognized the need to achieve a rapprochement with Asia's Communist giant, the PRC. Nixon expressed these views in a number of public forums in the mid- and late 1960s. Her self-proclaimed "naiveté" is an unconvincing explanation. It is understandable, but not excusable, that the spectacle of American politics would dazzle someone accustomed to witnessing single individuals (like General Chennault) effect historical change and mold events and outcomes.

Nixon, had he ever admitted complicity, might have given an altruistic explanation for his actions as well—he sought to end the war sooner than Humphrey either by being a tougher negotiator or a more aggressive commander-in-chief. But neither the final peace settlement nor Nixon's broadly illegal and unethical behavior support such arguments. And Kissinger, who acted from naked personal ambition, similarly lacked a defense grounded in the national interest or benign objectives. Therefore the "October surprise" of 1968 illustrates how informal diplomacy can negatively affect America's foreign relations. It also served as a catalyst to launch Anna Chennault into the highest circles of informal diplomacy. However, learning from the lessons of her 1968 experiences, she would turn her energy in succeeding decades toward more positive aspects of unofficial diplomacy, particularly in the business and social arenas.

Notes

1. *New York Times*, October 27, 1966; "Asia after Vietnam," *Foreign Affairs* (October 1967).

2. Chennault, *Education of Anna*, 170.

3. Ibid., 185.

4. GVN and DRV were the common U.S. government designations for the names adopted by each nation.

5. Chennault, telephone interview by author, July 3, 1996.

6. Chennault, *Education of Anna*, 174.

7. Ibid., 175; Bui Diem with David Chanoff, *In the Jaws of History* (Boston: Houghton Mifflin Co., 1987), 236.

8. Diem, *Jaws of History*, 236.

9. Chennault, *Education of Anna*, 174; Diem, *Jaws of History*, 236.

10. Diem, *Jaws of History*, 236.

11. Chennault Papers. Bui Diem described a single meeting; Diem, *Jaws of History*, 236.

12. Chennault, *Education of Anna*, 175–76; Diem, *Jaws of History*, 237.

13. Chennault, *Education of Anna*, 175–76.

14. Diem, *Jaws of History*, 245; Nguyen Tien Hung and Jerrold L. Schecter, *The Palace File* (New York: Harper & Row, 1986), 23.

15. Chennault, *Education of Anna*, 185; Peter M. Flanigan to Rose Woods, October 2, 1968, White House Central Files, Social Affairs, Nixon Project.

16. Chennault, *Education of Anna*, 184.

17. Ibid., 178; Republican National Committee Papers.

18. Chennault, *Education of Anna*, 179.

19. Diem, *Jaws of History*, 239.

20. Hung and Schecter, *Palace File*, 22.

21. George C. Herring, *America's Longest War: The United States and Vietnam, 1950–1975*, 2d ed. (New York: Alfred A. Knopf, 1986), 210, 217.

22. Hung and Schecter, *Palace File*, 21.

23. William Safire described letters from her to Nixon on June 24, June 28, August 19, and October 15, 1968. See Safire, *Before the Fall* (Garden City, NY: Doubleday, 1975), 88–90.

24. Nixon to Chennault, September 28, 1968, "Vietnam Correspondence," Chennault Papers.

25. Chennault to Nixon, October 15, 1968, "Vietnam," 1, Chennault Papers.

26. Ibid.

27. Ibid., 1–2.

28. Ibid., 2.

29. Walter Isaacson, *Kissinger: A Biography* (New York: Simon & Schuster, 1992), 129.

30. Richard Nixon, *RN: The Memoirs of Richard Nixon* (New York: Grosset & Dunlap, 1978), 400–401; Seymour M. Hersh, *The Price of Power* (New York: Summit Books, 1983), 20.

31. Briefing Paper, October 28, 1968, 1, National Security Files—Files of W. W. Rostow, box 6, "Vietnam: July–December, 1968," Lyndon Baines Johnson Library, Austin, Texas, 3–4.

32. Diem, *Jaws of History*, 239; "Special Daily Report on North Vietnam for the President's Eyes Only," October 18, 1968, National Security Files—Memos to the President—Walt Rostow, vol. 100, box 40, LBJ Library.

33. Nixon, *RN*, 402.

34. Ibid.

35. Clark Clifford with Richard Holbrooke, *Counsel to the President, A Memoir* (New York: Random House, 1991), 583.

36. Notes, 10/29/68, 2:30 A.M. Meeting with Foreign Policy Advisory Group, p. 21, National Security File, Special Files: Tom Johnson's Notes of Meetings, set III, box 4, LBJ Library.

37. Rostow to Johnson, October 29, 1968, 6:00 A.M., National Security Files—Memos to the President—Walt Rostow, vol 102, box 41, LBJ Library.

38. Author's confidential background interview with a former Johnson administration official, May 18, 1995. The surveillance was also confirmed by a former FBI official in an unattributable interview, July 18, 1994.

39. Rostow to Johnson, November 3, 1968, National Security Files—Memos to the President, Walt Rostow, vol. 103, box 41, LBJ Library.

40. Rostow to Johnson, November 4, 1968, page 2, National Security Files—Country File, Vietnam, box 137 (2 of 2), "Memos to the President/Bombing Halt Decision, 11/1–5/68, vol. 4, 1 of 3," LBJ Library.

41. Diem, *Jaws of History*, 240.

42. Clifford, *Counsel to the President*, 583.

43. Diem, *Jaws of History*, 244.

44. Memo—Bombing Cessation, November 10, 1968, page 8, Diary Backup—11/11–11/21/68, Box 115, "November 11, 1968," LBJ Library.

45. Meeting notes, October 29, 1968, 1:00 P.M., page 4, Tom Johnson's Notes, set III, box 4, "Tuesday Meeting with Foreign Policy Advisory Group," LBJ Library.

46. Meeting notes, October 14, 1968, page 8, Tom Johnson's Notes, set III, box 4, "Meeting with Foreign Policy Advisory Group," LBJ Library.

47. Nixon, *RN*, 405; Meeting notes, October 25, 1968, 12:38 P.M., Tom Johnson's Notes, set III, box 4, "Meeting with Foreign Policy Advisory Group," LBJ Library.

48. Meeting Notes, October 29, 1968, 2:30 A.M., page 14, Tom Johnson's Notes, set III, box 4, "Meeting with Foreign Policy Advisory Group," LBJ Library.

49. Rostow to Johnson, October 29, 1968, 2:50 P.M., National Security Files—Files of W. W. Rostow, box 6, "Vietnam: July–Dec., 1968," LBJ Library.

50. Lyndon Baines Johnson, *The Vantage Point* (New York: Holt, Rhinehart & Winston, 1971), 521.

51. Rostow to Johnson, October 31, 1968, 11:50 A.M., National Security Files—Files of W. W. Rostow, box 5, "Nixon, Richard—Vietnam," LBJ Library.

52. Clifford, *Counsel to the President*, 593.

53. Ibid.

54. Chennault, *Education of Anna*, 190.

55. Ibid., 190–91.

56. *Washington Post*, February 18, 1981.

57. Hung and Schecter, *Palace File*, 26.

58. Nixon, *RN*, 406.

59. Hung and Schecter, *Palace File*, 27.

60. Ibid., 26–27.

61. Cable, Rostow to Johnson, November 2, 1968, page 2, National Security Files—Memos to the President, Walt W. Rostow, vol. 103, box 41, LBJ Library.

62. Thomas Powers, *The Man Who Kept the Secrets: Richard Helms and the CIA* (New York: Alfred A. Knopf, 1979), 199.

63. Cartha "Deke" DeLoach, *Hoover's FBI: The Inside Story by Hoover's Trusted Lieutenant* (Washington, DC: Regnery Publishing, 1995), 399–406.

64. Rostow to Johnson, November 3, 1968, National Security Files—Memos to the President, Walt W. Rostow, vol. 103, box 41, LBJ Library.

65. Quoted in Stephen Ambrose, *Nixon*, Vol. 2, *The Triumph of a Politician, 1962–1972* (New York: Simon & Schuster, 1989), 212–13.

66. Partial transcript of "Meet the Press," November 3, 1968, National Security Files—Files of W. W. Rostow, box 5, "Nixon, Richard—Vietnam," LBJ Library.

67. Ambrose, *Nixon*, 2:213.

68. Defense Communications Operations Unit, Communications Branch, Presidential Calls List, November 3, 1968, Presidential Appointment File—Diary Backup, box 114, 10/23–11/10/68, "Appointment File 11/3/68"; President's Daily Diary Cards, entries for Richard Nixon, 11/3/68, LBJ Library.

69. Ambrose, *Nixon*, 2:213–14.

70. Theodore H. White, *The Making of the President—1968* (New York: Atheneum, 1969), 446–48.

71. Cited in ibid., Appendix A, 509–10.

72. Lewis Chester, Godfrey Hodgson, and Bruce Page, *An American Melodrama* (New York: Viking Press, 1969), 734

73. Clifford, *Counsel to the President*, 583.

74. Hung and Schecter, *Palace File*, 485, note 31.

75. Interview with James H. Rowe, Jr., November 10, 1982, page 21, LBJ Library.

76. Chennault, *Education of Anna*, 193.

77. Ibid., 194.

78. Ambrose, *Nixon*, 2:214.

79. Thomas W. Ottenad, January 1, 1969, *St. Louis Post-Dispatch*, 1.

80. Chennault, telephone interview by author, April 4, 1995

81. Walt Whitman Rostow, interview by author, March 16, 1994, Austin, Texas, LBJ Library.

82. George Christian, Austin, Texas, letter to author, St. Louis, Missouri, April 26, 1995.

83. January 13, 1969. Thomas Ottenad, who wrote both stories, was the Washington correspondent of the *Post-Dispatch*.

84. John W. Kole, "Zablocki Calls for Investigation of Reports on Mrs. Chennault," *Milwaukee Journal*, March 5, 1969.

85. Safire, *Before the Fall*, 90.

86. Ambrose, *Nixon*, 2:216, 207.

87. Chennault, interview by author, December 9, 1991.

5

Mastering the Milieu

Socializing and Politics in Foreign Relations

On March 21, 1975, Gerald L. Warren, deputy press secretary to President Gerald R. Ford, sent a brief note to Dr. Frederick Chien, the director of Taiwan's Government Information Office in Taipei: "I wanted to let you know how much . . . I enjoyed being with you last Tuesday at Anna Chennault's dinner party. Thank you very much for the two books. It was very thoughtful of you and I look forward to reading them."[1] Mrs. Chennault often brought together American and Asian leaders when she entertained during her travels abroad. It is an example of her mastery of *guanxi*, a Chinese term that William Safire defined as "the network of personal, familial and commercial relationships used by East Asian men to advance their interests." Among Asians, *guanxi* is usually considered "a benign connotation [of the] interplay of favors, jobs and status among the upwardly mobile," but often its "clear connotation" among Westerners implies "bribery, political fixing and general corruption."[2] This difference provides some explanation of how Chennault was successful as an informal diplomat while at the same time engendering hostile feelings among those who deemed her a manipulator.

Anna Chennault conducted parallel careers in politics and business in which her role as a facilitator made her a powerful player. Just as Republican Party liaisons connected her to American policymakers, the aviation industry connected her to Asian leaders. Moreover, as a successful hostess, she tied business and politics together in ways that enhanced her relationships and increased her prestige. This social aspect of informal diplomacy, often dismissed as merely the stuff of newspaper society pages, has been underexamined and underestimated as a part of foreign relations. In fact, this network of activity lubricates the wheels of diplomacy with its most essential elements—communication and influence.

Her personal influence can be shown in two ways: her contact with wide public audiences, and her access to a high-level bureaucratic constituency. Beginning in the 1950s through her speeches and writings, Chennault developed a reputation as an astute observer and chronicler of Asian and American affairs. She garnered respect for her ability to assess both American and Asian—particularly Chinese—perspectives, motives, and reactions. In addition, to the public at large she represented a voice of experience because of her firsthand knowledge of both societies.

As a prominent member of the Republican Party, Anna Chennault enlarged her contacts and expanded her influence into the late 1980s. She held various positions—short- and long-term, highly visible and behind the scenes—and used them to strengthen the party's electoral and financial power. Much of her political career was spent building bridges from a partisan power base, using her business and social connections, to reach international leaders.

This career must be viewed within the framework of U.S. foreign relations. General Claire Chennault's staunch anti-Communist rhetoric during his last dozen years of life echoed the anti-Communist policies of the American government immediately following the end of World War II. Anna embraced those same beliefs in her articles, books, and lectures (mostly to women's groups) of the 1950s. After the General died, Mrs. Claire Chennault (as she was usually called then) continued to warn Americans about the Communist threat in Asia, although her audience had widened beyond luncheon and coffee clubs. Once the United States opened relations with the PRC, Chennault's views slowly softened, like those of the policymakers with whom she associated. Her philosophical turnaround mirrored that of the government in Washington and many American and Chinese-American citizens.

Political and social environments created the atmosphere in which Anna Chennault operated. From that base, her career blended both elements and joined key figures from many circles at dinners and parties that furthered the goals of her guests and herself, all in the name of advancing U.S. Cold War foreign policy. Her ideological evolution from the 1960s to 1981 took place within this sphere, and her initial boost up the Washington social ladder came when Richard Nixon was elected.

A New Social Force in Washington

Several months after the 1968 election, Anna Chennault went to see President Nixon at the White House, where he took her aside to thank her for her help in the campaign. She commented that she had "paid dearly for it," to which Nixon replied uneasily, "Yes, I appreciate that. I know you are a good soldier."[3] Her reputation had been tarnished in the press for her suspected role in the "October surprise" affair, and no defense except denial was possible—certainly not a satisfactory response for either the public or Chennault.

Following his 1968 victory, the new president wanted to avoid any further focus of the press or Congress on Chennault. Her activities were already a source of speculation in various domestic and foreign publications. Had she desired a high-level appointment, Nixon would have been in a difficult position. Neither one relished the prospect of confirmation hearings before Congress where uncomfortable questions about Nixon, Anna, and the South Vietnamese government might be raised. And, luckily for Nixon, she was too devoted to her daughters and her work for Flying Tiger Lines to be very interested in any post in the administration. For her, "the election had been a bitter lesson," and Nixon's immediate switch to support of the Paris peace talks and of GVN participation in them after the election further dampened any "desire to serve" on her part.[4]

The *Washington Post*, following news stories about her participation in the "October surprise," noted: "If Mrs. Chennault does ultimately become known principally as a party-giver during the next four years, Nixon's foreign affairs advisers will probably breathe a sigh of relief. . . . [A] figure of glamour and mystery in the Nation's Capital . . . [she] has already caused Nixon aides to fear . . . she might become a political embarrassment."[5] Even before his inauguration, the Nixon camp's denial of any connection to Anna Chennault's reported role in the peace talk incidents pushed her out of the political limelight. Once his need for her was over, Nixon seemed to follow his earlier declaration—expressed to his aide during the 1964 Taiwan visit—that he wanted no obligations to her. Having created a debt that she could never publicly call due, Nixon had, however, given her the upper hand. The tie between them, despite denials, gave her prestige and access to political and international circles, even if it precluded any role in the new administration. Estranged from Nixon, she nonetheless maintained and expanded her position in the Republican Party over the next twenty years.

Senator John Tower speaks to the gathering at Anna's Watergate penthouse in honor of his birthday, September 29, 1971

Her growing reputation as a Washington hostess of note brought her an assignment for which she was well suited. A month after the election, she was named a "Special Adviser" to the chairman of the 1969 Inaugural Committee, J. Willard Marriott.[6] It was an easy job that allowed the Republicans to give Chennault some visible—yet limited—reward for her campaign efforts and to use her skills, but it simultaneously kept her away from close press scrutiny. With the many details involved in the inaugural festivities, especially following the Republicans' eight-year absence from the White House, she was a good choice because of her wealth of connections. In particular, she handled press relations for the Governors' Reception Committee and assisted with a luncheon for the governors and their wives.[7] (She would hold the same position again in 1973, "Special Adviser" to that year's chairman, Jeb S. Magruder.[8]) Thus, when it suited national political leaders, Chennault's role was shifted from the political to the social, conveniently pushing her from the newspapers' front pages to the society pages before she flew off to Asia on her next business trip for Flying Tiger Lines.

Yet, to consider Chennault's greatest talent as that of social hostess would be a very short-sighted view of her. She hated that label; nonetheless, it furthered her political and business careers from the beginning. The social and political were often tied together in a very public record of her activities. Press descriptions of her life cannot be accepted as a truly accurate gauge of how she was perceived by the general public. While stories described her variously as a Republican hostess, dynamic businesswoman, widow of the famous Flying Tigers' leader, beautiful exotic Asian, multitalented author, or any combination thereof, it is impossible to know exactly what people thought of her. For example, her distinctive eye makeup (which highlighted her almond eyes) has been described by interview subjects as either beautiful or hideous. But among a certain generational group—those whose life experience included the World War II years—it is uncommon to find anyone who has never heard of her.

Her cycle of entertaining spiraled upward after Nixon's election. Each time gatherings at her luxurious Watergate penthouse were covered in the Washington social pages, she was able to bring in more powerful players, such as National Security Adviser Henry Kissinger, Secretary of Transportation John Volpe, Attorney General John Mitchell, Republican National Committee Chairman Senator Robert Dole, Air Force Secretary Robert C. Seamans, Jr., Chairman of the Joint Chiefs of Staff Admiral Thomas Moorer, Vice President Gerald Ford, and Taiwan Ambassador Konsin Shah. The *Cleveland Plain Dealer* speculated that "if Mrs. Chennault invites the President and his wife to a party, it's a pretty good bet they will attend. And in Washington, if a hostess snares the President for a party, she becomes a social lioness."[9] This example shows the high level of access that many people believed Anna Chennault had, although due to Nixon's desire to keep his distance, he did not attend.

Suppositions similar to those of the *Cleveland Plain Dealer*'s left the public and Washington watchers believing in Chennault's connections at the top. Even broader press coverage kept her name in front of the cognoscenti beginning in the late 1960s and continuing into the 1990s. Stories about her appeared in *U.S. Transport, Air Transport World, Palm Beach Life, The Washingtonian, Parade, Vogue, Ladies' Home Journal, Life, Time,* and *People.* In the late 1960s and early 1970s newspaper articles reported on her almost every week, featuring stories about her apartment decor, wardrobe, lifestyle, and entertaining (even printing her recipes). When she lectured out of town, local newspapers usually mentioned her speech and often included items about her lifestyle as part of their coverage; and surprisingly, for the era, her business or political ventures often received as much space as the hostess tales. Chennault's clipping files from the 1970s indicate that newspaper articles about her appeared in cities such as Chicago, Milwaukee, San Diego, Boston, San Francisco, Fort Worth, Dallas, Orlando, Honolulu, Manila, Bangkok, and Hong Kong. This coverage gave her a public platform from which to propound her ideology and build her reputation as a woman with connections and clout.

Perceptions of her influence were reinforced by articles such as "Singing for Their Supper at Mrs. Chennault's," in the *Washington Post,* which featured her in a photo with General William Westmoreland and former Korean prime minister Chung Il-Kwon. The variety of guests who attended parties at her home is obvious in this excerpt from the *Post* article:

> A politically powerful chorus sang for its supper . . . at Mrs. Claire Chennault's dinner party . . . Gen. Kim Kye Won, former director of Central Intelligence of Korea, led the assembled generals and diplomats and statesmen in a chorus of 'Old MacDonald . . .' Seven generals joined in. . . . Gen. Charles H. Bonesteel III . . . commander of all the American forces in Korea, the United Nations forces and the 8th U.S. Army until his retirement in 1969 explained the situation. . . . Rep. Gerald R. Ford . . . joined in on the chorus. . . . Sen John G. Tower . . . recite[d] a few lines of Hamlet's soliloquy. . . . Secretary of Transportation John A. Volpe sang a tarantella, in Italian. . . . The chain reaction of clapping and toe-tapping . . . originated in the corner containing Gen. Westmoreland, Gen. Benjamin O. Davis, Jr. USAF Ret., and Yung You Chen, Korean ambassador-at-large.[10]

The guests all toasted Mrs. Chennault's comment at the end of the evening, "I always resent it when they say Republicans give a dull party."[11]

Below the surface of this gay evening, serious informal diplomacy was conducted. Guests were introduced, wined, and dined in the company of others with common interests and goals who might be useful in future endeavors. Such an agenda was implicit for many social gatherings in Washington. Chennault's guests that evening included military officials, elected leaders, cabinet members, foreign diplomats, and policymakers, the standard mix at her dinners; absent that evening were business leaders. She did research on the backgrounds of prospective guests to make decisions on whom to invite to any given event.

The connections between guests at this particular party illustrate how social and informal diplomatic activities connect to foreign relations. The dinner was given in honor of two visiting Korean leaders: former prime minister Chung Il-Kwon, and former intelligence director General Kim Kye Won. Chennault's objective was to strengthen U.S.-South Korean relations. Having several generals present along with the House minority leader (Ford) and the ranking Republican senator (Tower) on the Armed Services Committee allowed the Korean guests of honor to emphasize the importance of maintaining strong U.S. military ties to their country. The Korean ambassador-at-large benefited from keeping up his acquaintances with American congressional and cabinet leaders on whom he might need to call in the future. Transportation Secretary Volpe and General Davis, director of civil aviation security, both had connections with international aviation and with Mrs. Chennault's interests at Flying Tiger Lines, but they might also be useful to former prime minister Chung and General Kim in future dealings with the United States involving aviation, either civilian or military.

Even though the two guests of honor were not in office at the time of the party, their connections and influence in Korea would be of use to the Americans with whom they spoke. The Koreans could report on conditions, describe policy initiatives, and generally keep their nation's agenda before U.S. policymakers. When schedules permitted, Chennault often held parties in honor of sitting foreign officeholders during their state visits. Similarly, she was invited to formal White House functions honoring them; for example, she attended a 1969 dinner for the prime minister of Japan, a 1975 state dinner for the emperor and the empress of Japan, and a 1984 dinner for Premier Zhao Ziyang of China.

Many people believed that she was the model for artist Milton Caniff's evil "Dragon Lady" character in his syndicated cartoon strip, "Terry and the Pirates." On that subject, Caniff said that "I first drew the Dragon Lady in December 1934. That's long before I met Anna. . . . We have this half-joking thing about her being the Dragon Lady and I have done a portrait of her that she has in her apartment in Washington. It's just one of those legends that grows up."[12] She and Caniff met shortly after World War II, when his cartoon was already well established. The name "Dragon Lady" has often been applied to powerful Asian women such as Empress Cixi and Madame Chiang Kai-shek of China or Madame Ngo Dinh Nhu of Vietnam.

"Dragon Lady" traits—demanding, dangerous, manipulative—were often attributed to Anna Chennault, mostly by those who were the object of her attention. In the final document of a series about finalizing her appointment to the UNESCO advisory board by the Nixon administration, a memo inquired, "Is it time to ask Mr. Hastings [Wilmot R. Hastings, executive assistant to the undersecretary of state] *on what day* the 'Dragon Lady' will receive her UNESCO appointment?" The handwritten response was, "This has been done. She has accepted. Several drinks have been had by all." Apparently, the persistence with which Chennault pursued this post, and the persistence of administration leaders such as Bryce Harlow (counselor to the president), Peter Flanigan (an assistant to the president), and Elliot Richardson (undersecretary of state) who secured it, engendered some negative feelings about her within the Nixon staff.[13]

Unpleasant opinions did not stop her. Even those who were not her friends or allies gave her a kind of grudging respect, possibly mixed with some fear or disdain, expressed in statements like "she's someone I would never want as an enemy." David Laux, the Reagan administration's National Security Council director of East Asian Affairs, acknowledged that she had "been effective in Washington, a town where parties and dinners are important." He thought that such events "provide a forum where ideas can be aired and effective proponents can make their points . . . because in real policy-making so much is in private conversation and connections made."[14] The diversity of guests that Chennault cultivated led to what Senator Mark Hatfield (R-OR) called a "salon atmosphere" reminiscent of an earlier era.[15] They gathered in elegant and comfortable surroundings—her antiques-filled Watergate penthouse or a favorite restaurant—ate extravagant meals, and engaged in lively discussions of the topics of the day.

A Republican Party Animal

Chennault's cultivation of congressional Republicans aided her position as vice president of international affairs for Flying Tiger Lines. She engaged in some congressional lobbying since her office was located in Washington, rather than in California, where FTL was headquartered. Although she was not FTL's formal lobbyist, her expanding connections were useful in influencing legislation on international aviation.

Her files of congressional correspondence begin around 1969–70 and include hundreds of letters on a variety of topics: invitations and thank-you notes for social events, fundraising, her Asian trips, upcoming legislation, and political campaigns. On Capitol Hill her contacts included anyone whose help she needed, particularly for the issue she cared most about—continued support for the ROC. And her allies were not limited to Republicans. The most obvious example was long-time Democrat Thomas Corcoran, Mrs. Chennault's political mentor, friend, and frequent companion. Her ability to "cross the aisle" was noted in a *Washington Post* article that included her in a list of fifteen people who gave money to both Democrats and Republicans.[16] In addition, the *Washington Evening Star* noted her attendance at a January 1971 Texas party for the state's new Democratic senator, Lloyd Bentsen: "hundreds of Texans and equally as many Washingtonians, . . . all viable Democrats, converged on the club." Secretary of Transportation John Volpe was there, and "another GOP face in the throng was that of Nixon administration hostess Anna Chennault."[17] Her allies were found primarily at the conservative end of the political spectrum, and all favored U.S. support of the ROC. Early in Nixon's first administration, endorsement of the ROC was still widespread despite the president's slowly softening position toward the PRC.

Unlike some people in the Nixon administration who welcomed the president's moves toward the PRC, Anna Chennault was angered by its entry into the United Nations that followed in the wake of thawing Sino-American relations. She found a sympathetic ear among supporters such as Congressman John Buchanan, Jr. (R-AL), with whom she exchanged letters in late 1971. On November 5, Buchanan thanked her for pointing out a front-page item in the *Washington Daily News*, "Anna Chennault: Reappraise U.N. Support."[18] In the article, she criticized the expulsion of the ROC from the United Nations (to allow in the PRC) and included separate photos of her and UN Ambassador George H. W. Bush. Mrs. Chennault, "long . . . regarded as Taiwan's most powerful advocate in Washington," expressed several concerns: "I consider this an anti-American vote, and I question [if] the American public will continue to give . . . financial support to this world organization." She was also "very disappointed that our friends let us down.

Particularly all those nations that have been getting aid from us." Finally, she declared, "let's hope the [United Nations] will not end up like the League of Nations. . . . [Its] effectiveness is in grave doubt. . . . Fortunately, the big events can't be settled in the [United Nations] anyway."[19] As the only individual quoted in the article, she summed up the main arguments that ROC supporters were raising in opposition to the vote expelling Taiwan from the United Nations.

Several days later, Congressman Buchanan wrote her again, enclosing a copy of his remarks in the *Congressional Record*.[20] There, he stated that "a thoughtful examination of the issues which have been raised in the wake of the [United Nations'] tragic ouster of Taiwan was recently given by a lady who is certainly one of the world's loveliest and most effective ambassadors for freedom, Mrs. Anna Chennault."[21] The newspaper article's full text was included in the *Record*. Chennault thanked him, saying, "I am most appreciative of your time and effort on my behalf."[22] Despite Buchanan's fulsome phrase—and many others like it in the public record—Anna herself never saw her gender as a liability. Instead, she believed that her femininity only made it "harder for people to say no" to her.[23]

Over the years, statements by or about Mrs. Chennault were often included in the *Congressional Record*. An examination of some of these entries and their sponsors illustrates the wide range of her activities and friends in the U.S. government. The earliest example was her statement before the Subcommittee on Escapees and Refugees of the Senate Judiciary Committee in 1962 on behalf of Chinese Refugee Relief, which was entered into the *Record* by Congressman John McCormack (D-MA) on June 12. Senator Strom Thurmond (R-SC) included her article about the plight of returning Vietnam veterans that had appeared in a St. Louis newspaper in 1967 in addition to her 1970 speech to the Union League Club of Chicago entitled, "The Spirit of the 70s—U.S. and Free Asia." Speeches that she gave to the Los Angeles Breakfast Club and the Commonwealth Club of San Francisco in 1969 both appeared in the *Record*, again thanks to Congressman McCormack. In 1972 she spoke to the National Planning Conference of the Chinese American Citizens Alliance and appealed for Chinese-American involvement in the political process and inclusion in administration "appointments of significance." This speech was entered into the *Record* by Senator Hiram Fong (R-CA), who also highlighted her effort to influence the 1976 Republican national platform by opposing de-recognition of Taiwan or abrogation of the mutual defense treaty between the United States and the ROC. Long-time ROC defender Senator Barry Goldwater (R-AZ) cited a letter sent in 1977 to President Jimmy Carter, signed by Anna Chennault and eighty other prominent Chinese Americans, decrying the absence of human rights on the Chinese mainland.[24] She cultivated political allies along issue as well as partisan lines, and both Democrats and Republicans increased her notoriety by such entries in the *Congressional Record*.

Anna Chennault also drew on her wide-ranging connections to influence legislation on non-Asian matters. In the fall of 1981 the Senate deliberated an AWACS (airborne warning and control system) plane sale to Saudi Arabia. She received a letter from Assistant Secretary of State for Congressional Relations Richard Faribanks that included a list of eighteen Republican senators whom he wished her to approach about voting in favor of the sale: "Any help that you could give us to change their mind [*sic*] would be greatly appreciated."[25] In a followup letter, she wrote Counselor to the President Ed Meese to advise him of her progress: she had called on and phoned some senators. In addition, she contacted fellow members of the Republican Senatorial Trust, the Republican Eagles, and President's Club (all fundraising groups) from "around the country to ask our own members to urge their Senators to support the President." As a result, she believed that some senators "have . . . changed their position in favor of the AWACS sale."[26] Meese thanked her for her help in securing a winning vote: "Winning . . . was no easy task, and it was only with the support of people like you that our efforts were successful."[27]

Her renown as a GOP fundraiser clearly allowed her to gain leverage in the Senate. Her ability to bring in funds and the history of her own contributions to Republican campaigns secured the attention of many political leaders over the years. Moreover, her positions in the 1968 campaign as co-chair of Women for Nixon-Agnew, chair of the Republican Women's National Finance Committee, and member of the Republican National Finance Committee provided access to major contributors, some control over the use of campaign funds, and the grateful appreciation of candidates. A list of her contributions for Nixon's 1972 Committee for Re-Election of the President showed a total of over $90,000, equivalent to over $370,000 in today's dollars.[28] More than $30,000 of this sum came from her friends, and about $8,000 went directly to senators and congressmen.

By the 1980s, her financial support of her party's candidates included both broad-brush backing and a focus on individual legislators whom she knew and admired. One list of her contributions—both personal and those she brought in—for the 1980 election totaled almost $675,000, or over $1.41 million in today's dollars.[29] This amount included over $50,000 from her personally to the Republican Party, its subordinate organizations (such as the Republican Eagles and Senatorial Trust), and presidential and congressional candidates.[30] Her membership in the Eagle and Trust groups required a $10,000 annual contribution each. In addition, she contributed personally to congressional candidates as well as to some state legislators' campaigns, particularly those of women and ethnic candidates, regardless of party. Correspondence acknowledged her gifts (generally $1,000) in the 1980s to the congressional campaigns of Ted Stevens (R-AK), William Armstrong (R-CO), Charles Percy (R-IL), Guy Vander Jagt (R-MI), Spark Matsunaga (D-HI), Gordon J. Humphrey (R-NH), Mark Hatfield (R-OR), Larry Pressler (R-SD), Rudy Boschwitz (R-MN), Roger Jepsen (R-IA), and S. I. Hayakawa (R-CA).[31]

Chennault co-hosted a 1981 fundraiser for Senator Orrin Hatch (R-UT) that was dubbed "The Catch for Hatch" by the *Washington Post* and brought in $500,000. At the event, she told a reporter, "Be careful how you refer to me. I'm a business executive, not a Washington hostess. I just do fund-raising for my friends."[32] More than a decade after her rise in Washington political circles, she was still trying to get beyond the hostess label and be recognized for her activities in the business world.

As her business career grew, however, so did her position within the Republican Party. In addition to fundraising, she became prominent in ethnic minority organizing, or working with "heritage" groups, as the party called them. The National Republican Heritage Groups (Nationalities) Council (NRHGC) was the umbrella organization within the party that coordinated fundraising, recruitment, candidate development, and election activities for Chinese-American, Italian-American, Polish-American, and other groups of ethnic Republicans. The NRHGC was started in 1968 on a shoestring but grew to claim a membership of 50,000 by 1972. Within the Republican National Committee there was a Heritage Groups Division that served as the Council's connection to the GOP.

Chennault founded the Asian-American Republican National Federation in the 1970s, and it became part of the NRHGC during her efforts to reelect Richard Nixon in 1972. Early that year, she hosted a reception as co-chair of the NRHGC Century Club founding members ($100 donors).[33] Such social events, as well as activity summaries of regional affiliates and policy items of interest to ethnic Americans, were a mainstay of the reporting in the *GOP Nationalities News*, a monthly publication of the Republican National Committee. The April 1972 issue featured a photo of Chennault as co-chair of the NRHGC, and an article about her candidacy for the District of Columbia's Nixon delegate to the Republican National Convention. The article stated that "the area of party [GOP] activity that interests her most is her work in the ethnic area" and quoted her as saying: "the party leadership is aware of the potential presented by ethnic Americans in the political process. My selection as a member of a delegate slate pledged to the President confirms that awareness."[34] Elected twice as NRHGC chairman in 1979 and 1987, she considered her NRHGC work the best way to bring Asian Americans into the political process.

Her desire for ethnic voters' involvement in American electoral politics went beyond getting them to the polls. Within the NRHGC, she worked to develop a strong statement of the important issues concerning ethnic voters, particularly as they related to U.S. foreign policy. At the NRHGC's third annual convention in 1973 (where Anna Chennault was reelected co-chair), twenty resolutions were passed covering both domestic and foreign policies and then were submitted for ratification to member organizations (such as the American Hungarian Republican National Federation and the Lithuanian Women's Club). The platform then became "the official ethnic voice of the GOP, expressing the collective opinion of 32 nationalities from more than 20 states."[35] The Council represented over "1000 nationality clubs, state councils and national federations."[36] This work with the NRHGC gave Chennault yet another avenue of access to political leaders, especially those whose reelections depended on ethnic votes. Her writings and position as General Claire Chennault's widow had established her standing among Chinese Americans, but the NRHGC gave her a wider and deeper platform from which to encourage all Asian Americans to become involved in politics and to influence policy formation.

In her highly visible and effective role as an advocate for ethnic Republicans, Anna pushed for the creation of an executive branch-level position in the Nixon administration to represent the concerns of all ethnic Americans. The NRHGC also advocated its establishment. Her long-standing friendship with Congressman Gerald Ford helped shape his "understanding, appreciation and recognition of our pluralistic ethnic society in America," and, as president, he established the position.[37] Ford recalled his initial meeting with Chennault during his first term as a congressman in 1949. "Impressed by her background in China and her marriage to the General," he immediately recognized her views as "important"—ones to be "listened to," "considered seriously," and "respected." Thirty-five years later, the former president declared that "history will see her as a factor in Asian-Pacific Basin politics."[38]

Meeting with President Gerald Ford at a White House briefing on the ethnic community in 1976

Thereafter, the Ford White House actively pursued ethnic support, with Anna Chennault and the NRHGC as important vehicles for doing so. For example, the president sent her a copy of his 1975 "message to citizens of Chinese ancestry" on the occasion of the Chinese New Year. She advised him that the message was read in all major U.S. Chinese communities and printed in Chinese papers in Taiwan, Hong Kong, and elsewhere.[39] In addition, when the Chinese-American Republican Federation gave a dinner in New York to honor Chennault, Ford sent a telegram. The president joined the guests "in saluting the dedication and outstanding achievements of this fine American. . . . As a successful business executive, she has displayed the kind of resourcefulness and ability that has made our country a leader in commerce all over the world."[40] Thus, Ford earned recognition from the Chinese community and reinforced her public standing.

Because of her longtime friendship with South Vietnam, her ties to the Ford administration, and her role as an ethnic advocate, Chennault was approached by several Vietnamese leaders for assistance in gaining entry to the United States following the Communist victory. In May 1975 she met with South Vietnam's former prime minister, Tran Thien Khiem, in Taiwan. He gave her a memo outlining his requests for his family and those of his staff who were stranded in Taiwan where they, and many others, had escaped after the capture of Saigon by the North Vietnamese.[41] Chennault conveyed this request for help to her friends in the Ford administration. Then in June 1975 she wrote to Special Assistant to the President Theodore C. Marrs, asking for his help in securing entrance to the United States for former president Thieu's daughter and son-in-law. [42] By July, she received a letter from Khiem advising her that he was still in Taiwan waiting for permission to enter the United States. She forwarded a copy to Ted Marrs and General Brent Scowcroft, assistant to the president for national security.[43] Khiem's family and those of his staff members arrived in the United States shortly after he wrote her in July, and Scowcroft contacted her directly about the other persons whom Khiem hoped to bring into the country.

The fact that a person of Khiem's rank appealed to her for assistance illustrates some interesting points about both Anna Chennault and American foreign policy. Khiem, his wife, and others developed a deep friendship with her after years of her visits to Vietnam when she was interviewing leaders for various Chinese newspapers and promoting her aviation clients. Through dinners, meetings, receptions, and negotiations, a mutual respect grew between Chennault and many of South Vietnam's top officials. Thus, she was determined to help them in their hour of disaster—a disaster that she believed stemmed from Nixon's decision to end U.S. military involvement in Vietnam without somehow guaranteeing the security of the GVN. She sent Flying Tiger Lines planes into Saigon until the very end to aid fleeing South Vietnamese. She also used her influence with the Ford administration to help men who, in her estimation, were America's allies in the Cold War fight against communism.

The fact that she had to intervene for the officials or use FTL's resources demonstrated both the lack of American preparedness for the fall of South Vietnam and the nation's desire to leave behind it the bitter legacy of U.S. defeat. America was not gladly opening its arms to the former allied government officials, many of whom faced persecution under the new regime. Instead, Chennault and others with influence had to prod Washington to admit such refugees. Still a strong anti-Communist despite the thaw in U.S.-PRC relations, Anna saw herself as something of a conscience for American actions in Vietnam.

In the 1970s and 1980s, her activities on behalf of ethnic minorities became the most important part of her Republican Party involvement. This role kept her in contact with likeminded individuals in government who recognized the potential strength of ethnicity in American politics. Her NRHGC position enhanced her ties to Taiwan's supporters and American anti-Communists. It also helped her reach a wider Asian-American audience to appeal for expanded ethnic involvement in the political process. She worked to help Asian candidates run for office, to elect more Asian delegates to the party conventions, to expand and strengthen local and national Asian political organizations, and to keep her constituency's interests in front of political leaders. To Chennault, this was her most important legacy to the American political system.

Anna Chennault also built a successful and effective business career in conjunction with her powerful base of influence and connections made in the political and social spheres in U.S. foreign policy. The three areas of business, politics, and society interacted to strengthen her influence as an informal diplomat. As separate fields of operation, each area carried its own weight and power, but she combined them all in a way that made her career unique among citizen-diplomats. As a woman, her role as hostess gave her an edge that no man could match in American society. Thus, where gender might have limited someone else, she capitalized on it, tied it to her political activities, and added it to the growing base of her influence in the business world.

Notes

1. Warren to Chien, White House Central Files Name File, "Anna Chennault," Ford Library.

2. *New York Times Magazine*, December 15, 1996, 26–27.

3. Chennault, *Education of Anna*, 197–98.

4. Ibid., 197.
5. Maxine Cheshire, "Next Perle Mesta?" *Washington Post*, January 12, 1969.
6. Press Release, December 6, 1968, "1969 Inaugural Committee Press Releases," Republican National Committee (RNC) Library, box 5, RNC Papers and "Official Guide Book—Inaugural 1969," page 6, RNC Papers.
7. Press Release, December 16, 1968, "1969 Inaugural Committee Press Releases," RNC Library, box 5, RNC Papers.
8. "The Spirit of '76—1973 Inaugural Guide," Convention Office, box 53, page 7, RNC Papers.
9. Mary Strassmeyer, "Mrs. Chennault . . . Party Queen," *Cleveland Plain Dealer*, January 26, 1969.
10. Jeannette Smyth, "Singing for Their Supper at Mrs. Chennault's," *Washington Post*, January 19, 1971.
11. Ibid.
12. Lars-Erik Nelson, *Washington Daily News*, January 11, 1981.
13. Memorandum, Lamar Alexander (aide to Bryce Harlow) to Jon Rose, April 28, 1970, White House Central Files, Ex IT65, "UN Education, Science, & Cultural Organization, 1969–70," Nixon Project, National Archives and Records Administration.
14. David Laux, interview by author, Washington, DC, July 21, 1994.
15. Mark Hatfield, interview by author, Washington, DC, July 22, 1994.
16. "Large Political Gifts by Lobbyists, Others Listed," *Washington Post*, January 31, 1971.
17. *Washington Evening Star*, January 21, 1971.
18. John Buchanan to Anna Chennault, November 5, 1971, "Congress House of Representatives 1972," Chennault Papers.
19. Judy Luce Mann, *Washington Daily News*, October 26, 1971.
20. John Buchanan to Anna Chennault, November 9, 1971, "Congress House of Representatives 1972," Chennault Papers.
21. Congress, House, Congressman John Buchanan, 92d Congress, 1st sess., *Congressional Record* (November 4, 1971), vol. 117, pt. 30, 39508.
22. Chennault to Buchanan, November 29, 1971, "Congress House of Representatives 1972," Chennault Papers.
23. Interview by author, July 26, 1994.
24. October 12, 1967 (A5042), June 5, 1969 (H4533–35), May 28, 1970 (S8011), August 3, 1972 (26666), July 30, 1976 (24664), and July 11, 1977 (22293).
25. Richard Fairbanks to Chennault, September 22, 1981, "Senate Office '81–'86," Chennault Papers.
26. Chennault to Meese, October 27, 1981, White House Office of Records Management—Alphabetical Name Files, "Anna C. Chennault, 3 of 5," Ronald Reagan Library.
27. Meese to Chennault, November 3, 1981, ibid.
28. According to the Federal Reserve Bank of Minnesota, "What is a Dollar Worth?" Rob Grunnewald, http://minneapolisfed.org/economy/calc/cpihome.html the value of $1.00 in 1972 is equivalent to approximately $4.12 in 2000, making Chennault's contribution to Nixon's reelection campaign equal to $370,800 in 2000 dollars. This estimate is based on the Consumer Price Index.
29. A 1980 dollar is equivalent to $2.09 in 2000. Ibid.

30. "Finance Report Grand Total 1980," n.d., "Anna C. Chennault, 4 of 5," White House Office of Records Management—Alphabetical Name File, Ronald Reagan Library.

31. Various letters and check copies from "Congressional Correspondence," "House of Representatives '82–'86," and "Senate Office '81–'86," all in Chennault Papers.

32. "The Catch for Hatch," *Washington Post*, October 1, 1981.

33. "Vice President Agnew Joins," *GOP Nationalities News* 2, no. 2 (April 1972): 1.

34. *GOP Nationalities News* 2, no. 2 (April 1972): 3.

35. "Council Convention A Success!" *GOP Nationalities News* 3, no. 5 (June 1973): 1.

36. Ibid.

37. "Ethnic Leaders Meet at White House," *GOP Nationalities News* 6, no. 2 (April 1976): 1.

38. Gerald R. Ford, telephone interview by author, September 7, 1994.

39. Chennault to President Ford, February 19, 1975, General Subject File: Ethnic Affairs, box 8, "Flying Tiger Line," Theodore C. Marrs Collection, Ford Library

40. Telegram to Josephine Hong (chairman of the Chinese-American Republican National Federation) from President Ford, January 8, 1975, "Anna Chennault," White House Central Files—Name File, Ford Library.

41. "Memo for Mrs. Chennault," Tran Thien Khiem to Chennault, Taipei, Taiwan, May 5, 1975, FG 1-2/CO 21-CO 43-2, box 13, White House Central Files, Ford Library.

42. Chennault to Marrs, June 13, 1975, "Anna Chennault," White House Central Files—Name File, Ford Library.

43. Packet of letters and internal memorandum under cover memo to Ted Marrs from Jeanne Davis regarding proposed reply to Chennault, September 9, 1975, "Khiem, Tran Thien," White House Central Files, IM/K (Exec.), box 3, Ford Library.

6

The Business of Influence

Aviation Connections to Asia

In Washington, Anna Chennault's name was practically synonymous with the Republican Party and fundraising, an identity she did not want. Her work for Flying Tiger Lines (as vice president of international affairs) and consulting for such clients as Pan American Airlines, Northrop Corporation, General Electric, Norden Systems, Grumman Corporation, GTE, and Lockheed Corporation were worthy of more respect, she believed, than that accorded merely a wealthy socialite. Chennault considered herself on the "front line" in Asia, helping American businesses do their part to advance the broader national security goals of U.S. foreign policy. These efforts, as a facet of informal diplomacy, expanded her connections in Asia by adding another dimension to her political and social activities. Unfortunately, all it did for her public persona was widen the base from which she operated—by providing more diverse guest lists and deeper pockets to "pick" for the Republican party—because of the behind-the-scenes nature of the aviation business. On the private side, however, it made her a more valuable asset to those policymakers who took advantage of her appraisals of Asian or American politics and society. But, developing that more rounded image (if only to those who really knew her) took serious work in the aviation industry's "trenches."

Flying Tiger Lines

In May 1969, Anna Chennault received a letter from Director of Vietnamese Civil Aviation Nguyen Dinh Lan.

He expressed his great pleasure at meeting with her and other executives from Flying Tiger Lines (FTL) to discuss the expansion of their all-cargo air transport business into South Vietnam.[1] Her role in the process of obtaining FTL landing rights was described by *Business Week* as "swe[eping] away the typical Oriental delays and paperwork . . . [and obtaining] a Vietnam [landing] certificate, relatively speaking, overnight."[2] This was an early example of her role on behalf of the aviation corporations for whom she consulted over the next two decades.

In the highly charged Cold War years of the Vietnam War era and beyond, Washington's interests in Asia centered on its commitments to maintaining strong "free" regional allies to counterbalance the Communist governments of China and North Korea. Thus, support for the ROC (Taiwan), South Korea, South Vietnam, the Philippines, and Thailand was an important part of American foreign policy. Chennault's work for her aviation clients over the years also advanced that diplomatic goal. Her knowledge of Asian business styles, *guanxi*, and her acquaintance with many leaders in Asian aviation were very useful for FTL and other aviation clients in the 1970s and 1980s.

Negotiating rights for FTL's operations in various countries required a delicate balancing act between U.S. national security interests, overseas American industrial expansion, and encouragement of the growth of strong, friendly Asian governments. Anna Chennault elaborated on this theme in a 1970 memo to FTL's top executives on the "political outlook" in Asia. She defined "a U.S. rock-bottom position" as "trying to prevent any single power [from] mobilizing and consolidating all the people and resources of any entire continent, whether Europe or Asia. Because that single power, to keep its diversities under control, will have to be totalitarian and therefore against freedom in America." Her analysis went beyond just seeing the American side of the equation. She represented the Asians as wanting "1) security against aggression; 2) economic cooperation with stabilized countries; [and] 3) creative and mutual friendship with the United States."[3] This kind of analysis made her useful to American policymakers.

She also recognized some of the past problems encountered by American political and business leaders in Asia: "We who do business with the Asians, must realize . . . the days of Colonialism and Imperialism [are] over. . . . When we [Americans] tend to think of a U.S. form of democracy as the panacea to all problems somehow we have ignored the background, the need, the culture of the peoples we deal with and they know it." Her recommendation was that "more and more we have to do business *the Asian way*. . . . The business know-how of those like us who are involved in Asia will have . . . to be permeated with a kind of 'bipartisan' political wisdom to meet the increasing challenge of coming years. Figures alone won't determine decisions and bullying and high pressure will be *effectively* resented." Cutting through the Cold War rhetoric of the time, she told her superiors that they needed to have a "*feel* of the Asian situation in planning future operations [and] assist our people at all levels to better understand their [Asians'] problems." She finished by summarizing in detail the political and economic environments in Vietnam, Korea, Taiwan, the Philippines, and Japan, including FTL's options and prospects in each country.[4]

U.S. policymakers considered the establishment of a core group of economically viable, anti-Communist nations essential to the Cold War balance of power in Asia; any business enterprise that furthered that end was welcome. Anna had experienced the power of commercial ties to build alliances and worked very hard to do the same for America and American companies. The links that she forged within international commerce gave her (and businesspeople generally) the strength to make business a useful adjunct to official U.S. foreign policy. Thus, FTL's operations, and her role in making them successful, exemplify an informal diplomatic tool for furthering U.S. policy goals in Asia, thereby enhancing Washington's national security mission.

Initially, her efforts were focused on securing landing rights for FTL in various Asian nations. When the U.S. Civil Aeronautics Board (CAB), first with President Johnson's approval and later with Nixon's, opened up new routes to Asia for American airlines, it was only the first step of the project for FTL and others. In order to begin flights to Asian cities, airlines had to negotiate and secure landing rights at various airports. Between 1969 and 1971, Chennault helped obtain permission for FTL to land in South Korea, Taiwan, South Vietnam, Thailand, and the Philippines.

With expanding American military operations there by the late 1960s, South Vietnam naturally became a high priority for further U.S. business connections because of Washington's desire for a stable and economically strong, non-Communist Vietnamese regime. Following a polite exchange of letters with Nguyen Dinh Lan in May 1969, Chennault delivered FTL's formal request to him for "temporary authority to engage in scheduled air transportation between the [United States] and the Republic of Vietnam, in both directions . . . [carrying] military cargo and military mail . . . not . . . the delivery or uplift of commercial cargo."[5] Her letter declared that FTL's service "would in no way compete with . . . Air Vietnam," and she outlined the "aid and assistance" that FTL would offer Air Vietnam if it were granted the authority to operate:

> [FTL] will exert its best efforts to assist Air Vietnam in obtaining . . . aircraft presently held as surplus by the [U.S.] government. . . . [If] such aircraft cannot be obtained . . . [FTL] will provide [them]. [FTL] will assist in the recruitment . . . of qualified and rated flight crews for the [above-mentioned aircraft. If requested] . . . [FTL] can obtain and import for Air Vietnam an aircraft loader and certain other ground equipment . . . to be paid for by Air Vietnam. . . . [If Air Vietnam wants to] request authority from the [U.S.] Civil Aeronautics Board to operate to the [United States] . . . [FTL] will assist [with the] preparation, filing and prosecution of Air Vietnam's request.[6]

Such an offer of assistance to Vietnam's national airline was meant to reduce its concern about competition from FTL.

As a shrewd negotiator, Chennault knew the importance of placating a sovereign nation's domestic industrial sector. Particularly in Asia, a Western company trying to enter a national market needed to be appropriately humble and solicitous. In her letter, she added, "It is expected that [FTL's] . . . service would further benefit Air Vietnam by virtue of handling fees earned for Air Vietnam's handling of scheduled flights."[7] Knowing how best to manage Asian business dealings, using the lawyers and marketers of Chennault's corporate clients, made for a powerful tool in the service of American diplomatic policies. While not generally controlled by any specific governmental directive, American business executives were happy to take advantage of her political connections to benefit their own commercial operations, which ultimately advanced U.S. policy goals in Asia.

It was not always easy to obtain permission for FTL to do business or to maintain positive working relationships once operations began. A mid-1969 telex from an FTL executive indicated the often fragile nature of such negotiations: "I have pushed as hard as possible for the time being but a harder push may be necessary in coordination with Mrs. C. if approval is not forthcoming in next day or so."[8] FTL and other employers relied on her to navigate the often treacherous waters of internal governmental egos in their negotiations with Asian clients. In Korea, she helped resolve difficulties between FTL and Korean Air Lines (KAL), whose chairman acknowledged the value of her assistance when he wrote: "Your most considerate arrangements for our meeting with Mr. Healy [FTL executive] will remain as a monumental achievement in the annals of [KAL]. . . . Once again, I am deeply moved by your superb troubleshooting at a time when both Tigers and [KAL] were seeking a breakthrough on the problems of mutual concern. I appreciated very much your post-meeting comments—humble attitude and virtues cherished by Orientals."[9] Chennault's Chinese upbringing and background were incalculable assets to her American clients who, because of the cultural differences between the hemispheres, operated in unfamiliar territory and were thus at a disadvantage when they sought Asian business opportunities.

Touring the Cuu Long livestock distribution center in Saigon as the sponsor of the Helping Hand Foundation, a joint U.S.-Vietnamese program to improve the living standards of Vietnamese naval personnel, 1971

Her personal style also made her successful. As the lone woman at business meetings, her ability to put a roomful of men at ease and deal forthrightly with business and government leaders was a great asset. As a skilled hostess and diplomat, long familiar with protocol and etiquette, she often reminded traveling FTL executives to send thank-you notes to the government officer or businessman whose hospitality they had enjoyed. One such letter to FTL's president following a trip with Chennault included not only the list of those whom they had met, but also some reminders and personalizations for his use in composing the letters.[10] She knew the value of courtesy, in business generally and in Asia particularly.

John Alison, a retired Army Air Corps general who had flown with Claire Chennault's Fourteenth Air Force and a former Northrop Corporation vice president with whom Anna frequently worked during her years of consulting for Northrop, testified to the value of her services. She often reported directly to the president or chairman of the board of her various corporate clients, in addition to higher-level officers such as Alison. He asserted that she knew everything that was needed to do business in Asia: she "had all the contacts and [was] a scholarly observer of the politics of Asia."[11]

Alison recalled that she not only knew most of the U.S. ambassadors in Asia, which "got you in to get [their] counsel and advice," but also "her presence made it a pleasant personal meeting" especially since often the "Ambassador would look to her for advice due to her knowledge of their country's political situation and also that at home." In one instance, Alison and Chennault worked on negotiating a large contract to sell planes to South Korea. He characterized Korea as "a very male society," yet "she was bright, interesting to have around, a good conversationalist and never made any feminine advances. She could flatter men in other than feminine ways. Anna did all the toasts and speeches [required in Korea] and I don't know any other girls who were accepted that way." For Alison, Chennault's skills made her "worth everything we paid her and we probably didn't pay her enough. She knew how to get the job done."[12]

The itineraries for her trips to Asia covered a wide range of events and contacts. Her March-April 1972 Asian tour provides a representative example. The Japan visit included a speech at a breakfast meeting of the U.S. Chambers of Commerce-Japan, lunch with members of the Asian-Pacific Council of American Chambers of Commerce, followed by an afternoon meeting with the chairman of Fuji Bank (who was also the chairman of the U.S.-Japan Advisory Council). The agenda for another trip to Korea listed a dinner attended by the Korean minister of transportation, the Chinese ambassador to Korea, and the chief of the U.S. Military Assistance Group in Seoul and other generals, and a meeting with the prime minister. During a trip to Taiwan, Chennault met with U.S.

Ambassador Walter McConaughy and had dinner with the ROC minister of economics. She was commonly a houseguest of U.S. Ambassador Henry Byroade on visits to the Philippines. In Hong Kong she was a guest at a reception given by U.S. Consul General David Osbourne. While in Saigon, she routinely met with both President Thieu and Prime Minister Khiem. Her frequent visits to Vietnam, Thailand, and Singapore always included meetings with the American ambassadors there.[13]

If the press, public, and some politicians in the United States still viewed her as just a social butterfly, others saw her differently. One president of FTL wrote to thank her: "I appreciated all your efforts in making possible my meeting [with the] Republic of China Minister of Communications and Transportation."[14] Indeed, many FTL executives requested Chennault's intercession. For instance, a senior vice president, Russ Emerson, wrote: "I would like to ask you to correspond with Mr. Saw Huat Lye [the general manager of Malaysian Airline System], urging his approval or hopefully his endorsement of the conversations I will have [with him]."[15] In her letter to Lye, Chennault started with general pleasantries, the current difficulties in the United States and Malaysia, and then a personal comment—"I do hope you are well and your two girls have adjusted to their schooling in England"—before getting to the matter at hand. This was the Asian style of conducting business, unlike the more direct American way. Emerson's meeting was to discuss and get approval for FTL to begin operations in Malaysia. Chennault wrote on Emerson's behalf: "He hopes to have a chance to get together with you and talk in detail about FTL operations in Malaysia in the near future. . . . I will appreciate your giving him some of your time."[16] She suggested that Emerson notify her office of his exact trip dates so she could telex Lye and arrange the meeting.[17]

Chennault's FTL superiors acknowledged her value in letters, contract renewals, and salary increases. Her compensation rose from a base of $36,000 per year plus expenses and stock options in 1969 to $42,500 in 1975, and $80,000 in 1986.[18] In 1980 an executive praised her assistance in negotiating a contract with China Airlines for FTL to handle its materials at Los Angeles International Airport: "Thank you for your help. . . . I think we'll get an agreement even though we are high bidder on the contract."[19] Of course, Asian aviation administrators also understood the value of her connections. A Chinese aviation official thanked her for facilitating a visit from American Federal Aviation Administration (FAA) experts to assist the ROC in improving their system of aviation safety. He acknowledged, "I am pretty sure without your great effort in pushing the whole thing, the arriving of the two gentlemen could not be so soon [*sic*]. I certainly appreciate all your kind assistance."[20]

Another example was a 1982 effort to sell a special 707 airplane to Mrs. Imelda Marcos, the wife of the the president of the Philippines. In her attempts to make the sale, Chennault met with Ferdinand and Imelda Marcos, a senior official in the Central Bank of the Philippines, the president of a plane sales company, the FTL executives, and General Fidel Eddie Ramos, deputy chief of staff of the Filipino Armed Forces. She covered all angles of the deal, which in the end was foiled when Mrs. Marcos was "told by the Central Bank and the other officials in charge of the Philippine economy that they could not afford to pay for it due to the recession in the Philippines and . . . also some political considerations."[21] Even in defeat, the president of TigerAir (an FTL subsidiary) wrote Chennault to "extend our gratitude to you for your continuing efforts to overcome the many obstacles which have ultimately prohibited the sale of this aircraft."[22] For many men at FTL, Chennault was the one who could sweep aside any obstruction, contact any official, make any sales pitch where Asian business was concerned, and its operations in Asia were very profitable. FTL's chairman of the board linked a compensation increase to this, in "recognition of your outstanding contribution to the success of the company."[23]

Chennault maintained strong ties to American ambassadors and diplomatic representatives in Asia. In 1972 her report to FTL executives on her recent Asian tour noted that "our U.S. Embassies . . . had some frank discussions with me, and I told them the time for equal competition is here . . . the only way for U.S. industry to survive overseas is for the U.S. government and U.S. industry to work together."[24] She knew the value of open access at the top of American representation in Asian nations and used her access to push her agenda.

The president of Northrop Airport Development Corporation, in a 1972 letter thanking her for a social event, added: "Your rapport with Secretary [of Transportation John] Volpe and the many ambassadors was most helpful."[25] General Alison's notice of Chennault's friendship with diplomats was confirmed by former ambassadors and foreign service officers. She was considered "one source, with good access" in Taiwan by former National Security Council senior staffer and Assistant Secretary of State for East Asian and Pacific Affairs John Holdridge.[26] The former U.S. ambassador to the PRC, Arthur Hummel, recalled meeting with Chennault often between 1981 and 1985. He believed that "on the whole, [she provided] a positive connection and [unlike others] she didn't see [PRC-ROC relations] as a zero-sum game. Her objective was good [U.S.-PRC, U.S.-ROC, and PRC-ROC] relations."[27] Former diplomats agreed with this last observation. However they assessed her methods, her ability to self-promote, or her level of reliability, her desire to promote positive U.S.-Asian relations was undeniable.

As in politics, part of her value to her business clients came from her successful entertaining. Whether in Washington or in Asia, Anna brought together a variety of people with common interests and goals. In the first six months of 1969 she hosted fifteen luncheons, teas, dinners, or receptions on behalf of the FTL in Seoul, Taiwan, Saigon, and Washington. Honorees at her parties included Korea's Prime Minister Chung Il-Kwon; the Philippines' Ambassador and Mrs. Ernesto V. Lagdameo (twice); Secretary of Defense Melvin Laird; Transportation Secretary Volpe; the secretary-general, commerce secretary, and ambassador of Korea; Mrs. Imelda Marcos and Madame Nguyen Cao Ky, the wife of the former president of South Vietnam; the ROC chief of the Chinese Aviation Administration; Lynn Jones of the FAA; the Chinese air attaché and General S. K. Hu of the Chinese Government Procurement and Service Mission; National Security Adviser Henry Kissinger; and CIA official Ray Cline.[28] For some of these events she requested reimbursement since "part of FTL's present good will and good relationships here in Washington and in Asia are the result of time and expense on my part."[29] The entertaining was an integral part of her job.

She forged another important link between U.S. business and foreign policy that began with President Kennedy but accelerated under Nixon. The Defense Department's work to increase the sales of American manufactured arms abroad reflected a strategy partially formulated to counter the nation's growing trade deficits and to stimulate the domestic economy and defense manufacturers. The Northrop Corporation, a major defense contractor for the U.S. government, benefited greatly from such policies, only to have entertaining (broadly defined) as a business practice—which often increased foreign arms sales—called into question.

In the fall of 1975 the *Washington Post* and *Washington Star News* both reported that "Northrop billed the government for the costs of lavish parties given by Washington hostess Anna Chennault and attended by some top Pentagon brass—held for the purpose of selling the aerospace firm's F5 jet fighters to Asian governments."[30] As early as 1971, Alison had instructed Chennault to note the reason for any entertaining in submitting expenses to the company. He suggested, "It would perhaps be advisable to add to each item that the purposes of these conferences was to discuss with these officials matters pertaining to the use of Northrop products now being operated in Southeast Asia and to discuss improvements and additions to these products."[31] She followed Alison's instructions when completing her expense reports, but was unable to control the misuse of the information by Northrop's internal accountants, who submitted the information to the government.

Such detailed reporting certainly aided the Defense Contract Auditing Agency in its review of Northrop's records, which determined that in 1972 "at least some of the $11,000—and possibly more" paid to Chennault "went for large parties." Senator William Proxmire (D-WI), who was investigating Northrop's dealings with the Pentagon, was outraged and declared that such figures amounted to a "Defense Department subsidy of the Washington cocktail circuit."[32] Congressman Milton Robert "Bob" Carr (D-MI) agreed and castigated Northrop on the floor of the House of Representatives. "Just think of it," he fumed, "top military brass, powerful U.S. and foreign officials and Senators and Congressmen drinking expensive liquor and munching on imported caviar paid for by you—the taxpayer—while Northrop executives make sales pitches for their airplanes. That is sheer gall."[33] Eventually, Northrop repaid some of the billed expenses to the government and settled the case.

Charges of misclassification and incorrect reporting were also brought against FTL and its top executives, including Anna Chennault, by the CAB in the late 1970s. Part of the problem stemmed from gifts valued at almost $8,000 that she distributed over a three-year period to various foreign VIPs and airline officials.[34] Again, as in the Northrop case, her reimbursement for the items was "improperly charged by FTL" to the wrong accounts under the CAB's system of accounting and reporting, not reported incorrectly by Chennault to FTL. In the initial decision, the judge ruled that since there was "no allegation that the gifts were unlawful," he would allow FTL's defense that the expenses were legitimate operating costs because "the gifts were of a character usually and ordinarily incurred in the performance of foreign air transportation in the region."[35] Chennault was not penalized for any of her actions with FTL or Northrop. Over time the practice of currying favor in Asian capitals with gifts diminished as a standard way of doing business because it was considered unacceptable by Western authorities. As a result, the value of personal connections became even more important.

Trade Missions to Asia

Final recognition of Chennault's advancing status beyond that of "Republican hostess" came with her appointment to the President's Export Council (PEC) in 1981. Her 1970s involvement in international business organizations broadened her connections and experience in the commercial field. For example, her service as a special assistant to the chairman of the Asian-Pacific Council of AmChams (American Chambers of Commerce), vice chairman of Republicans Abroad, and chairman of U.S. Citizens in Asia for Nixon took her beyond the aviation industry. Since much of this work was closely tied to activities in the Republican Party, her efforts were obvious to party leaders. Much self-promotion was needed to gain this recognition, which she hoped would move her beyond the hated "hostess" label. Her rising GOP influence and expanding business success culminated in the PEC appointment.

Within three days of Ronald Reagan's election as president in 1980, Chennault sent a memo to three members of the new administration's top transition team. Shrewdly basing her appeal on both party welfare and her qualifications, she recounted her efforts for Reagan and the party—particularly among women's and Asian groups. She asserted that "for the first time [Asian Americans] have come out from isolation [and] voted Republican," and she suggested that "if we start from the beginning to pay some attention and give them some recognition, we need not work as hard to get them [to become Republican voters] as we did with the Blacks and Hispanics." She followed her analysis of ethnic voting with a request for an (unpaid) appointment in the administration working on ethnic issues. Such recognition for her would look good to all those newly minted Republicans: "For an Asian woman with experience and ability to be appointed to a special position will help not only our new President's image but will be following the line of the Republicans advocating broadening the base and giving women equality."[36]

Later in November 1980 she expanded the scope of acceptable appointments to include positions such as ambassador-at-large, special assistant to the president on Ethnic Affairs, trade negotiator, undersecretary of transportation, or United Nations representative.[37] Over the next five to six months, many of her political and business friends and associates wrote to various White House staffers on her behalf, including NRHGC officers, Thomas Corcoran, senior Republican senators, presidents and chairs of several state and national Chinese- and Asian-American organizations, and major business donors to the Republican Party. Some echoed her earlier plea that rewarding her with a position would redound to the benefit of the Republican Party by showing its support for an ethnic woman. Others cited her twenty years of dedicated work for the GOP, her business experience, and/or her high level of international expertise. She also wrote several more times to key individuals seeking a response. Finally, in April 1981, these efforts proved successful when she was appointed to membership on the PEC and became its vice chairman.

Formed in 1973, the Council included both public- and private-sector representatives and was charged with advising the president on matters pertaining to U.S. exports. In 1984 the Council published a multivolume report, *Coping with the Dynamics of World Trade in the 1980s*; it included "plans and actions for expanding U.S. exports and . . . identifying the needs of business, industry and agriculture in effecting successful export programs."[38] Chennault's principal interest in exports centered on the aviation industry, and her position as co-chairman of Aviation/Aerospace Industries for Reagan-Bush in the 1980 campaign confirmed that focus. But her most visible role in the PEC was to facilitate and lead trips to Asia for various groups of American business leaders in search of export markets. John Autin of the Commerce Department wrote that "although the PEC was originally called into existence . . . to advise the President on export promotion, it had never before taken a direct role in mounting a U.S. trade mission. The idea originated with Mrs. Chennault."[39]

As she announced at the PEC's first Reagan administration meeting, Chennault envisioned "a working organization."[40] At this gathering, she outlined her broader PEC agenda. The Council needed to foster "better cooperation" between the government, its agencies, and the private sector in exchanging ideas and experience; U.S. companies (large and small) had to "reappraise their methods, techniques . . . to deal with foreign governments and people" and learn about the countries with which they were negotiating; U.S. companies' internal processes, such as the "relationship between . . . executives and . . . middle level workers," input from marketing people to chief executives, or simplification and improvement of inside bureaucracy, should be directed toward successful international competition; small businesses called for greater PEC attention since they required as much help "as the large companies"; the PEC and other government agencies needed to foster cooperative and harmonious relations; and the Departments of State and Commerce as well as the White House must afford the PEC strong support.[41] Chennault clearly had a wide-ranging vision for the success of American business in the global market, and the PEC provided a perfect platform from which to expound her views.

Her push for a PEC-sponsored trade mission resulted in its first delegation of American business executives traveling abroad. A group went to the Philippines, Malaysia, Indonesia, and Thailand to explore trade opportunities in May 1983. The fact that the first-ever PEC mission went to Asia rather than to Europe or elsewhere is testimony to the strength of Chennault's influence in the PEC as well as the growing recognition of the area's importance for trade expansion. She projected: "Between 1982 and 1992, we estimate that the two-way business could total between 2.5 and 3 trillion dollars. This mission is only the beginning of an unprecedented growth in relationships between the United States and Southeast Asia." To start its tour, the delegation began with a meeting, arranged by Anna Chennault, with Philippines' President Ferdinand Marcos.[42] By its end, members of the mission had met with dozens of business and government leaders in a number of countries, established considerable goodwill, and garnered concrete leads for future trade transactions.

Following her return, Chennault sent President Reagan an eleven-page report in which she listed the mission members (fourteen total, one-third of whom were women), covered highlights of the trip in each nation visited, and summed up the basic reasons for its success. The mission comprised only "a small, select group," it represented a variety of industries, her own contacts secured entrée to not only high-level government officials but also to important business leaders, and it was supported by U.S. embassies and the Commerce Department.[43] Chennault added that mission members not only paid their own expenses but also contributed an additional $2,000 each to the Commerce Department to cover extra expenses, thereby eliminating reliance on taxpayers' money for the trip. She took credit for personal "arrangements" that "upgrade[d] the mission from just any trade mission [to something] considered a high level group representing [Reagan's] administration to extend goodwill, friendship and trust between the United States and the ASEAN [Association of Southeast Asian Nations] organization."[44]

The PEC mission received good press coverage in Asia and the United States and encouraged continuing positive relations with those nations visited. A front-page article in the *Business Times*, Malaysia's financial newspaper, reported the mission's arrival and goals. The *Times* asserted that the Americans sought to counter "the Japanese export blitz in the [ASEAN] region" and cited Anna Chennault's view that "American businessmen were beginning to realize they would have to be more aggressive and work as hard as the Japanese to get a share of the lucrative export and investment markets in the region."[45] Her report to Reagan also quoted an editorial in the *Philippines Times Journal* that urged "Philippine businessmen [to] take advantage of the presence here of a dozen American businessmen who are seeking to enter into joint venture partnerships with them."[46]

The *Kuala Lumpur Star* printed the comments of the Malaysian housing minister's beliefs that "the delegation's visit had helped to further strengthen the 'old ties' between the two countries [and] would open new avenues for cooperation and the promotion of better understanding between Malaysia and the U.S."[47] This sentiment for expansion of business relations in the nations visited was exactly the response that Chennault had hoped for, along with the hope of "upgrading the image of the American business executive abroad." John Autin in a published article articulated Chennault's goal for the mission: "Our first priority was to market friendship and good will. . . . we want first to understand each other more and to have a closer dialogue . . . [we each] have our problems . . . let us get together to . . . help each other. . . . Americans are really not 'ugly' Americans. We just need to learn about other people . . . and they don't know us all that well either!"[48] In one step, she hoped to improve personal and business relations between Americans and Southeast Asians, recognizing that one follows the other.

These same objectives motivated another PEC-led mission that featured a visit to the PRC in 1984. This trip, which included stops in Japan, Hong Kong, Thailand, Indonesia, and Singapore, followed President Reagan's state visit to the PRC in 1984, when the Chinese government agreed to receive a commercial mission. Because of its importance for Chinese development and U.S. exports, the aerospace industry was specified as one of the proposed areas for discussion. Recognizing the magnitude of this opportunity, President Reagan dropped in on the mission group's White House briefing luncheon to show his support and sent along personal letters to Chairman Deng Xiaoping and Premier Zhao Ziyang.

The trip was a major success. An article by Olin Wethington, deputy undersecretary of commerce for international trade and a member of the PEC mission, described its accomplishments. The main purpose of the trip had been "to strengthen the contract negotiating and sales position of U.S. aerospace manufacturers and suppliers through an aggressive use of U.S. Government support in the highly competitive China market." The effort had created a Joint Work Program for Aerospace Cooperation between the two nations, negotiated several contracts for aerospace and aviation exports to China, and generally advanced "U.S. trade promotion and policy goals."[49]

The American embassy in Beijing sent a lengthy wrap-up report to the Department of Commerce summarizing the "extremely successful" mission. In addition to detailed descriptions of the various meetings during the Beijing visit, the embassy noted how the

> mission co-leaders [including] Chennault diligently and skillfully pursued the basic objectives of the mission . . . [which were] to stress the strategic importance of our bilateral relations in connection with China's ambitious program of economic modernization, to underscore the importance of the aerospace industry to China's modernization and the predominant role of U.S. companies and technology in that field, to demonstrate [U.S. government] support for the U.S. aerospace industry . . . [and help with] potential sales to China, and to increase our understanding of China's aerospace needs, priorities and customers.[50]

The mission had set a very ambitious agenda and attained many of its goals. The agenda coincided with the then-current American policy of expanding free market connections to China. The embassy report also cited stories about the mission in the leading English- and Chinese-language papers in Beijing. The *People's Daily* included a photograph of Anna Chennault with Premier Zhao and a companion story on the front page, which quoted Zhao's comments on the programs established under the Joint Work Program that echoed her long-standing beliefs about international commerce: "[E]fforts of both countries [*sic*] industries and governments to strengthen industrial and commercial ties . . . help create stable relations which contribute to world peace."[51]

Autin's article identified one of the best assets that Chennault had brought to this aspect of her PEC work when he said that "her many contacts in Southeast Asia contributed as much as any other factor to the [mission's] success."[52] In one brief article, he had summarized her "calling" (as she saw it) with the PEC, her philosophy of improving personal as well as business relations, and her great gift of access in contributing to the organization's goal. In many ways, this was a synopsis of her business career and service to the United States. One of the members of the first mission, Rosemary Mazon, vice president of Wheelabrator-Frye, Inc., noted that the "diplomatic aspects of the mission [were] high-level contacts . . . high-level people felt they were meeting with their peers."[53] In concluding its analysis of the 1984 mission to the PRC, the embassy stated that Anna Chennault, "in particular, deserves thanks for her knowledgeable guidance to the mission."[54] That final recognition by the U.S. government's representatives spoke volumes about the important part that she played in this informal diplomatic arena of business. Her push for PEC trade missions, emphasis on the importance of trade with Asia, recognition of the critical person-to-person aspect of successful international commerce, and unfailing support for the expansion of American business abroad made her a highly successful appointee to the President's Export Council.

Anna Chennault's contributions to informal diplomacy significantly influenced both American politics and American business abroad. Her friendships in the Republican Party, on Capitol Hill, within the State and Commerce Departments, and among business leaders have been deep, strong, and often long-lasting. She was clearly considered a source of valuable information by both American and Asian leaders. Some put more stock in her analysis than others, but all recognized her unique mixture of experience in American and Asian cultures and societies. She called on, entertained, strategized with, and served presidents, ambassadors, institutional leaders, and corporate executives according to the dictates of her beliefs. In combining aspects of the milieu of foreign relations without carrying the weight (or burden) of formal government employment, she utilized business enterprise to carry forward the diplomatic interests of the United States in Asia.

Notes

1. Nguyen Dinh Lan to Chennault, Saigon, May 9, 1969, "Vietnam—Correspondence," Chennault Papers.

2. "A lion's share for Flying Tigers," *Business Week* (May 22, 1971): 72.

3. "Report on Asia, 1970/1971," Chennault to Robert Prescott and Wayne Hoffman, December 31, 1970, "Asian Reports FTL," Chennault Papers.

4. Ibid.

5. Chennault to Nguyen Dinh Lan, July 23, 1969, "FTL-Vietnam, 1969–72," Chennault Papers.

6. Ibid., 2.

7. Ibid.

8. Telex from Wayne Partridge to unknown, undated, "FTL-Vietnam, 1969–72," Chennault Papers.

9. Choong Hoon Cho to Anna Chennault, February 2, 1979, "Flying Tiger 1979," Chennault Papers.

10. Chennault to Joseph Healy, April 19, 1979, "Flying Tiger 1979," Chennault Papers.

11. John Alison, interview by author, Washington, DC, July 14, 1994.

12. Ibid. In the 1960s and 1970s, "girl," meaning woman, was not necessarily a negative term.

13. "Appointment Schedule" for Chennault, March 26–April 22, 1972, "Asian Reports FTL," Chennault Papers.

14. Thomas Grojean to Chennault, December 18, 1979, "Flying Tigers 1979," Chennault Papers.

15. Russ Emerson (senior vice president of scheduled services) to Chennault, January 29, 1979, "Flying Tigers 1979," Chennault Papers.

16. Chennault to Saw Huat Lye, February 5, 1979, ibid.

17. Chennault to Emerson, February 5, 1979, ibid.

18. Chennault to Prescott with Letter Agreement, December 19, 1969, "FTL-Prescott 1969–72," Wayne Hoffman (chair, FTL Board of Directors) to Chennault, December 31, 1974, "FTL," and Lewis Jordan (FTL executive vice president) to Chennault, April 9, 1986, ""FTL-Agreement(s) Fedex," all Chennault Papers.

19. Michael Gurley (FTL vice president, Western Region) to Chennault, June 17, 1980, "FTL 80," Chennault Papers.

20. T. M. Liu (ROC Civil Aeronautics Administration) to Chennault, May 1, 1982, "Flying Tiger Lines 1981," Chennault Papers.

21. Chennault to George Gross, April 20, 1982, "TigerAir," Chennault Papers. Other letters from the same file on this episode include Gross to Chennault, May 3, 1982; Chennault to General Ramos, February 1, 1982; Gross to Ismel Mathay, Jr. (vice governor of Metropolitan Manila), December 21, 1982; Chennault to Gabriel L. Singson (senior deputy governor of Central Bank), December 15, 1981; Morres Fostrey (president of Jet Trader, Inc.) to Chennault, December 17, 1981; Gross to Chennault, November 6, 1981; and Chennault to Gross, December 14, 1981.

22. Gross to Chennault, May 3, 1982, "TigerAir," Chennault Papers.

23. Wayne Hoffman to Chennault, December 13, 1973, "FTL," Chennault Papers.

24. "Asian Report, March 23–April 23, 1972," Chennault to Prescott and Hoffman, n.d., 5, "Flying Tiger Line, Inc. 1972 Miscellaneous," Chennault Papers.

25. Glenn R. Lord to Chennault, June 12, 1972, "Northrop Airport Development Corp.," Chennault Papers.

26. John Holdridge, interview by author, Washington, DC, July 26, 1994.

27. Arthur Hummel, interview by author, Washington, DC, July 26, 1994.

28. Chennault to Robert W. Prescott (FTL president), June 3, 1969, 6–7, "Expense Accounts F.T.L.," Chennault Papers.

29. Ibid., 2.

30. Peter Gruenstein, "Northrop Billed U.S. for Chennault Parties," *Washington Star News*, September 15, 1975, and *Washington Post*, September 16, 1975.

31. Alison to Chennault, July 26, 1971, "Northrop Corp. Exp.," Chennault Papers.

32. Gruenstein, *Washington Star News*.

33. *Congressional Record*, 94th Cong., 2d sess., vol. 122, pt. 8, April 7, 1976, 9784.

34. Complaint Before the Civil Aeronautics Board, Flying Tiger Line, Inc., Wayne Hoffman, Robert Prescott, Joseph Healy, Charles Hopkins, Rudolph Valenta and Anna Chennault, Respondents, n.d., "FTL-Anna Chennault," Chennault Papers.

35. Initial Decision of Administrative Law Judge Burton S. Kolko, Enforcement Proceeding Docket #30254, Served September 15, 1977, "FTL," 10, Chennault Papers.

36. Memorandum, Chennault to Ed Meese, Bill Casey and Pendleton James, November 7, 1980, "Anna C. Chennault, 2 of 5," White House Office of Records Management—Alphabetical Name File, Reagan Library.

37. Chennault to George Bush, November 21, 1980, "Anna C. Chennault, 2 of 5," White House Office of Records Management, Reagan Library.

38. President's Export Council, *Coping with the Dynamics of World Trade in the 1980s*, vol. 1 (Washington, DC: Government Printing Office, 1984), 1.

39. Memorandum, Autin to Chennault, with attached article on PEC mission, August 1, 1983, "President's Export Council," Chennault Papers. See article, John Autin, "Trade Mission Marketing," *Executive Female* (September–October 1983): 10–12.

40. "Anna Chennault's Remarks," October 15, 1981, "President's Export Council," Chennault Papers.

41. Ibid., 1–2.

42. Ibid., 2.

43. Chennault to Reagan, May 23, 1983, 3–4, "President's Export Council," Chennault Papers.

44. Ibid., 2.

45. Ho Sook Han, "Americans are fighting back," *Business Times*, May 13, 1983.

46. "U.S. Trade Group Paves the Way," *Philippines Times Journal*, n.d., cited in Chennault to Reagan, May 23, 1983, 5, ibid.

47. *The Star*, May 14, 1983.

48. Autin, "Trade Mission Marketing," 11.

49. Olin Wethington, "Presidential Trade Mission Reflects New Era in U.S.-China Trade," *Business America* (a publication of the Department of Commerce), October 15, 1984, 3–4, 6.

50. Telegram, American Embassy in Beijing to Department of Commerce in Washington, August 14, 1984, 1–2, "China-US Pres. Trade Mission-1984," Chennault Papers.

51. Ibid., 1.

52. Autin, "Trade Mission Marketing," 11.

53. Ibid.

54. American Embassy to Department of Commerce, 5, ibid.

7

A Personal Rapprochement

Working Both Sides of the Taiwan Strait

In April 1971 an American table tennis team traveling in Japan was suddenly invited by the government of the People's Republic of China (PRC) to visit Beijing. This move represented another volley in the diplomatic game between the United States and the PRC on their path to normalization of relations. Upon the team's arrival in Beijing, President Nixon announced the end of the general trade embargo against the PRC that had existed since the Korean War.

Anna Chennault gave her views on this monumental change in Sino-American relations in a *New York Times* article, "The Perils of Trade with China." She expressed the desire of "three generations of [her] family . . . to transform China politically, educationally and economically into the kind of modern nation in which one of the truly great peoples of history could have . . . freedom of speech and expression, freedom of worship, freedom from want and freedom from fear."[1] Echoing President Franklin D. Roosevelt's Four Freedoms made her emotional appeal attractive to a wider audience, many of whom were members of her wartorn generation.

Trade was "primarily a political weapon" in Communist countries, she believed, but she was skeptical that such trade would ever "yield a business profit to [a] competitive free enterprise counterpart." She nonetheless recognized that her "best interests" as well as those of her children, the United States, and "all the people of my brilliant, hardworking and deserving Chinese race whether in Taiwan, Overseas China or on the Mainland, are linked to the United States." Therefore, she thought that the "best hope" for the Chinese and Americans to "live together in a long future [was] through Chinese men and women who understand . . . America's political and economic language."[2] She regarded American democracy and capitalism as tools to recast China into a First World nation.

This statement, made when she perceived the steadfast U.S. position toward the PRC to be crumbling, indicated her ability to transcend the boundaries of her anti-Communist past. Her assertions are ambiguous when read with hindsight. While on the surface she expressed caution and doubt about the future possibilities of trade with China relative to "U.S. economic and military interest[s]," her words still hinted at the power of commerce to transcend politics. Her experiences with American companies in Asia demonstrated the impact that commercial connections had on peoples and political systems. Nonetheless, she retained a long-held distrust and dislike of the Chinese Communists.

The power balance in Asia—in place since 1949—changed dramatically in the 1970s. With Henry Kissinger's 1971 secret mission to Beijing, Richard Nixon's visit there in 1972, the 1971 expulsion of Taiwan (Republic of China, or ROC) from the United Nations, the gradual expansion of U.S. trade with the PRC, and finally Washington's recognition of the PRC in 1979, America's China policy completely reversed itself. Eventually, so did Anna Chennault's. She surmounted her own rhetoric of anticommunism to tread a fine line between the two Chinas and maintain her position as a leading Chinese-American activist in U.S.-Asian affairs.

Chennault's metamorphosis occurred over a decade and after a number of developments that cumulatively convinced her that change was necessary and right. She acted on her own oft-repeated "ideology of commerce" that business was a universal language that improved relations between nations. During the 1970s, her activities in a variety of international forums brought her into contact with Chinese Communists; she realized that they "weren't monsters." Moreover, she perceived through the glitter of the alleged ROC economic miracle that "prosperity was coupled with great corruption." These realities forced her to recognize that "confrontation wasn't the answer; . . . people with different philosophies sometimes have to compromise."[3] The personal mission that had driven her career—building personal and commercial ties between Americans and Asians—was, at last, applicable to her own relationship with her homeland. Before Chennault was comfortable enough to travel to the PRC as often as she did to the ROC, however, she underwent a difficult process that reconfigured her anti-Communist stance.

Her anti-Communist views were not jettisoned completely; instead, she altered them in ways that mirrored the changed perspectives of American policymakers as well as those of many Chinese living outside the mainland. As other individuals interested in the U.S.-China relationship modified their positions after observing hers, she served as a model for both Chinese and Americans to transcend the animosities engendered by the 1940s civil war. She thus played an important role in changing public opinion concerning the Nixon overtures to China. Some Chennault-watchers viewed her evolution as a sign of maturity in the aggressive businesswoman/socialite who was willing and able to gauge the direction of the political winds.

Others, however, considered the change as a betrayal of their long-held hopes for a "free" China. Although the vast majority of former anti-Communists eventually revised their views, a small group could not surmount their antipathy toward the PRC. Senator Goldwater best represented this group. After describing some of her activities in the 1980s, he wrote that he "had to leave her alone."[4] Prior to his death, he would not speak about her, despite a friendship that dated to 1960. Other legislators such Senator Jesse Helms (R-NC) still remain vocal critics of China, its government, and warmer U.S.-PRC relations. A former staff member in Helms's office declared Chennault's change of position as an effort to remain "queen bee in the center of attention—and that's a moderate assessment."[5] Nonetheless, Chennault's leadership in reshaping America's relationship with the PRC enabled her to continue as a significant practitioner of informal diplomacy in U.S.-Asian relations.

Nixon's Apparent Sell-out

Prior to a 1971 routine business trip to various capitals in Asia, Anna Chennault received a pre-trip briefing from Henry Kissinger —a fairly common occurrence for the administration's friends. The meeting was later interpreted by a reporter to mean that part of her mission was to give Asian allies assurance that the new Nixon policy of supplying military and economic aid instead of troops to help allies (later known as the Nixon Doctrine) would not lead to abandonment of U.S. friends there.[6] A society page item referred to her interview with Kissinger as "a rarefied meeting of two powerful swingers."[7]

Following the trip, Chennault wrote President Nixon requesting "an opportunity to report to you about my trip" and "convey personal messages" from Presidents Marcos (Philippines), Thieu (South Vietnam), and Chiang (ROC) as well as from the prime ministers of Thailand and Korea.[8] Although she often made observations on Asian affairs to policymakers after such trips, Nixon was reluctant to see her. Only after a series of internal memos, including one in which Kissinger remarked that "[h]er connections with many key Asian leaders are, in fact, quite good," did the president agree to receive her.[9]

The invitation to the American table tennis team to visit China preceded the Chennault-Nixon April meeting by less than a week, which conveniently advanced Nixon's secret plans to open relations with the PRC. She underestimated the depth of the president's conviction to seek this rapprochement with China. At the meeting, Nixon inquired how she thought the ROC would respond to a friendly American approach to the PRC. She pleaded that abandoning Taiwan would "be tantamount to the United States telling the Free World that it can no longer depend on it for support . . . [and] would shake the confidence and trust of our other allies in Asia and . . . would prolong the Vietnam War because the Communists, both Russians and Chinese, would consider it an admission of weakness."[10]

When, shortly thereafter, Nixon announced his own visit to Beijing, Chennault was shocked and felt betrayed—just as she had after the 1968 election—since he had given no hint of the secret plans when they spoke in April. She recalled that at the end of their meeting, Nixon invited Kissinger into the office for a few words and then a photo-op with the White House photographer. Chennault joined the two men in cheerful expressions for the camera but was horrified later—after Nixon's big news break—to see the photo used in a context that made it appear she had been in on the secret all along.[11]

During the months before Nixon's historic July 1971 China-visit announcement, Chennault's views on changing U.S. policy toward the PRC were reported in many newspapers. An account of her April meeting with Nixon appeared in the *Washington Post*. When asked what her credentials were for her meeting with the president, his press secretary, Ronald Ziegler, replied that she "reported 'in her capacity as Mrs. Anna Chennault.' "[12] Her comments on Nixon's strategy of opening trade and travel relations with the PRC, published two days later in the *Post*, were characterized as "surprisingly kind" coming from "one of Nationalist China's strongest supporters in America."[13] She observed that "no president has tried as hard as President Nixon to bring peace and peace with strength. The new arrangement doesn't mean he is weakening" his support

With President Nixon and National Security Adviser Henry Kissinger not long before Nixon's first trip to China is announced, 1971

for the ROC. Rather, Nixon was working to improve communications and "eliminate [the] conflict and . . . confrontation" that had long existed between the United States and the PRC, which she did not think threatened American support of the ROC.[14]

Chennault's comments in a *Washington Daily News* article were more cautious and expressed the concerns of the Asian leaders with whom she had met on her 1971 trip. The new Nixon policy sought "to encourage America's friends to 'take more responsibility'; it was not meant to abandon them." She understood Nixon's overall policy but reported that resentful Asian leaders had the impression that "the United States is promoting Japan to take over as the leader of Asia," and she was unable "to assure them otherwise." Finally, she acknowledged that Nixon "appear[ed] to be moving toward a two-China policy" but claimed that he wanted her to assure Chinese people everywhere that he was not "abandoning our long-time friends" in Taiwan. Although she still opposed recognizing the PRC, she was "not closed-minded."[15] Already, Chennault was softening her views toward the PRC, a process that continued throughout the decade.

With Sino-American relations changing rapidly under Nixon's guidance, Chennault felt the need to consolidate and tighten her legislative friendships in order to ensure that her ideas about Asia, and China in particular, received a hearing. Her April 22 article in the *New York Times* brought her views on evolving American policy to a large and diverse audience. In particular, it helped her secure congressional favor for continued American support of the ROC. She sent a copy to several friends on Capitol Hill, and Colorado Senator Peter H. Dominick introduced it into the *Congressional Record*.[16] Congressman Gerald Ford thanked her for sending him a copy and added: "I am not sure that the Editorial Board . . . will be converted, but I am sure your impressive grasp of the situation in China will be welcomed by open-minded readers as it was by me."[17]

When Nixon announced his proposed visit to Beijing, Chennault was visiting Orlando, Florida, to speak at the seventeenth annual Sino-American Cooperative Organization convention. She "dashed water on hopes that President Nixon's trip to Red China could lead to normal relations between nations right away," calling it "wishful thinking." She would "neither oppose nor endorse" the changing Sino-American relationship but hoped that "the U.S. [would] follow the old British diplomatic foreign affairs tactic: 'Recognize no eternal enemies, recognize no eternal friends but keep an eternal interest in all countries.' "[18] Her subsequent comment to the *San Francisco Examiner*—"Nothing surprises me anymore . . . I've lived in Washington for twelve years"—summarized her feelings.[19]

Her analysis of Nixon's decision was conducted in a very public manner. In addition to coverage of her views in many major newspapers, she appeared with the ROC ambassador to the United States, James C. H. Shen, on the "Issues and Answers" television program and on a Public Broadcasting Service panel discussion restating the views she had expressed since the beginning of the year.[20] Participating in these forums confirmed and enhanced her reputation as an expert on Sino-American relations with the general public. Her audience here was not limited to elected officials and policymakers.

Two major issues were the focus of her Nixon policy analysis. The first was expanded trade with China—the ever-alluring "China market"—as a motive for changing Sino-American relations. She asserted that the hope of lucrative trade with China "had something to do" with Nixon's decision, but she believed that it would prove disappointing because the United States could not "compete with the cheap labor there."[21] Here, she perceptively identified a major and ongoing issue in Sino-American trade.

She also discussed America's international prestige and standing with its Asian allies, the second issue. Nixon visiting China, as opposed to a Chinese leader visiting Washington, "enabled Chou [En-lai, the premier] to gain 'face' in Asia."[22] Because Nixon had asked to visit Beijing, the *Honolulu Star-Bulletin* argued that "the United States . . . lost face—an important consideration in the Orient." Thus, she thought that "Chou En-lai and the Chinese government have the upper hand."[23] Moreover, there was "unanimous" feeling among the Asian leaders she had recently met on opposing closer American ties to the PRC. "They were deeply concerned . . . because they know . . . communist expansionist power has been restrained to a certain extent by the [United States]. Those people won't have such firm trust in the [United States] in the future," she said.[24] Nixon tried to allay such fears by including in his announcement of the forthcoming visit a reassurance to America's friends in Asia that his efforts to establish more friendly relations with the PRC would not be "at the expense" of U.S. support for their independence and survival.[25]

Even if Chennault were disillusioned with or angered by Nixon's planned trip to Beijing, her political loyalty did not waver. Her public statements of support for her party's leader illustrated her ability to move beyond any feelings of betrayal that she might have felt toward Nixon. The *Los Angeles Times* reported that she was "living proof that President Nixon need not worry about all his conservative followers deserting him over his bold new China policy."[26] However, her public stance also reflected an understanding that her own business interests in Asia would require her flexibility on U.S. policies concerning the PRC and the ROC.

She conceded, moreover, that conservatives really had no one to support other than Nixon. When asked if he would be reelected (in 1972) with her help, she replied, "Yes, there are only two parties, aren't there?"[27] No matter what Nixon's China policy was, it was clear that Chennault and others had nowhere else to go. She echoed commentaries of the time and observations later by historians that only an established Cold Warrior such as Nixon could have courted the PRC without being buried beneath charges of selling out or being soft on communism. Conservatives who could accept Nixon's actions recognized the pragmatism of opening ties with the world's most populous nation, and they were confident that Nixon (thanks to his right-wing stripes) would not go too far in abrogating American responsibilities to its non-Communist Asian allies in an effort to befriend or appease Beijing. This certainty was not something they could trust to the Democrats. Anna Chennault was not happy with Nixon's policy reversal, but she was politically astute enough to know that the winds were changing and that she must bend in order to survive the new world order being created around her.

The Last Act of an Anti-Communist

Following the excitement generated by Nixon's announcement of his intended trip to mainland China, Chennault continued her multifaceted work. She helped Flying Tiger Lines secure permission to operate in the Philippines, geared up her GOP activities for the 1972 election, and increased her influence among American businessmen operating in Asia. The last was accomplished through such roles as special assistant to the president of the Asian-Pacific Council of the American Chambers of Commerce and chair of U.S. Citizens in Asia for Nixon in the 1972 election. In particular, the *New York Times* wrote that she "reportedly suggested to President Nixon" a meeting between Americans operating in Asia with several cabinet members concerned with issues relating to foreign trade.[28] Her 1970 appointment by the Nixon administration to the United Nations Educational, Scientific, and Cultural Organization (UNESCO) Advisory Council also widened the range of her Asian contacts.

Her expanded roles in the 1970s helped to reshape her previously strong feelings against mainland China. Anna was reminded of the agony of families separated by the Taiwan Strait when she renewed contact, after almost forty years, with her mainland "uncle," Liao Chengzhi.[29] Liao, whom Chennault had last seen in 1938 in wartime Hong Kong, had risen to a position of authority in the Chinese Communist Party. After being jailed with Deng Xiaoping during the Cultural Revolution, by the late 1970s Liao had become director of the Office of Overseas Chinese Affairs and a member of the CCP's Central Committee and Politburo.[30] Renewed ties to his now well-known Chinese-American cousin Anna were an asset of inestimable value. The ties of blood were strong enough for Chennault to want to establish some connections with the remnants of her family on the mainland. In the 1970s she corresponded occasionally with Liao Chengzhi and his son Liao Hui, who succeeded him as head of Overseas Chinese Affairs.

Also over the years, Chennault had come into contact with several Chinese Communists who had defected to the United States. At the request of the CIA she helped debrief them and assisted them in getting settled. These direct and close contacts with current and former Communists—both family members and strangers—strengthened her growing belief that "the way to change the people in power was not by fighting, but contacting."[31] People-to-people connections afforded the greatest opportunity for change.

Although her attitudes toward the PRC were evolving over the 1970s, when the ROC faced a crisis, Chennault came to its aid in the best way she could. President Jimmy Carter made the announcement in December 1978 that the United States would formally recognize the PRC on January 1, 1979. It came as a surprise to everyone, but, according to Thomas Corcoran, who shared her support for the ROC, "through her Republican contacts, Anna was the first to get a whole three hour notice of what was really going on."[32] Corcoran described her reaction to the announcement. With her "instinct for the jugular," she recognized the need to "support increasing Free China sentiment [by] preserv[ing] the symbolic 'apparatus' of continuity of Free China in Washington."[33] The symbol he referred to was Twin Oaks, the landmark mansion on ten acres that served as Taiwan's embassy in Washington. Chennault understood that if the ROC could hold onto the property, it would "keep Free China visible and viable," confirmed "by the very strength of [the anticipated] Communist protest against the non-cession to them of Twin Oaks."[34]

Corcoran credited Anna Chennault with a plan that would prevent Twin Oaks from passing to the PRC upon U.S. recognition of its regime as the sole government of China. He wrote that "at [her] suggestion there was organized the transfer of the [Twin Oaks] . . . title [from] the Republic of China into the title of the Friends of Free China," thus preventing the automatic property transfer to the PRC at the time of recognition.[35] As described by its director, Jack E. Buttram, the Friends of Free China (FOFC) was "a private non-profit organization of Americans interested in maintaining contacts and good will with the Republic of China."[36] FOFC stepped forward to act as the instrument through which Taiwan would maintain possession of Twin Oaks. The precedent upon which Mrs. Chennault based her suggestion was the 1949 maneuver that Corcoran, along with General Chennault and Civil Air Transport, executed to keep Nationalist Chinese Air Force planes from being transferred to the new PRC government.

Mrs. Chennault convinced ROC ambassador James Shen "to get authority from Taiwan to make such [a] transfer."[37] The deal was approved and finalized when the FOFC's executive director gave Corcoran (representing the ROC) ten dollars for consideration and took possession of Twin Oaks. Bipartisan congressional friends of Anna Chennault, Corcoran, and the ROC—such as House Speaker Thomas "Tip" O'Neill (D-MA), Congressman Clement Zablocki (D-WI), and Senators Strom Thurmond (R-SC) and Jennings Randolph (D-WV)—included specific language in the subsequent Taiwan Relations Act (TRA), passed in April 1979, to counteract any attempts to nullify the arrangement. To finally secure the FOFC deal, the TRA stipulated: "For all purposes under the laws of the United States, including actions in any [U.S.] court," withdrawal of diplomatic recognition of the ROC government "shall not affect in any way the ownership of or other rights or interests in properties, tangible and intangible, and other things of value, owned or held on or prior to December 31, 1978."[38] It was presumed by ROC supporters that this clause protected not only the Twin Oaks transfer but also other legal operations of the ROC government at the time of derecognition.

Corcoran and Anna worked through their congressional allies on both sides of the aisle to formulate a much stronger TRA to protect the ROC and U.S.-ROC relations than the one originally proposed by the Carter administration. In addition to generalized guarantees of American support for a determination of the future status of the ROC "by peaceful means" and continued ROC access to U.S. "arms of a defensive character," the TRA's most prominent feature was the creation of an "instrumentality" for unofficial, nondiplomatic relations between Washington and Taipei.[39] This was achieved by creation of the American Institute of Taiwan (AIT), a nonprofit corporation through which would be funneled all "programs, transactions and other relations conducted or carried out by the President or any agency of the [U.S.] government with respect to Taiwan."[40] In addition, the ROC established its own "instrumentality" that would handle all relations with the United States: the Coordination Council for North American Affairs (CCNAA).[41] Essentially, AIT and CCNAA functioned as the American and Taiwanese embassies in the respective host countries.

Following the hastily arranged sale of Twin Oaks to the FOFC, Chennault, a member of the board of the District of Columbia National Bank, "put [FOFC] in touch with people at the bank who enabled [them] to secure a loan" to cover maintenance and property taxes for the estate.[42] The plan included FOFC holding the property "to let the situation lie quiet until [they] disposed of any move of the Communists to take [it] over," then to have it "re-occupied by [ROC] personnel who will carry on relations with their supporters as before."[43] Finally, four years later, FOFC transferred Twin Oaks to the CCNAA, which had been using the buildings and grounds all along.

Chennault's lobbying efforts on behalf of the TRA (much of which, she said, was drafted by Corcoran, Senator Goldwater, and Iowa's Senator Jack Miller) were recognized by several policymakers in and out of Congress.[44] John Holdridge recalled that she worked along with Senators Helms and John Glenn (D-OH) "complicat[ing] the lives" of those in the State Department trying to reconcile provisions of the TRA with President Carter's recognition agreement with the PRC government.[45] Senator Alan Simpson (R-WY) said that Chennault worked very hard on the content and passage of the TRA, and Senator Percy remembered consulting with her on his inclusion of certain language in the TRA.[46] Percy wanted the stated importance of a peaceful resolution of ROC-PRC differences to be expanded beyond that of a "grave concern" to become an issue of "national security."[47] The final language reflected Chennault's efforts: "peace and stability in the area are in the political, security, and economic interests of the [United States]," and determining the ROC's future by any other than "peaceful means" is considered by the United States "a threat to the peace and security of the Western Pacific area and of grave concern to [Washington]."[48]

Aided by crucial allies, Chennault helped secure the most important and valuable symbol of ROC resistance to the PRC government.

She embodied the cause of "Free China," providing leadership with others such as Corcoran to ensure support for Taiwan. Her impact through the Twin Oaks-TRA episode had lasting, unmistakable repercussions on Sino-American relations. Indeed, Washington was the only city in the United States where the PRC did not obtain the former diplomatic property of the ROC.

While these events appear to indicate Chennault's continued anti-PRC outlook, they were in fact the climax of her activities exclusively on behalf of the ROC. She had reexamined her own attitudes toward the PRC since Nixon's 1972 visit. Even though she made a substantial effort on behalf of the ROC, she was at the same time advocating the "one China-two governments" model that many people supported as "a workable formula" for dealing with both the PRC and ROC.[49] The common ethnic link was perhaps the strongest stimulus to Chennault's growing acceptance of the PRC. She wrote in 1971, "I can appreciate all points of view of all loyalties of Chinese [*sic*] . . . against exploiters and China's hereditary real enemies we are all in heart Chinese together, whether Nationalist, Mainlander or Overseas."[50] This sentiment stimulated contacts with Liao and his son and in 1986 prompted her suggestion to the ROC's Chiang Ching-kuo (who succeeded his father Chiang Kai-shek as president after the latter's death in 1975) that he consider allowing Taiwan residents to visit the mainland.[51] The sad plight of separated Chinese families, whether in Taiwan or the United States, weighed more heavily on her than many of her anti-Communist allies realized.

A Personal Journey

In 1980, Chennault was given the opportunity to visit mainland China for the first time since her departure in the late 1940s when the first PRC ambassador to the United States, Chai Zemin, delivered an official invitation from Deng Xiaoping. It was transmitted secretly in the fall of 1980. She accepted, but she told the ambassador that she could not go until after the American presidential election in November. She later concluded that the PRC was very aware of her position and visibility in both the United States and the ROC and recognized the public relations benefits that would accrue to the PRC from her Beijing visit.

Her invitation dovetailed with another one from Deng to then Republican Senate leader Howard Baker (R-TN) and his wife Joy (the daughter of Senator Dirksen) to discuss prospects for Sino-

American relations in the newly elected Reagan administration. Despite oft-quoted press statements that they were not representing Ronald Reagan or carrying any messages from or to him, both Republican whip Ted Stevens (AK) and Chennault years later said that their visit was an effort by the Republicans to assure the Chinese leadership that the GOP hoped for continued healthy relations under the incoming administration. She claimed privately that President-elect Reagan did send a message to Deng through her to convey how much he believed in the importance of U.S.-PRC relations.[52]

Candidate Reagan's rhetoric had been very pro-ROC, denouncing the Carter administration's recognition of the PRC and its abrogation of the U.S.-ROC Mutual Defense Agreement. Chennault was convinced that Reagan's pro-ROC position had derived in part from his acceptance of campaign funds from the Taipei government. Given accusations of PRC contributions to 1996 American political campaigns, her admission of similar ROC activities in the past is instructive. Perhaps the PRC learned about influencing American democracy from its cross-Strait relative.[53]

Once elected, Reagan moved quickly to exploit the new realities of U.S. policies in Asia and endorsed the Baker trip. When Joy Baker became ill, the Tennessee senator asked Stevens to go in his stead. According to Stevens, the Chinese leadership was "nervous" about Reagan: "They thought a revolution [in political leadership] had taken place and were full of questions."[54] Although the original invitation had gone to Baker, Stevens believed that the Republican National Committee (RNC) also wanted Anna Chennault to participate in the visit.[55] She already had her own invitation from Deng, but the RNC recognized the potential GOP bonus with Asian voters if her return to the PRC were linked to a partisan excursion such as this one, rather than being a personal or business trip.

The Stevens-Chennault visit was given front-page coverage in the *New York Times* and stirred up extensive media interest both in the United States and in Asia.[56] All the publications recognized the significance of her return to the mainland, likening it to Nixon's 1972 visit, which represented the turnaround of a staunch anti-Communist. She acknowledged the parallel when she said:

> In politics and . . . international affairs, you must keep an open mind and keep on learning and look at the world in reality. . . . My way of looking at the world in the '60s was different from the'50s, and in the'70s it was different from the'60s, and now we are coming into the'80s. We have to reassess our positions,

> broaden our base, be humble enough to learn and have the courage to change. . . . If you don't learn, you stay put in the same positions and look at the world in an unrealistic way.[57]

She again expressed a desire "to play an intermediary role in bringing Taiwan and China together."[58]

The Chinese played gracious hosts to Chennault and Senator Stevens, who turned the last-minute trip into a honeymoon with his new wife. Chennault visited her "uncle" Liao and appeared with him in an Associated Press photograph on the front page of the *Los Angeles Times*.[59] She represented not only the Chinese on Taiwan but also many people like herself who were too young to fully understand the Communist-Nationalist feuds of the 1930s, or who had little or no direct contact with the Communists. Liao, who had fought those battles with the Nationalists, represented the Chinese on the mainland. Stevens believed this pairing represented "the bridge of heredity spanning those [Taiwan] Straits [*sic*]."[60] Chennault also met with Li, her former third-grade teacher and now an old man, who so long ago had encouraged her writing. Stevens, a former pilot with the Fourteenth Air Force under General Chennault, returned to the scene of his war years and thereby rebuilt Chinese-American ties on another level.

There were also several meetings with Deng Xiaoping to discuss Sino-American diplomatic and economic relations. Chennault was part of the conversation at all three meetings and acted as Stevens's and Deng's interpreter. She recalled Deng saying to Stevens, "In the U.S. there are 100 senators but there is only one Anna Chennault," and asking if Stevens minded if she sat next to him.[61] Stevens confirmed to the *Christian Science Monitor* that topics of discussion included "Taiwan . . . , defense problems, [Soviet] aggressive designs, energy and pollution." And he declared that Chennault's very presence stated "symbolically that the people who had supported Nixon, and now supported Reagan, had in mind a more open dialogue with the PRC."[62]

Stevens had returned to China twice in the 1970s. Compared to those visits, he noticed a decided difference that illustrated the "seeds of private enterprise and change from the grassroots level."[63] Such improvements made a strong impression on Chennault and all but eliminated any opposition to PRC relations that she might have still harbored. Instead, she focused her attention on the potential for change that existed on the mainland.

After their three days in the PRC, she and Stevens stopped in Taiwan on their way back to the United States in response to an invitation from ROC leaders to visit Taipei. President Chiang Ching-kuo received them in a very short public meeting but later held a lengthy private conference with Chennault alone. He was "very curious about the people" on the mainland, she said, but also concerned about Reagan's position. He was displeased with the trip that she and Stevens had made to the PRC but admitted that if anyone had to go on behalf of the Reagan administration, he preferred that it be she. Her visit to China, she realized, had elicited a mixed response from people in the ROC: "many of them saw [her] as their own, but many others were glad" she went. The time had finally come for her to see what the mainland was like, find her own facts, and make her own judgments.[64]

Chennault reaped personal, political, and commercial benefits from this trip. The most visible outcome was to see her name in the headlines, not just on the society pages. Her visit to the mainland created a huge new Chinese audience for her books, which numbered over thirty by then, all but three in Chinese. Particularly the younger generation, to whom she was virtually unknown at the time, sought out her books as a point of contact with their own literature and history. In addition, Chennault found an enormous new group of people who could benefit from her charitable donations, including from her own educational and cultural foundation. The trip greatly enhanced her prestige in Asia, giving her connections in both Chinas, and made her a more valuable consulting resource for business clients wishing to expand into mainland China. For the remainder of the 1980s, she helped to broaden U.S. ties to the PRC, primarily in the areas of investment and trade. Her years in business had fostered and sustained the U.S.-ROC relationship. Negotiating joint ventures between the United States, the PRC, and eventually between Taiwan and the PRC engaged her seemingly boundless energy.

A Bridge over the Strait?

After her visit to Beijing in 1980, Chennault's career entered another stage. Combining long-developed skills, connections, and instincts with a belief in the promise of American ideals and a deeply felt loyalty to China and other Chinese, she summoned all her talents to improve the relations of both Chinas with one another and with the community of nations. In a variety of ways, that goal has been the basis of her remaining career.

She led the President's Export Council trade mission to the PRC in 1984, displaying the enthusiasm with which she had embraced her old homeland. Indeed, her general business efforts focused more and more on the PRC during the 1980s, and in the 1990s it became almost her sole focus. Part of this change was explained by the relative prosperity of Taiwan versus the mainland. The PRC's less-developed economy provided more opportunities for commercial investment. Her emphasis on the PRC also derived from her frustration over the high level of corruption she witnessed in the ROC, where such behavior had become a higher art than in the PRC and thus a greater hindrance. The mainland was itself still mired in bureaucracy, however, and it took all her connections to hack through those tangled thickets.

Certainly, America's China policy, even though focused on the PRC, still advocated a strong ROC as a pivotal capitalist force in Asia. Deteriorating U.S.-Soviet relations in the early 1980s also caused President Reagan to retreat from his previous denunciations of the PRC. He all but embraced the former enemy with its prospective markets and political cooperation and followed a relaxation of his hostile rhetoric with a visit of his own to Beijing in 1984. Nonetheless, throughout the 1980s, through the "informal embassies" that AIT and CCNAA established under the Taiwan Relations Act, the United States and ROC completed numerous trade and commercial agreements bent on strengthening their relations.

A 1982 U.S.-PRC communiqué, in which the Reagan administration agreed to limits on its arms sales to the ROC, also stated that the United States planned to continue its "historic obligations to the people of Taiwan," balanced against the "important and growing relations with the [PRC]."[65] The administration's concern over ROC security—despite U.S. aspirations to further PRC relations—was evident when members of the Joint Chiefs of Staff met in Chennault's home with officials from the ROC to work out details of the communiqué's language before it was finalized.[66] With the American guarantee of arms to Taiwan weakening, Chennault knew that despite a newfound preoccupation with the PRC, she could not abandon her interests in the ROC. What appealed most to her was finding ways to tie the two interests together.

Her continued employment as a consultant for Flying Tiger Lines kept her in regular contact with ROC officials handling FTL's extensive operations in Taiwan. Shortly after her return from Beijing in January 1981, she reported to FTL's vice president of public relations that it "was not a business trip but a political assignment. However, it is the general opinion that Tiger has been benefitted by my visit to both Peking and Taipei. Since Washington, the People's Republic and Taiwan are happy with my trip, I presume we can say we have another breakthrough."[67] Although her correspondence with FTL executives and other corporate clients clearly indicated a continued emphasis on business with the ROC, FTL and others were quite interested in exploring the opportunities for doing business in the PRC, especially since their consultant was developing connections there in her usual aggressive way.

Less than a year later, Chennault took part in plans for FTL negotiations in the PRC, and a senior FTL executive expressed his appreciation for her assistance in preparing "for the Civil Air Negotiations with the [PRC]." Even though the talks were not initially productive, FTL thought it "had made significant progress in beginning a dialogue with [the Civil Aviation Administration of China]."[68] Despite several setbacks over the next few years, FTL kept up its efforts to start operations in the PRC.

When Federal Express (Fedex) purchased FTL in 1989, Chennault's existing consulting agreement stated that she would "provide advice and counsel . . . regarding . . . the Company's business in Asia, including but not limited to the [PRC]."[69] Budget constraints led Fedex to sever the relationship. Still, the notification letter sent by Fedex recognized her valuable expertise. A Fedex vice president wrote that in his "investigation concerning consultants who had been supporting Tiger over the years, your name was always mentioned with a tremendous amount of respect. . . . I recall [the] statement that if you need something accomplished in Taiwan, Anna Chennault's participation is critical. [I] clearly understand the support at the very highest levels of government which you have been able to pursue for [Fedex] in matters involving Taiwan, Hong Kong, and as well in mainland China."[70] Even while she was shifting her energies to bring more business opportunities to the PRC, she maintained her contacts in Taiwan and the rest of Asia, and clients from Korea, Indonesia, and Thailand continued to thank her for her efforts.

She gradually became more interested in bridging the gap between the PRC and ROC through corporate consulting. She hoped to play the role of mediator and help reconcile the two nations. No matter how much ill will might have been generated by her

PRC visit, many in the ROC could not abandon ties to Anna Chennault. She continued to be courted by ROC leaders who feared the loss of her influence with Congress and the Reagan administration and the possibility that American funding would flow to the PRC if she switched loyalties.[71] Chennault hoped to take advantage of this remaining attachment to help effect an ROC and PRC rapprochement.

As the 1980s wore on, however, the possibilities for improved PRC-ROC relations seemed to wane. Many political changes occurred within Taiwan that included more open elections, legalization of opposition parties, and travel to and investment in the mainland. Those improvements, combined with continued economic prosperity and social stability, strengthened the movement for an independent Taiwan. Evidently, there were few negative repercussions on the ROC from its loss of formal diplomatic recognition around the world. Many people in Taiwan thought of themselves as citizens of a separate country and believed a path to nationhood, rather than any form of reunification with the mainland, was in their best interests. This growing attitude worked against efforts to bridge the divide with China and diminished the desire to have Chennault (or anyone) play the role of peacemaker.

Instead, what seemed to be a better role for her was one tying together the United States, ROC, and PRC in a "complicated triangular relationship," as it was described by the president of the Taiwan Central News Agency.[72] He viewed her 1981 PRC trip not only as the "beginning of the end of her close relationship" with the ROC but also the beginning of her new role among the three nations. Since the 1981 visit, he believed she had developed ties to PRC leaders comparable to her friendships in the ROC. Former ROC ambassador Konsin Shah agreed with that assessment and thought that she could be a further bridge, but "Taiwan [was] not using her talents." Shah, like Anna, thought that "increased cultural and economic ties" would bring the Chinas together. But unlike him, a diplomat whose "footsteps [were] restricted," Chennault "as an American . . . [could] move easily between" the ROC and PRC.[73]

Following the deadly demonstrations in Beijing's Tiananmen Square in June 1989, Chennault described an episode that, like the "October surprise," was a model of the pitfalls of informal diplomacy for the citizen-diplomat. Denial allows formal diplomats to disavow an individual who has undertaken a task that, if a failure, might draw negative criticism to policymakers for even attempting it. Such was the situation in which Chennault put herself in an effort to maintain smooth Sino-American relations in the aftermath of the PRC government's harsh reprisals against peaceful students who were seeking a more democratic voice in their nation.

Soon after the student deaths in Tiananmen Square, the PRC sent Chennault an invitation through its ambassador to visit Beijing so that she could convey an explanation for its actions to American policymakers. The PRC was very concerned over "domestic and international repercussions" and about losing U.S. support over the incident. Her visit was reported in the *Washington Post* where she said that Chinese leaders "acknowledged . . . a lack of experience in handling large protests." Beijing's mayor told her that "the army was called in because there were not enough police to quell the protest."[74] In addition to justifying its actions to Washington leaders, she clearly served as a messenger from the PRC to the American public.

When Chennault saw President George Bush at a GOP meeting shortly after receiving her invitation and told him of her upcoming trip, he asked her to explore the situation and report back to him. According to her account, Bush instructed her that if she spoke with Deng Xiaoping and could deliver the message that the United States would maintain its support despite its displeasure at the events in Tiananmen Square, he would acknowledge her as his representative.

During her visit, Chennault met with many top PRC government officials, expressed her own horrified reaction to the incident, and listened to their explanations. In particular, she visited the coastal resort of Bei Dai Ho (Peh Tai Ho), which was favored by party leaders, and talked with some of them informally at the beach. Deng was the only leader she did not meet during her stay. While still in China, news of her arrival was publicized in the United States. The *Washington Post* quoted her as declaring that "she carried a message to Chinese leaders from President Bush saying that the [United States] would like to maintain the close ties to Beijing that have been developed over the last decade." James Lilley, ambassador to China at the time, reported hearing that she had spoken to the White House about her trip, although he knew of no specific message from the president.[75]

Considering her high-level ties to the GOP, reporters covering Bush at his Kennebunkport, Maine, summer home asked him if Chennault was carrying any messages to the Chinese leadership. He denied any knowledge of her visit or her mission. Bush was likely not prepared to acknowledge his administration's still-favorable disposition toward the Beijing regime. Angered that the president did not reply with "no comment," this categorical disavowal led her finally to realize that politicians would continue to use her as long as she let them. She subsequently had little to do with the Republican Party, neither actively supporting Bush's 1992 reelection bid nor making or soliciting any major donations. The episode did not, however, dampen her enthusiasm for improved ROC-PRC ties.

These events raise two important issues. The first is the tenuous nature of relations among the United States, PRC, and ROC. Within the span of several weeks in 1989, the PRC's standing with many nations, especially the ROC, was shaken dramatically. Tiananmen Square harmed Sino-American relations so severely that President Bush sent administration officials on their own "secret" mission in the month after the incident to try to repair the damage. Chennault believed that Bush's denial of her earlier efforts stemmed from an inability to give credit to a woman. PRC critics in the ROC took advantage of the events to decry the progress made toward building ties between the two Chinas. She saw much of the recent work undone in one horrible moment in Tiananmen Square. The road to amicable three-way Sino-American relations continued to be a very rocky one.

Second, Chennault's break with the GOP and President Bush reflected the changing world of international relations outside the sphere of governmental politics and, in particular, her own role. She conducted her American-Chinese relations further outside the realm of politics than ever before after the summer of 1989 and suffered no loss of prestige in either China as a result. Her standing among American politicians and business leaders was also undiminished. As connections between nations became less state-oriented and more individualized and skill driven, the role of informal diplomacy expanded. In the global marketplace, the place of partisan politics decreased because of the feasibility of more direct commercial relations. The rising importance of nonstate relations thus spotlighted informal diplomatic connections and increased the activities of citizen-diplomats who could follow Anna Chennault's career as a model.

In the years after she first returned to mainland China, businessmen in the ROC often approached her to help them make connections in the PRC. Finally, in 1989 she decided to take advantage of the recent legalization of indirect investment by ROC citizens in the PRC. Following her experience with trade missions for the

President's Export Council, she organized a similar mission for ROC businessmen to the mainland. Planning for the trip was done privately to protect the participants from political fallout in Taiwan. Even though travel to the mainland was legal, it was supposed to be primarily for the purpose of visiting one's family. The ROC government was still very sensitive about expanding ties to the PRC. In public, Chennault denied that the trip was for business purposes. Indeed, at a press conference in Taipei, she refused to answer reporters' questions on the subject. The *China News* commented that she "said reports of her organizing the tour are not true [and] hinted that she had experienced heavy pressure in connection with the matter."[76] Some men who originally planned to participate left the group following coercive efforts to force them out. According to Chennault, someone in the group who sought publicity for himself leaked the names of the participants to the press. She continued to publicly deny the trip's purpose in order "to help protect" the businessmen.[77]

For her efforts she was initially rewarded with some scathing criticism in the ROC. Her explanation that she "was in favor of separating economics from politics" was largely misunderstood. Her comment was not the naive oversimplification attributed to her because she certainly realized the connections between the two. Instead, she had come to recognize the importance of commercial exchange despite divergent political viewpoints as a way of bringing two political systems closer together. Nonetheless, an editorial in the *China News* after the trip attributed her motives to "personal financial considerations," even though she made no money from it. She earned no commissions or fees, but many of the businessmen started commercial relations that later made them multimillionaires.[78] She remembered that visit as being much more difficult than her return to the PRC in 1981 because of the advance public scrutiny. But she recognized that the ROC had "capital, manufacturing expertise, technology, and a shrinking labor pool" that could best be used in a market such as that of the PRC.[79]

Despite the objections raised over the trip, shortly thereafter many people in Taiwan were calling for changes in trade and business practice regulations in the ROC. One newspaper reported that the ROC's "Ministry of Economic Affairs ha[d] crafted a three-pronged proposal that would further liberalize [ROC] trade policies with the China mainland."[80] These included lifting the ban on business trips such as the one Chennault had just conducted. The article stated that "recent trends have proven it is impossible to entirely prevent local businessmen from investing in the mainland."[81] Another report described "a group of prominent [ROC] industrialists [who were] preparing for a meeting . . . to strongly urge the government to repeal its ban against local businessmen visiting the . . . mainland."[82] In addition, that article noted the trend of businessmen "under the pretense of visiting relatives on the mainland" who go instead "for the strict purpose of evaluating or establishing subsidiary plants or marketing facilities."[83] Calls arose for the ROC to relax its regulations and allow open commercial exchange across the Strait since it was already occurring and would benefit Taiwan as much as Beijing.

In late March 1990 the *China Post* reported that Anna Chennault would soon lead another group of ROC businessmen to study "the investment climate on the mainland."[84] Thus, despite some negative fallout from the December 1989 trip, she followed her instincts and proceeded with efforts to reconcile the ROC and PRC. Again, her belief in the power of contact and commerce was put into practice.

Her changed viewpoint in the 1980s had a profound long-term, multilayered impact on Sino-American relations because of its ripple effect within her many spheres of operation. Her informal diplomacy remained within the altered directions of U.S. foreign policy, her own ideology mirroring its changes. Even her efforts to save Twin Oaks did not contravene the broader American policy goals for Asian relations. When Nixon went to China, she urged caution, but she did not cut her ties to the GOP. It was in her interest to retain those connections. Chennault slowly perceived possibilities in relations with the PRC and eventually received an invitation to visit there in 1980 that she could not refuse. Once she crossed the line of physical contact with her homeland, her wider vision of the possibilities for American-Asian relations overtook her anti-Communist tendencies. Opportunities on the mainland could not be ignored. Chennault dedicated herself to improving ties to China through joint-venture operations with American businesses, and later those in Taiwan. If the possibilities of PRC-ROC commercial relations would bring the two Chinas closer together, then she promoted them. In the final analysis, therefore, her informal diplomatic career allowed her to make a contribution to the Asian policy of the United States while revealing the methods and limits of unofficial diplomacy for those willing to observe closely.

Notes

1. *New York Times*, April 22, 1971.
2. Ibid.
3. Anna Chennault, interview by author, July 25, 1994.
4. Goldwater to author, June 2, 1994.
5. Statement to author, August 2, 1994.
6. Ted Knap, "Mrs. Chennault reports to Nixon Asia fears U.S. 'bugging out,' " *Washington Daily News*, April 13, 1971.
7. Ymelda Dixon, "Your Date with Ymelda," *Washington Evening Star*, April 15, 1971.
8. Chennault to Nixon, March 12, 1971, part of briefing packet in "4/1/71–4/30/71," White House Central Files-Subject Files, Ex FO8, Nixon Project, National Archives.
9. Memorandum, Kissinger to Nixon, March 29, 1971, part of briefing packet, Nixon Project.
10. Chennault, *Education of Anna*, 236–37. There is currently no available record of Nixon's response.
11. Ibid., 237.
12. Chalmers M. Roberts, "Nixon Sees Mrs. Chennault and Taiwan's Ambassador," *Washington Post*, April 13, 1971.
13. George Lardner, Jr., "Anna Chennault Praises President," *Washington Post*, April 15, 1971.
14. Ibid.
15. Knap, *Washington Daily News*.
16. 92d Cong., 1st sess., vol. 117, pt. 15, June 10, 1971, 19214–15.
17. Ford to Chennault, May 6, 1971, "Congress House of Representatives 1972," Chennault Papers.
18. "Chennault's Widow Begs U.S. Caution," *Orlando Sentinel*, July 17, 1971.
19. "The Goal: China, Nixon's 2 1/2 Years of Secret Effort," *San Francisco Examiner*, July 17, 1971.
20. "Issues and Answers," July 25, 1971; PBS broadcast of a panel discussion on the PRC from the International Platform Association Convention, July 30, 1971.
21. "Mrs. Chennault Wary of Nixon's Peking Trip," *Evansville Press*, July 24, 1971.
22. Ibid.
23. "China and the Anna-Watchers," *Honolulu Star-Bulletin*, July 26, 1971.
24. " 'Flying Tiger Lady' Opposes Peking Trip," *Washington Daily News*, July 24, 1971.
25. Statement by Richard Nixon, July 15, 1971, *U.S. Department of State Bulletin*, Vol. 65, July-September 1971, 121.
26. "Mrs. Chennault Still a Nixon Supporter," *Los Angeles Times*, August 8, 1971.
27. "China and the Anna-Watchers," *Honolulu Star-Bulletin*.
28. "U.S. Businessmen in Asia to Meet Cabinet Officers," *New York Times*, October 12, 1971.
29. Even though by strict familial descent Liao Chengzhi was Chennault's cousin, the traditional title for him in Chinese culture was "uncle,"

a term of respect for elderly relatives. She referred to his son, however, as her cousin.

30. Wolfgang Bartke, *Biographical Dictionary and Analysis of China's Party Leadership, 1922–1988* (Munich: Saur Verlag Gmlott & Co. KG, 1990), 115–16; Howard L. Boorman and Richard D. Howard, *Biographical Dictionary of Republican China*, vol. 2 (New York: Columbia University Press, 1968), 363–64.

31. Anna Chennault, interview by author, July 25, 1994.

32. Thomas Corcoran to ROC Vice Minister of Foreign Affairs Frederick Chien, December 29, 1978, box 112, folder 1, Corcoran Papers.

33. Thomas Corcoran to Anna Chennault, March 27, 1979, 3, container 112, folder 1, Corcoran Papers.

34. Ibid.

35. Thomas Corcoran to George Yeh, July 2, 1979, container 112, folder 2, Corcoran Papers.

36. Jack E. Buttram, "Georgia's Place in the History of Friends of Free China (FOFC): The Viewpoint of Its Executive Director," 1, published in booklet form by Friends of Free China, Washington, DC, September 1991, Anna Chennault Papers, National Central Library, Taipei, Taiwan.

37. Corcoran to Chennault, March 27, 1979, 3, container 112, folder 2, Corcoran Papers.

38. Taiwan Relations Act, Section 4 (b)(3)(B), Public Law 96-8, approved April 10, 1979, hereafter TRA.

39. Ibid., Section 2 (b)(3) and (5).

40. Ibid., Section 6 (a).

41. Ibid., Section 10.

42. Buttram, "Georgia's Place," 5.

43. Corcoran to Chennault, March 27, 1979, 3, container 112, folder 2, Corcoran Papers.

44. Anna Chennault, interview by author, July 26, 1994.

45. John Holdridge, interview by author, July 26, 1994.

46. Senator Alan Simpson, telephone interview by author, July 21, 1994.

47. Senator Charles Percy, interview by author, August 2, 1994.

48. TRA, Section 2 (b) (2) and (4).

49. "A Proposal for U.S. Policy on China," statement presented to the GOP Platform Committee by Anna Chennault, *Congressional Record*, 94th Cong., 2d sess., 1976, pt. 116, S12896.

50. Madame Claire Chennault, "China," *Reporter* (Official publication of the Minnesota Republican Heritage Council), vol. 7, no. 10, October 1971, 1, Minneapolis.

51. In September 1987 the ban on such travel was eliminated for some ROC citizens.

52. Chennault interview, July 25, 1994.

53. Ibid.

54. Ted Stevens, interview with author, June 27, 1994.

55. Ibid. Senator Baker and other leaders of the RNC declined interviews with the author, so this cannot be substantiated.

56. *New York Times*, January 5, 1981.

57. "Anna Chennault Given Warm Peking Welcome," *Los Angeles Times*, January 3, 1981.

58. "New Views Hinted by Mrs. Chennault," *New York Times*, January 5, 1981.

59. *Los Angeles Times*, January 4, 1981.
60. Stevens interview.
61. Chennault interview, July 25, 1994.
62. Takashi Oka, "Deng plan to woo Taipei gets a boost from key member of Taiwan lobby," *Christian Science Monitor*, January 5, 1981.
63. Stevens interview.
64. Chennault interview, July 25, 1994.
65. Statement of John H. Holdridge, Assistant Secretary of State for East Asian and Pacific Affairs, Hearings before the Committee on Foreign Affairs, U.S. House of Representatives, 97th Cong., 2d sess., 1982, 1.
66. Chennault interview, July 27, 1994.
67. Chennault to Nissen Davis, February 1, 1981, "Flying Tiger Lines '81," Chennault Papers.
68. Cyril Murphy, Senior Vice President of Government and Public Affairs to Chennault, January 28, 1982, "Flying Tiger Lines '81," Chennault Papers.
69. Business Consultancy Agreement between FTL and Chennault, April 1, 1988, "FTL-Agreement(s) Fedex," Chennault Papers.
70. A. Doyle Cloud, Jr., to Chennault, December 13, 1990, "Fed Express-Doyle Cloud," Chennault Papers.
71. Chennault interview, July 25, 1994.
72. Kermin Shih, interview by author, November 15, 1994, Taipei, Taiwan, ROC.
73. Ambassador Konsin C. Shah, interview by author, November 10, 1994, Taipei, Taiwan, ROC.
74. Michael Weisskopf, "Chennault Meets With Chinese Leaders," *Washington Post*, August 27, 1989.
75. Chennault interview, July 25, 1994; *Washington Post*, August 27, 1989; James Lilley, interview by author, August 1, 1994.
76. "Chennault denies planning to lead group to mainland," *China News*, November 30, 1989.
77. Chennault interview, July 25, 1994.
78. "Friendship with a price," *China News*, December 13, 1989; Chennault interview, July 25, 1994.
79. Chennault interview, July 25, 1994.
80. Lu I-yu, "Mainland Trade Changes Eyed," *Free China Journal*, February 26, 1990.
81. Ibid.
82. "Government Urged to OK M'land Business Visits," *China News*, March 8, 1990.
83. Ibid.
84. *China Post*, March 29, 1990. The *China News* carried a similar story on the same date.

Conclusion

Anna Chen Chennault's career illustrates the role of informal diplomacy through the activities of one unofficial diplomat. Because this diplomat was a Chinese woman, issues of gender and ethnicity influenced the story but were generally incidental to an analysis of informal diplomacy itself and its contribution to American foreign relations. Her career revealed the connections between spheres of a hidden and forgotten world of international affairs that at various times confounded, conjoined, contravened, or consumed formal relations between governments with (and sometimes without) the knowledge and blessing of elected officials and citizens.

The informal diplomatic milieu includes many areas of human interaction—social, political, economic, and scientific. To exclude these realms from the study of foreign relations is to overlook a rich source of material and to forfeit an understanding of the more intimate areas of contact. The cultural contexts within which formal international affairs are conducted require the soil of familiarity to truly flourish. These areas of connection that foster comfortable relations between people are very often hidden from scholars' and analysts' scrutiny. The best way to peer into these reaches is to accompany a participant, especially one who interacts in several areas. Anna Chennault operated in areas important for their contribution to foreign policy, and her career illustrates the relationship of informal diplomacy to the conduct of foreign relations.

Chennault's background and upbringing in China were instrumental in developing her determination, vision, and passion. Her family's heritage of scholarship and diplomacy introduced her early to the world beyond the confines of the household. Experiencing firsthand the Sino-Japanese War and World War II during her formative years were adversities that helped form her strong convictions and personality. Working as a young journalist reporting the activities of the Fourteenth Air Force in China and its charismatic leader, General Claire Lee Chennault, exposed her to American values of individualism and personal liberty. The horrors and hardships of the war made her vow to never be cold or hungry again and left her sensitive to human suffering.

When World War II ended, Anna's tenacious nature advanced her journalism career and helped her capture the affections of General Chennault. The retired general's private airline venture in China after the war (Civil Air Transport) gave Anna an introduction to areas of informal diplomacy that she would cultivate following his death less than eleven years after their marriage. CAT was an informal diplomatic tool itself. Founded by the leader of the Flying Tigers as a secret effort against the Japanese invaders of China prior to Pearl Harbor, it also fell within the parameters of unofficial diplomacy. Anna's experiences with the General and CAT served as her baptism into the world of anticommunism and the China Lobby, the realm of political influence, and the arena of extralegal actions in support of a cause.

After General Chennault's death in 1958, Anna's career took on a life of its own beyond that of being the widow of a famed war hero. By settling in Washington, DC, Mrs. Chennault placed herself at a locus of international power and unofficial diplomacy. She became involved slowly through her political and social life, but her friendship with one of Washington's leading lobbyists and men of influence gave her a mentor with incomparable skill and contacts. After the widowed Anna moved to his hometown of Washington, Thomas Corcoran took her under his wing. From him, she learned her lessons well and applied them from the early 1960s onward.

Mrs. Chennault's political activities, supported by a speaking and publishing career, were enhanced by her role as a society hostess, all accomplished within her expanding circles of friends and associates in Washington and Asia. It was as a hostess that she became best known to the American public, but she developed a much broader reputation among political, business, and diplomatic leaders. Her career widened to include international refugee aid and consulting for American companies wishing to expand their operations in Asian markets. She augmented this work with her entertaining schedule—a frequent item in Washington's society columns. This pattern persisted as her political connections and international ties grew to include men at the highest levels of partisan politics and government.

Mrs. Chennault and Thomas G. Corcoran at a reception honoring the Deputy Secretary of Defense, 1978

All these areas of her life converged in the "October surprise" of the 1968 presidential election. This event thrust Anna Chennault further into the public spotlight and prompted a noticeable shift from her status as widow, "Mrs. Claire Lee Chennault," to that of a capable woman in her own right, "Mrs. Anna Chennault." Richard Nixon used her as a conduit to South Vietnam's leaders for many months before the election, all the while promoting the belief that, if elected, his administration would be more supportive of the South Vietnamese cause than a Democratic one and would negotiate for a stronger settlement on their behalf against North Vietnam. This informal diplomatic process was possible because of Chennault's top-level connections in Saigon, her frequent business trips there that provided access without arousing public attention, and her reputation for discretion. These elements are, not coincidentally, also essential for successful informal diplomacy.

In Saigon with General William Westmoreland, circa late 1960s

When, after the election, reports of the Nixon-Chennault-Thieu political triangle began to surface, everyone denied it, but Chennault's role in these events enhanced her political and business standing. As the 1970s progressed, her increasing focus on business dealings helped American corporate enterprises strengthen U.S. ties to non-Communist Asian nations, which simultaneously advanced Washington's diplomatic goals. These goals centered on building a large contingent of pro-American capitalist nations with strong economies in Asia to counterbalance the Communists on mainland China, in North Vietnam, and in North Korea. The process extended the post-World War II American policy of creating a powerful Japan as the major Asian Communist counterbalance. Chennault's ties to the Republican administrations of Nixon and Gerald Ford in turn improved her standing in Asia.

Her importance as a player on the diplomatic stage was reflected by the high regard that trans-Pacific leaders held for her access and influence. In Asia, Chennault was considered an expert on American politics and business who provided Asian policymakers with charts for navigating the choppy waters of U.S. public opinion, legislative maneuvers, and official contacts—all important facets of keeping up a positive and balanced relationship with the leader of the Western world. American customs and practices seemed as obscure and unfathomable to Asians as those of Asia appeared to American businessmen hoping to tap the resources and markets of the fastest-growing commercial region of the globe. For U.S. companies that wanted to facilitate negotiations or quickly reach the top bureaucrat in the ministry that governed their industry, Anna Chennault was known as the right person to see in South Korea, Indonesia, Thailand, the Philippines, and, most important, Taiwan.

As American relations relaxed to include dialogue and limited commercial relations with the PRC beginning in late 1971, the dynamics of Anna Chennault's role slowly began to change. Because she did not have the connections within the PRC at that time that she did in the ROC, she was not very involved in the developing U.S.-PRC relationship in the 1970s. But for the ROC, these years were fraught with uncertainty over its own status; thus, she was even more vital for any information or insight that she could offer about American intentions, actions, or attitudes. Former Washington officials involved with U.S.-ROC affairs all praised her efforts on behalf of ROC interests, particularly in the area of commerce.

Once Chennault initiated her own relations with the PRC following her 1981 visit, her role underwent its final metamorphosis—to a triangular function among the United States, PRC, and ROC. Former ambassador, State Department official, and American Institute of Taiwan (AIT) director Harry Thayer doubts public assertions that she carried messages between the PRC and ROC governments during the 1980s, an allegation that she also denied. Most certainly she carried her analysis and impressions of each side to the other, but Anna's discretion made it wholly inappropriate for her to confirm that she carried messages, even if she did so.[1] Given that working both sides of the Taiwan Strait is a "very delicate matter [because] it is hard to keep the trust of both sides," another official believed that she "has done better than most at keeping herself" in the favor of both Chinas.[2] During the 1980s her views commanded attention in the Reagan administration's National Security Council for the insights they offered on the bilateral China relationship.[3] As a group, former government officials viewed her contribution to American-Asian relations in a positive light. Some were more enthusiastic about her than others, but they all believed that she was an intelligent and knowledgable player with high-level connections and the sincere desire to favorably advance relations among the United States, PRC, and ROC—particularly the latter two. Officials acknowledged that sometimes Chennault had connections to leaders that they lacked, and several said that they often spoke with her about current events in order to add her analysis to the pool of information they drew upon for policymaking and advice to the State Department and the White House.

During the 1970s and 1980s, Chennault's activities in informal diplomacy increased dramatically. The bringing together of government, business, and political leaders in a social setting was a skill in which she excelled. As one official said, "she provided a forum where ideas [could] be aired and effective proponents could make their points [since] in real policymaking so much is in private conversation." Her importance came from facilitating the forging of connections.[4] But any view that defined her merely as a "hostess" (albeit an important one) underestimated her position. Because of her contacts not only with large numbers of American and Asian policymakers but also in numerous venues of informal diplomatic activity, Chennault serves as a useful model for a study of unofficial diplomacy. In the two decades following Nixon's opening of the door to the PRC, no single individual had the breadth of maneuverability in so many places and situations as did Anna Chennault. Whatever opinions she generated, whatever level of direct influence over policy she controlled, or whatever opinions her changing politics inspired in others, she must be included in any examination of this aspect of foreign relations.

The years since 1990 have been times of continued activity for Chennault, but also times when she moved in other directions—primarily outside the political realm. While maintaining her connections to various Asian-American organizations and others such as the Fourteenth Air Force Association, or the National Military

Families Association (which she helped found), she expanded ties to her homeland through her foundation, the Council for International Cooperation (CIC). CIC has worked to improve education in the PRC with funds for public and academic libraries and scholarships for students. Most notable among CIC's initiatives are the Anna Chennault Awards for Academic Excellence given in Beijing to outstanding teachers from across the country during Teachers' Week in September each year. While Chennault may be out of the diplomatic limelight, she has not stopped her life's work. China's policymakers recognize her value (diplomatic, cultural, commercial) even if U.S. policymakers have forgotten the assistance that Chennault provided in earlier years.

In her early career, her visible ties to the China Lobby labeled her ideologically, but it would be simplistic and confining to view her only in that light. Unlike some China Lobby members, Anna Chennault never accepted any payment for her advocacy of ROC interests, or later for those of the PRC. The China Lobby and its successor organization, the Committee of One Million, represented individuals such as General Chennault who brought their own prejudices to the subject of the PRC. Because of their wartime experiences and connections, they saw no redeeming or positive qualities in the Beijing government. Anna Chennault broke out of those ideological confines, as did Congressman Walter Judd (R-MN), another person very closely linked to the China Lobby. She recalled that Judd understood why she went to Beijing in 1980; he was a man who "really cared about the Chinese people." He appreciated "her courage [which] made a tremendous contribution to the Chinese people."[5]

Not all of her fellow ROC supporters were so forgiving, and some never accepted America's or her move toward the PRC. Because of her willingness to move beyond an anti-Communist view, David Dean, who helped establish AIT, believed it would be "selling her short" to see her as only a Cold Warrior of the China Lobby stripe.[6] Regardless of these diverse opinions, Chennault never abandoned her concern for the ROC and its people. She instead saw a different path for them—a path that included contact with their mainland neighbors, relatives, and fellow Chinese. The route to success and security, she believed, was one that included the PRC, the ROC, and Overseas Chinese people walking together.

Her first return trip to the People's Republic in 1980 focused her energies more on projects in mainland China—projects that eventually included imports and investments from the ROC.

Ambassador Nat Bellocchi, chairman of the AIT in 1994, observed that ROC businessmen who invested in the PRC "are very apolitical [with] only capitalist interests," an assertion proven by the fact that Taiwan has been the largest investor in the PRC.[7] Despite divergent political and economic systems, when presented with a business opportunity, political differences melt away. Chennault embraced that view and its friendship-building potential. She was also keenly aware of such interests when she took ROC businessmen on a trade mission to the PRC in December 1989. Since many of the participants became millionaires because of contacts made on that trip, she obviously gauged the situation accurately. Her efforts to tie the PRC and ROC together commercially illustrate her larger goal: reconciliation between the two Chinas.

American officials who acknowledge that Anna Chennault was a helpful source for them vary in their opinions of her usefulness to Asian policymakers. In the early years of U.S.-PRC relations, there were good reasons for the PRC to cultivate her as an Asian knowledgable about U.S. culture and politics. There were many Americans willing to explain what was going on in the United States, but if the Chinese wanted analyses from someone with high-level contacts *and* an Asian worldview, she was the best source. Likewise, in other Asian nations, Chennault was often the only connection to provide them with top-level policymaking perspectives. Once the Sino-American relationship included formal recognition, others could meet this need. Also, as older leaders died—"Uncle" Liao in 1983, for example—some of her contacts ended. This process was even more profound in the ROC as members of the World War II generation such as those who knew and respected General Chennault lost power. Younger leaders in the ROC were often unaware of Mrs. Chennault's historical connections; they were more familiar with her recent activities. Ironically, the important expansion of commercial and other ties that Chennault promoted between the Chinas diminished her importance as links between the two nations grew more extensive and varied.

Another measure of Chennault's influence can be seen in her standing among the Chinese public, in both the United States and the two Chinas. Her impact on differing Chinese audiences largely depended on their location. On the mainland, she was seen positively because she moved past relationships of old and worked with the PRC. Most informed PRC citizens know her name (most commonly her Chinese name, Chen Hsiengmei, whether on the mainland or in Taiwan) and are most likely to recognize her as an author. She is also visible through her foundation, CIC. Those benefiting from her efforts to bring commercial operations and educational assistance to the nation generally know and appreciate that facet of her career. In 1994 two members of the PRC embassy staff praised her willingness to bring the United States, PRC, and ROC together. One claimed she was well known and loved on the mainland because of General Chennault's efforts to aid China against Japan and added that her knowledge of Chinese history helped her to understand events and communicate with all sides.[8] Ambassador Konsin Shah viewed her efforts to perpetuate the name of General Chennault in the PRC as "pav[ing] the way for greater future friendship between a democratic China and the U.S." Even in the April 2001 clash over a downed U.S. reconnaissance plane, Beijing's leaders met with Anna Chennault.

Views of her in Taiwan span a wider range of attitudes. While most people know her and many (but not all) accept her changed position, some of those same individuals do not consider her relevant to contemporary concerns. With the opening of ROC society to more political options has come an increased call for an independent Taiwan. Looking to such a future, some Taiwanese found no useful role for Anna Chennault in the more autonomous ROC international position that evolved after the U.S. derecognition in 1979. Still, her access to ROC leaders remained, and the Taiwan general public were not always aware of the level of such connections between Chennault and their own government.

On the other hand, her place in the perception and judgment of Chinese Americans toward the changing relationships of the two Chinas has been very important. Initially, her acceptance of the PRC and her willingness to work with its leaders went a long way toward helping Chinese Americans come to grips with the changing Asian scene. As with some American policymakers, there were some Chinese Americans who viewed her changes as an abandonment of the ROC. There is, here, a most apt comparison to be made between Nixon and Anna Chennault. Both were able to go to the PRC and not be charged with selling out to the Communists because both were such well-known, ardent anti-Communists. An ROC scholar observed that in this comparison with Nixon, Chennault's place was most important as a "model for changing the minds of Chinese-Americans much more than the minds of the people of Taiwan."[9] She continually encouraged Chinese Americans (and

Asian Americans generally) to get involved in the U.S. political process, raise their voices, and make the system work for them.

A prominent member of the Chinese community in Washington described Chennault's extensive activities on behalf of Chinese Americans in business and politics. She helped start an Asian bank in the District, found government jobs for young Asians, obtained Small Business Administration loans, but especially encouraged and supported Chinese involvement in politics. Dr. Bill Chin Lee, who served more than once with Chennault as a delegate to the Republican National Convention,[10] believed that most people saw her "as a leader with respect for them and as an example of what Chinese can achieve in America."[11]

Washington Chinese restaurateur and businesswoman Linda Lee saw Anna Chennault as a mentor and role model for herself and other Chinese women. Lee was particularly impressed when she met Chennault in the mid-1960s after she forced the Chinese American Citizens Alliance chapter in Washington, which was all male at the time, to admit women members by refusing to accept their invitation to speak until they did so.[12] Lee and others considered Chennault to be ahead of her time on issues such as women's place in business and relations with the PRC.[13] Over the years, Chennault served as founder, co-founder, president, director, or regional chair of over a dozen local and national Chinese organizations. Thus, it seemed reasonable for Chinese Americans to look to her, as other Americans looked to Nixon, for guidance in changing Sino-American relations. With the potential strength of organized ethnic voters to influence U.S. foreign policy (Cubans being perhaps the best example), Chinese Americans' acceptance of broader U.S. connections to the PRC was a welcome nonissue for Washington policymakers—one that was certainly facilitated by Chennault's influence within the Chinese-American community.

One of the few areas where her credibility has come under fire is over the question of the level of seriousness with which she is taken by either Chinese government. In the ROC, Anna Chennault was perceived as a somewhat controversial figure due to the mediating role that she hoped to assume. While Kermin Shih of Taiwan's Central News Agency believed that she played a part in the triangular U.S.-PRC-ROC relationship, he did not see her as a liaison between the two Chinas because the ROC "rejects any longstanding friend who tries to play a mediating role."[14] According to others, she was not alone in being rejected for attempting to facilitate those relations. They believe that the ROC and PRC have to

The first female member of the Washington Gaslight Club receives her key, 1972

find their own way to any kind of reconciliation. Several former State Department officials suggest that Chennault lost some credibility with ROC leaders through her attempts at peacemaking. They recalled their own ROC contacts expressing doubts about her sincerity and loyalty to Taiwan. Some men with contacts in the PRC noticed a similar loss of credibility for her reports relative to PRC-ROC reconciliation issues. These Americans (who otherwise had positive overall opinions of Anna Chennault) believe that her desire to be a mediator was perceived by some ROC and PRC officials to color and cloud her assessments, which may have led her to offer overly optimistic reports. These viewpoints require consideration of the connection and contradiction between influence and self-promotion.

One cannot succeed in her arenas of activity without self-promotion. Access, which is critical to gauging influence, is aided by self-promotion, and higher levels of influence often engender not only admiration and respect but also jealousy and enmity. This complicated issue was at work throughout Chennault's career. She herself admits to being a self-promoter; her desire to succeed and her self-confidence (the result of her wartime experiences) drove her ambition in politics and business. But what successful politician or business leader is not a self-promoter? Certainly, Ronald Reagan, Bill Clinton, Ross Perot, and Donald Trump have been self-promoters. The trait should not be viewed negatively unless the person's aims are purely selfish. For Anna Chennault, that was not the case. Whatever benefit she drew from her efforts (as a business consultant she was compensated but not on a commission basis), the larger impact of her activities furthered the goals of American foreign policy, improving U.S.-Asian relations in general. Even former State Department officials who had negative comments about her summed up her career in positive terms. And these negative comments were made only upon assurance of anonymity—a fact that by itself indicated a desire to stay in the good graces of a woman who still had powerful connections.

History must be circumspect about the memories and statements of its characters, but history must be equally circumspect about the refusal of others to speak. Several notable persons declined to be interviewed or answer questions about Anna Chennault. This refusal could be attributed to a number of reasons. One possibility, suggested by Chennault herself, is that they did not want to support a project that centered on a Chinese woman's contributions to American foreign policy.

She refused, however, to allow her gender to keep her from achieving her goals. In the United States she was part of a postwar generation of women who pushed societal boundaries. Her belief that "being a woman only made it harder for others to say no" to her illustrated her view of her gender and of the men around her.[15] The statements of male policymakers who extolled her skills while often including observations about her appearance demonstrate how gender played a part in others' responses to her. A *Washington*

Post article about her fundraising activities reported her techniques and accomplishments along with comments about her appearance. She was quoted as saying, "I travel mostly in a man's world, but no matter what you do, you can be business-like and not forget you're a woman. The men will treat you with dignity and kindness."[16] She was certainly willing to use her femininity as well as her business acumen to land either a donation or a deal.

For some people around her, however, Chennault's gender might have produced more negative reactions. During the 1960s and 1970s, when she rose to prominence, powerful women were not always accepted. In that light, it is understandable how the "Dragon Lady" label stuck to her. It is also easy to see how some individuals, regardless of gender, might have resented her position, access, and accomplishments, especially in the political sphere. Here was a diminutive woman, and Chinese at that, who saw, in an ordinary day, administration officials at the highest level; phoned their counterparts in Asian capitals; advised, negotiated for, and consulted with a major corporation on an important commercial deal; strategized with leaders of the GOP about fundraising, policy, and electoral tactics; and then gave a smashing dinner party for high-ranking military, political, and business leaders. To some, this level of proficiency in informal diplomacy was suspect, particularly when women were rarely seen in such highly visible roles.

As a Chinese woman, Chennault brought another factor to her persona that was vital to her success. Had she married an American whose interests and career gravitated toward Europe, for example, she would likely still have been successful, but not on a comparable scale. Ambassador Shah believed that her outspoken nature would have been a liability had she remained in Asia; however, it served her very well when negotiating and conferring with American leaders. She was considered pragmatic and straightforward and was valued for that reason. For American policymakers, her Chinese heritage gave her useful insight into the character of Asian allies and opponents, especially since she could place it all in the context of American interests, which she understood equally well.

Her well-developed observation, analytical, and communication skills were the basis of her most important political contributions. With these skills, she was an effective extra set of eyes and ears for both American and Asian policymakers. More significant for the American political system was her emphasis on the importance of ethnic voters. Not only was she a force in organizing Asian-

American voters, but she was also instrumental in the creation of a powerful ethnic voice within the GOP. According to Nixon, "In this new era of building bridges of peace and friendship with all the peoples of the world, more than ever before we will be calling upon the special resources of Chinese-Americans to further expand cultural and economic relations between East and West."[17] New York's Governor Nelson Rockefeller was even more pragmatic about the prospects for the GOP when he wrote her that "I hope we can attract increasing numbers of the younger generation [of Chinese Americans] to the Republican Party."[18] Chennault agreed, but she also wanted more for Asian Americans than just to be counted as voters.

For over twenty years she persistently prodded Republican administrations to utilize the talents of Asian Americans through appointments in the federal government. While her success on that score was not what she hoped, her efforts did raise the consciousness of some elected officials. President Nixon assured her of his "own deep respect and admiration for Americans of Chinese descent and the remarkable way they have enriched our national life. This Administration is fully committed to . . . expanding opportunities for government service to those who can make a special contribution."[19] The issue was more concretely articulated by Senator Fong, who wrote Chennault that she "correctly said [in a speech he entered into the *Congressional Record*] that our Government has not made full use of the talents of the Chinese Americans. A few have been appointed to responsible posts . . . but the number is small and more should be done."[20] Senator Percy agreed "that our government has thus far failed to tap the talents of the Chinese-American community. Asian-Americans have made great contributions to American life and culture, and their active involvement in the governmental process is long overdue."[21] Chennault kept up her appeal during Nixon's second administration and the Ford, Reagan, and Bush presidencies, but with only limited success. She believed that in this singular situation, her voice—that of a woman—carried much less weight than if she had been a man. The failure of the GOP to move further than it did in this area was another factor contributing to her disengagement from the Republican Party after 1990.

Thus, as an unofficial diplomat, Anna Chennault had unique and varied attributes that made her career an especially appropriate one for exploring the American-Asian relations about which she cared so much. She worked widely varying venues to bring together American and Chinese cultures. She believed that each could benefit the other and help to further greater regional goals, including the reunification of mainland China and Taiwan. Few citizen-diplomats such as she operate so wholly in the private sector, without portfolio, yet have connections at the top in so many national governments. Or talk balance sheets and import-export quotas with corporate executives and commerce secretaries. Or share aircraft specifications with high-ranking military commanders in several different nations. Or bring them all back home for an impromptu evening of dining, dancing, and discussion.

Anna Chennault's career vividly demonstrates the value of examining the importance of informal diplomacy in the larger area of foreign relations. Within the general fields of business, politics, international organizations, and social gatherings, the content and outcome of U.S.-Asian relations are not fully revealed without the specific actions of an individual to make them relevant. If the interchange of formal and informal, official and unofficial diplomacy is more obvious and relevant and if the value of this forgotten realm of international contacts is now an obvious aspect of foreign relations, then studying Anna Chen Chennault's career has served its purpose.

Notes

1. Harry Thayer, interview by author, July 12, 1994.
2. David Laux, interview by author, July 21, 1994.
3. Ibid.
4. Ibid.
5. Chennault interview, July 25, 1994.
6. David Dean, interview by author, July 27, 1994.
7. Interview by author, July 8, 1994.
8. Interviews by author, July 28, 1994.
9. Dr. Chiu Kun-shuan, interview by author, November 10, 1994, Taipei, Taiwan, ROC.
10. Interview by author, July 27 and August 2, 1994.
11. Dr. Lee interview, August 2, 1994.
12. Anna Chennault was also the first female member of the Washington Gaslight Club.
13. Interview by author, July 27, 1994.
14. Shih interview, November 15, 1994.
15. Chennault interview, July 26, 1994.
16. Marie Smith, "A Wealth of Talent—GOP's Anna Chennault," *Washington Post*, November 1, 1968.

17. Richard Nixon to Chennault, August 3, 1972, "Chinese American Citizens Alliance," Chennault Papers.

18. Nelson Rockefeller to Chennault, August 4, 1972, ibid.

19. Nixon to Chennault, August 3, 1972.

20. Hiram Fong to Chennault, August 4, 1972, "Chinese American Citizens Alliance," Chennault Papers.

21. Charles Percy to Chennault, July 26, 1972, ibid.

Bibliographical Essay

Scholars have left largely unexamined both the general topic of informal diplomacy and the specifics of Anna Chennault's career. While the academy has broadened its characterization of diplomacy beyond the activities of the "men in striped pants" to include such actors as international businesses and nongovernmental organizations, diplomatic historians have infrequently addressed the experiences of citizen-diplomats. Thus, those interested in pursuing the subject must search broadly to understand the parameters, limitations, and possibilities of the field.

Most of the existing literature on informal diplomacy concentrates on the activities of international organizations and on international business leaders, journalists, or former politicians. Some important sources include Maureen R. Berman and Joseph E. Johnson, *Unofficial Diplomats* (New York, 1977), George L. Ridgeway, *Merchants of Peace: The History of the International Chamber of Commerce* (Boston, 1959), Oran R. Young, *The Intermediaries: Third Parties in International Crises* (Princeton, NJ, 1967), Robert O. Keohane and Joseph S. Nye, Jr., eds., *Transnational Relations and World Politics* (Cambridge, MA, 1972), Elmer Plischke, *Modern Diplomacy* (Washington, DC, 1979), James N. Rosenau, *National Leadership and Foreign Policy: A Case Study in the Mobilization of Public Support* (Princeton, NJ, 1963), David D. Newsom, ed., *Private Diplomacy with the Soviet Union* (Lanham, MD, 1987), Henry E. Mattox, *The Twilight of Amateur Diplomacy: The American Foreign Service and Its Senior Officers in the 1890s* (Kent, OH, 1989), Seymour Freidin and George Bailey, *The Experts* (New York, 1968), Raymond Cohen, *Negotiating across Cultures: Communication Obstacles in International Diplomacy* (Washington, DC, 1995), and Michael H. Cardozo, *Diplomats in International Cooperation: Stepchildren of the Foreign Service* (Ithaca, NY, 1962).

International relations scholars have examined some of the connections between diplomacy and business. See Ronald Rogowski, *Commerce and Coalitions: How Trade Affects Domestic Political Align-*

ments (Princeton, NJ, 1989), John M. Stopford and Susan Strange, *Rival States, Rival Firms: Competition for World Market Shares* (New York, 1991), Robert O. Keohane and Helen V. Milner, *Internationalization and Domestic Politics* (New York, 1996), Kim McQuaid, *Uneasy Partners: Big Business in American Politics, 1945–1990* (Baltimore, 1994), and Jack N. Behrman, J. J. Boddewyn, and Ashok Kapoor, *International Business-Government Communications: U.S. Structures, Actors, and Issues* (Lexington, MA, 1975).

Turning to the role of women in foreign relations, we find that more works exist on the subject of women in the formal diplomatic world than those who work outside it. Three good studies are Homer L. Calkin, *Women in American Foreign Affairs* (Washington, DC, 1977) and *Women in the Department of State: Their Role in American Foreign Affairs* (Washington, DC, 1978), in addition to *Women at State: An Inquiry into the Status of Women in the United States Department of State* (Washington, DC, 1984) by Mary S. Olmsted and others at the Women's Research and Education Institute of the Congressional Caucus for Women's Issues. Still within the formal governmental context, but on the periphery, are ambassadors' wives whose contributions are described by Jewell Fenzi in *Married to the Foreign Service: An Oral History of the American Diplomatic Spouse* (New York, 1994). Women ambassadors' views are developed in Ann Miller Morin, *Her Excellency: An Oral History of American Women Ambassadors* (New York, 1995). For a broader perspective on the varying roles of women in foreign policy, a number of books stretch the picture to include women outside the government: Edward P. Crapol, ed., *Women and American Foreign Policy: Lobbyists, Critics, and Insiders* (Wilmington, DE, 1992), Ellen Boneparth, ed., *Women, Power, and Policy* (New York, 1982), Nancy E. McGlen, *The Status of Women in Foreign Policy* (Ithaca, NY, 1995), Nancy E. McGlen and Meredith Reid Sarkees, *Women in Foreign Policy: The Insiders* (New York, 1993), Cynthia Enloe, *Bananas, Beaches, and Bases: Making Feminist Sense of International Politics* (Berkeley, CA, 1990), and Rhondri Jeffreys-Jones, *Changing Differences: Women and the Shaping of American Foreign Policy, 1917–1994* (New Brunswick, NJ, 1995). Two stories deserving mention for their contribution to the discussion of women in politics and foreign policy are Eleanor Lansing Dulles, *Eleanor Lansing Dulles: Chances of a Lifetime, A Memoir* (Englewood Cliffs, NJ, 1980) and Ingrid Winther Scobie, *Center Stage: Helen Gahagan Douglas, A Life* (New York, 1992).

Any examination of Anna Chennault must begin with her autobiographies, *A Thousand Springs: The Biography of a Marriage* (New

York, 1962) and *The Education of Anna* (New York, 1980). These are the only two in English; the remainder are in Chinese. Mrs. Chennault is a prolific writer in her own right, publishing over fifty books of fiction, poetry, biography, autobiography, short stories, anthologies, and commentaries. Her only other publications in English are *Chennault and the Flying Tigers* (New York, 1963), a story of her husband's military career; and her Georgetown University effort, *Dictionary of New Simplified Chinese Characters* (Washington, DC, 1962). Chinese scholars have begun analyzing her work. See Ma Shenbiao, ed., *Chen Xiang Mei San Wen Ping Lun Ji* (Taiyuan, Shanxi, PRC, 1998) and Yao Moyu, ed., *Chen Xiangmei Yan Jiu* (Hangzhou, Zhejiang, PRC, 2000).

Mrs. Chennault's papers are in her possession in Washington, DC. These materials include correspondence, memoranda, speeches, calendars, photographs, and extensive newsclipping files from domestic and international publications. Examining these materials was necessary for understanding the essential character of her connections and style of operation as well as for establishing the full extent of her activities. Some materials, mostly ceremonial and honorary items, donated by Mrs. Chennault to the National Central Library in Taipei, Taiwan, are also available.

The papers of others with whom she has worked also reveal her many connections. The papers of General Claire Lee Chennault, Hoover Institution, Stanford University, with a microfilm copy at the Library of Congress, Manuscript Division, Washington, DC, expose much about the famous multifaceted pioneer of warfare aviation but little about his wife. The Thomas G. Corcoran Papers, Library of Congress, Manuscript Division, include many references to Mrs. Chennault's career and demonstrate how a longtime friendship with Corcoran, her political mentor, contributed to her development as an informal diplomat. In addition, the Republican National Committee Papers, Office of Presidential Libraries, National Archives and Records Administration, Washington, DC, illustrate Mrs. Chennault's activities within the GOP at multiple levels. The Whiting Willauer Papers, Firestone Library, Princeton University, Princeton, New Jersey, are useful for the story of General Chennault in postwar China as well as for CAT and some of her personal activities.

Materials covering Mrs. Chennault's connections to several administrations can be found in the following presidential libraries: John F. Kennedy, Boston; Richard M. Nixon, Yorba Linda, California; Gerald R. Ford, Ann Arbor, Michigan; Lyndon Baines

Johnson, Austin, Texas; Ronald Reagan, Simi Valley, California; and George H. W. Bush, College Station, Texas. The presidential papers of Richard Nixon are still held by the National Archives in College Park, Maryland, and contain a number of references to Mrs. Chennault's activities during his administration; however, material on the 1968 election is still unavailable.

Within government sources, both Claire Lee and Anna Chennault are represented in the *Congressional Record* by their appearances before congressional committees or through inclusion of their speeches, letters, or other communications in the public record of the U.S. Congress. Anna's statements occur in the years 1962–1977, while Claire's in 1949 are most significant to this story. The vast majority of military paperwork from Claire's career is included in his papers at the Hoover Institution in California. Anna has been further documented by multiple branches of the U.S. government, including the State, Commerce, and Transportation Departments in addition to the President's Export Council (in the 1980s) and the Federal Bureau of Investigation. Because of its recent vintage, much of the departmental material is not easily obtainable. Freedom of Information Act processing is required to obtain it, and some requests remained pending as this manuscript was completed.

Memories of participants in and observers of the diplomatic process are necessary sources for the historian seeking a record of modern diplomacy. Many of Mrs. Chennault's contemporaries in the political and business worlds are still alive. Some will discuss her career; some will not. Senators, former senators, former diplomats, businessmen, and friends contributed information for this book. A partial list of those who spoke with the author include President Gerald Ford, General John Alison, General Alexander Haig, Dr. Kun-shuan Chiu, David Dean; former ambassadors Nat Bellocchi, Arthur Hummel, James Lilley, Konsin C. Shah, and Harry Thayer; Senators Mark Hatfield, Claiborne Pell, Charles Percy, Paul Simon, Alan Simpson, Ted Stevens, and Strom Thurmond; Dr. Bill Chin Lee, Colonel Henry Lee, Doug Paal, David Laux, Ms. Linda Lee, Mark Pratt, Colonel Ed Rector, Kermin Shih, Dr. Robert L. Thorp, and Louise Willauer.

In the absence of interviews, memoirs and biographies are useful for historical study, although, like interviews, memoirs must be treated carefully. The following memoirs proved particularly helpful: Claire Lee Chennault, *Way of a Fighter* (New York, 1949), Clark Clifford, *Counsel to the President: A Memoir* (New York, 1991), Bui Diem with David Chanoff, *In the Jaws of History* (Boston, 1987),

H. R. Haldeman, *The Haldeman Diaries* (New York, 1994), Cartha "Deke" DeLoach, *Hoover's FBI: The Inside Story by Hoover's Trusted Lieutenant* (Washington, DC, 1995), Lyndon Baines Johnson, *The Vantage Point: Perspectives of the Presidency, 1963–1969* (New York, 1971), Henry Kissinger, *White House Years* (Boston, 1979), and Richard Nixon, *RN: The Memoirs of Richard Nixon* (New York, 1978). These biographies by third parties are also valuable for the more detached views that they provide: Walter Isaacson, *Kissinger: A Biography* (New York, 1992), Seymour M. Hersh, *The Price of Power: Kissinger in the Nixon White House* (New York, 1983), Thomas Powers, *The Man Who Kept the Secrets: Richard Helms and the CIA* (New York, 1979), and Barbara W. Tuchman, *Stilwell and the American Experience in China, 1911–1945* (New York, 1972).

In addition to his own memoir, a whole body of literature exists on the career of General Chennault. Some of the most scholarly sources include Yonggang Huang, "Chennault and U.S. Air Support to China during World War II" (M.A. thesis, Baylor University, 1987), Boyd Heber Bauer, "General Claire Lee Chennault and China, 1937–1958" (Ph.D. diss., American University, 1973), Martha Byrd, *Chennault: Giving Wings to the Tiger* (Tuscaloosa, AL, 1987), and several works by historian William M. Leary, Jr., including *Perilous Missions: Civil Air Transport and CIA Covert Operations in Asia* (University, AL, 1984), and with William Stueck, "The Chennault Plan to Save China: U.S. Containment in Asia and the Origins of the CIA's Aerial Empire, 1949–1950," *Diplomatic History* 8, no. 4 (Fall 1984): 349–64. Other accounts have been written by Charles R. Bond, *A Flying Tiger's Diary* (College Station, TX, 1984), Duane Schultz, *The Maverick War: Chennault and the Flying Tigers* (New York, 1987), Maj. John M. Kelley, *Claire Lee Chennault: Theorist and Campaign Planner* (Ft. Leavenworth, KS, 1993), and Daniel Ford, *Flying Tigers: Claire Chennault and the American Volunteer Group* (Washington, DC, 1991).

Of the other historical figures with whom Mrs. Chennault was connected during her career, Richard Nixon is the one about whom the most literature has been generated. Some works include Joan Hoff, *Nixon Reconsidered* (New York, 1994), William Bundy, *A Tangled Web: The Making of Foreign Policy in the Nixon Presidency* (New York, 1998), Herbert S. Parmet, *Richard Nixon and His America* (Boston, 1990), Stanley I. Kutler, *Abuse of Power: The New Nixon Tapes* (New York, 1997), Tom Wicker, *One of Us: Richard Nixon and the American Dream* (New York, 1991), Jules Witcover, *The Resurrection of Richard Nixon* (New York, 1970), Anthony Summers, *The Arrogance of Power: The Secret World of Richard Nixon* (New York, 2000), Vamik K. Volkan,

Richard Nixon: A Psychobiography (New York, 1997), and Kenneth Franklin Kurz, *Nixon's Enemies* (Chicago, 1999).

An advantage—or distraction, some might think—of studying recent history is the wealth of popular published materials such as newspapers, magazines, and organizational and institutional organs. Many of these sources were invaluable to the author and are useful resources for this field. Most important for following Mrs. Chennault's activities are the newspapers in Washington, DC, where she lived and worked: *Washington Post, Washington Evening Star,* and *Washington Daily News.* Major daily papers in New York, Baltimore, Milwaukee, Taipei, and Hong Kong carried stories about her career over the years, in addition to the countless papers in cities, large and small, foreign and domestic, where she traveled, entertained, conducted business, and spoke publicly. Popular and women's magazines of the period—*Ladies' Home Journal, Vogue, Town and Country, Parade, Life, Time,* and *People,* among others—covered her in one or more aspects of her life as hostess, political activist, or businesswoman. Her name appeared in general business as well as in specific aviation trade publications. House organs for the National Republican Party and its Heritage Groups Division included coverage of her activities, as did similar publications for the U.S. Chamber of Commerce and the Departments of Transportation and Commerce.

Several authors have studied the presidential election of 1968. Useful to examine are Jules Witcover, *The Year the Dream Died: Revisiting 1968 in America* (New York, 1997), Lewis Chester, Godfrey Hodgson, and Bruce Page, *An American Melodrama: The Presidential Campaign of 1968* (New York, 1969), Kent G. Seig, "The 1968 Presidential Election and Peace in Vietnam," *Presidential Studies Quarterly* 26 (Fall 1996): 1062–80, and Theodore H. White, *The Making of the President—1968* (New York, 1969). Soviet involvement in the Vietnam peace process is best examined in Illya V. Gaiduk, *The Soviet Union and the Vietnam War* (Chicago, 1996), and Douglas Pike, *Vietnam and the Soviet Union: Anatomy of an Alliance* (Boulder, CO, 1987). A number of sources explore the general peace process. See Allan E. Goodman, *The Lost Peace: America's Search for a Negotiated Settlement of the Vietnam War* (Stanford, CA, 1978), Jeffrey P. Kimball, *Nixon's Vietnam War* (Lawrence, KS, 1998), and George C. Herring, ed., *The Secret Diplomacy of the Vietnam War: The Negotiating Volumes of the Pentagon Papers* (Austin, TX, 1983). Nguyen Tien Hung and Jerrold L. Schecter, *The Palace File* (New York, 1986), Marilyn Young, *The Vietnam Wars, 1945–1990* (New York, 1991), and Stanley Karnow, *Vietnam: A History* (New York, 1983) explore U.S.-Vietnamese relations.

An understanding of Sino-American relations specifically, and Asian-American relations generally, was necessary for this study. Scholarly works on these topics include Michael Schaller, *The United States and China in the Twentieth Century* (New York, 1990), Akira Iriye, *Across the Pacific: An Inner History of American-East Asian Relations* (New York, 1967), idem, *The Cold War in Asia: A Historical Introduction* (Englewood Cliffs, NJ, 1974), Michael Hunt, *The Making of a Special Relationship: The United States and China to 1914* (New York, 1983), Ernest R. May and John K. Fairbank, *America's China Trade in Historical Perspective: The Chinese and American Performance* (Cambridge, MA, 1986), Marilyn B. Young, *The Rhetoric of Empire: American China Policy, 1895–1901* (Cambridge, MA, 1968), Paul A. Varg, *The Closing of the Door: Sino-American Relations, 1936–1946* (East Lansing, MI, 1973), James C. H. Shen, *The U.S. and Free China: How the U.S. Sold Out Its Ally* (Washington, DC, 1983), Warren I. Cohen, *America's Response to China: A History of Sino-American Relations* (New York, 1990), and Harry Harding, *A Fragile Relationship: The United States and China since 1972* (Washington, DC, 1992).

On these same two topics, see Ramon H. Meyers, *A U.S. Foreign Policy for Asia: The 1980s and Beyond* (Stanford, CA, 1982), John F. Copper, *China Diplomacy: The Washington-Taipei-Beijing Triangle* (Boulder, CO, 1992), Tang Tsou, *America's Failure in China, 1941–1950*, 2 vols. (Chicago, 1963), Tan Quingshan, *The Making of U.S. China Policy: From Normalization to Post-Cold War Era* (Boulder, CO, 1992), A. Doak Barnett, *China Policy: Old Problems and New Challenges* (Washington, DC, 1977), Li Gang, *U.S.-China Relations since the End of the Cold War* (Washington, DC, 2000), Ralph N. Clough, *Reaching across the Taiwan Strait: People-to-People Diplomacy* (Boulder, CO, 1993), King-yuh Chang, *ROC-U.S. Relations under the Taiwan Relations Act: Practice and Prospects* (Taipei, Taiwan, 1988), Nancy Bernkopf Tucker, *Taiwan, Hong Kong, and the United States, 1945–1992: Uncertain Friendships* (New York, 1994), Murray L. Weidenbaum, *United States, China, Taiwan: A Precarious Triangle* (St. Louis, MO, 2000), and James Mann, *About Face: A History of America's Curious Relationship with China, from Nixon to Clinton* (New York, 2000).

The place and role of women in Chinese society were important to Anna Chennault's character and career. Several works useful in clarifying that perspective are Margery Wolf and Roxane Witke, eds., *Women in Chinese Society* (Stanford, CA, 1975), Li Yu-ning,

Historical Roots of Changes in Women's Status in Modern China (Jamaica, NY, 1981), and *Chinese Women through Chinese Eyes* (Armonk, NY, 1992), Esther S. Lee Yao, *Chinese Women Past and Present* (Mesquite, TX, 1983), Stacey Peck, *Halls of Jade, Walls of Stone: Women in China Today* (New York, 1985), Kay Ann Johnson, *Women, the Family, and Peasant Revolution in China* (Chicago, 1983), Bobby Siu, *Women of China: Imperialism and Women's Resistance, 1900–1949* (London, 1982), Jean Lyon, "New Horizons for the Chinese Woman," in Hollington K. Tong, ed., *China: After Seven Years of War* (New York, 1945), Lily Xiao Hong Lee, *The Virtue of Yin: Studies on Chinese Women* (Broadway, NSW, Australia, 1994), and Dorothy Ko, *Teachers of the Inner Chambers: Women and Culture in Seventeenth-Century China* (Stanford, CA, 1994).

Also valuable for a Western author are various sources on the American missionary movement in China, life in pre- and post-revolutionary China, and views of Chinese and Americans about each other. Sources include Harold Robert Isaacs, *Scratches on Our Minds: American Images of China and India* (New York, 1958), Paul A. Varg, *Missionaries, Chinese, and Diplomats: The American Protestant Missionary Movement in China, 1890–1952* (Princeton, NJ, 1958), James Reed, *The Missionary Mind and American East Asian Policy, 1911–1915* (Cambridge, MA, 1983), Jane Hunter, *The Gospel of Gentility: American Women Missionaries in Turn-of-the-Century China* (New Haven, CT, 1984), Robert McClellan, *The Heathen Chinee: A Study of American Attitudes toward China, 1890–1905* (Columbus, OH, 1971), James Claude Thomson, *When China Faced West: American Reformers in Nationalist China, 1928–1937* (Cambridge, MA, 1969), Marie-Claire Bergere, *The Golden Age of the Chinese Bourgeoisie, 1911–1937* (Cambridge, UK, 1989), George N. Kates, *The Years That Were Fat: The Last of Old China* (Cambridge, MA, 1952), Paul Chao, *Chinese Kinship* (London, 1983), Hubert Freyn, *Chinese Education in the War* (Shanghai, 1940), Frank Tao, "Student Life in China," in Hollington K. Tong, ed., *China: After Seven Years of War* (New York, 1945), Marianne Bastid, *Educational Reform in Early Twentieth Century China* (Ann Arbor, 1988), and Richard H. Solomon, *Chinese Negotiating Behavior: Pursuing Interests through "Old Friends"* (Washington, DC, 1999).

Several useful references on Chinese leaders and citizens include Alex Ramsay, *The Peking Who's Who 1922* (Taipei, Taiwan, 1971 reprint), *Who's Who in Communist China* (Hong Kong, 1969), H. G. W. Woodhead, *The China Yearbook* (Tientsin, China, 1912–1930), Howard L. Boorman and Richard D. Howard, *Biographical Dictio-*

nary of Republican China, 5 vols. (New York, 1968), Max Perleberg, *Who's Who in Modern China (From the Beginning of the Chinese Republic to the End of 1953)* (Hong Kong, 1954), and Wolfgang Bartke, *Biographical Dictionary and Analysis of China's Party Leadership, 1922–1988* (Munich, 1990).

The inner workings of American party politics and domestic political connections to foreign policy are an important part of painting the informal diplomatic picture. Helpful on this topic are Stanley D. Bachrack, *The Committee of One Million: "China Lobby" Politics, 1953– 1971* (New York, 1976), R. P. Anand, *Cultural Factors in International Relations* (New Delhi, 1981), Ross Y. Koen, *The China Lobby in American Politics* (New York, 1974), W. W. Rostow, *The Diffusion of Power: An Essay in Recent History* (New York, 1972), Yizhong Sun, "New China Lobby: China's Encounter with the U.S. Congress" (Ph.D. diss., University of Notre Dame, 2000), William Safire, *Before the Fall: An Inside View of the Pre-Watergate White House* (Garden City, NY, 1975), and Nancy Bernkopf Tucker, *China Confidential: American Diplomats and Sino-American Relations since 1945* (New York, 2000).

Index